Tool Kit For Human Resources

Tool Kit For Human Resources

Charles Anderson

iUniverse, Inc.
New York Lincoln Shanghai

Tool Kit For Human Resources

iUniverse, Inc.

For information address:
iUniverse, Inc.
2021 Pine Lake Road, Suite 100
Lincoln, NE 68512
www.iuniverse.com

ISBN: 0-595-32369-3

Printed in the United States of America

FROM THE AUTHOR

My heartfelt thanks are extended to Mrs. E. Ledford who patiently and lovingly edited this book for publication.

CONTENTS

ACKNOWLEDGMENTS

I offer my sincere thanks to everyone who helped with this project.

FOREWARD

Andy Anderson inspires me. He is a man of wisdom, determination and humor. Despite having to battle the challenges of Parkinson's disease for the past several years, he has put together a book of true value. This book represents the wisdom he accumulated over a career of helping others work more efficiently and effectively. I hope it will be as great a source of inspiration to its readers as Andy's friendship is to me. In the face of challenges many of us would find overwhelming, Andy has lived with courage and grace.

Life is not fair. We do not deserve the less than wonderful or wonderful things that happen to us. Life is difficult but whether we make sense of it or not depends on seeing it as grace rather than insisting on fairness.

Dr. Vic Greene, Chaplain
Angel Hospice and Palliative Care

Knowing Mr. Anderson's desire for excellence, I recommend this book as a book that reaches his desires and goals. Andy was my teacher at Webster University, my Mentor and is my friend. He was tough and demanding as a professor, an idealist and consistent as a Mentor/Advisor, and amusing, but supportive as a friend. He turned down my final paper in his class although I was State Director (Florida) of the Society for Human Resource Management at the time (something about wanting more!)

George L. Russell, SPHR

SURVIVAL OF HUMAN RESOURCES' FITTEST

Long ago, in the not too distant Business past, employees were hired on board a Company to be watched over and cared for initially by kindly "good ole boys" known as the "Personnel Manager" and the "Training Manager". These guys were usually "fairly quick-witted" older white males, not technically trained in their field but who had a graduate degree from the "School of Hard Knocks" in how to do the job. To a man they usually possessed the "gift of gab" and any job longevity they achieved was by being pretty adept at "pouring oil upon troubled waters".

A Personnel group, or Human Resources Management (HRM) team as it's now called, generally self-perpetuates its existence while housed underneath the Company's Administration umbrella. From this lofty Administrative perch, Personnel executes its authority and power to interview applicants, sometimes to test their skill levels (though more often not) and then to subjectively make hiring decisions regarding who comes on board. HRM also documents company policies and procedures while maintaining employee records (i.e., hours, attendance, performance, etc.). It further administers benefits and pension plans; coordinates safety; and if necessary, terminates and adjudicates employees.

Training, therefore, generally experiences a more "tentative" existence and is usually housed within Personnel. Sometimes Technical Training finds a temporary abode in places outside of Administration called Manufacturing or Operations. Training or Human Resource Development (HRD) usually reports to HRM but in certain technical training situations, HRD can report directly to Manufacturing. HRD has rarely, if ever, been given the status or respect to stand as its own entity within the organization.

Who you report to in a technical training position tremendously impacts how you are perceived and are treated on the operating floor. Technical trainers when reporting directly to manufacturing often sense a different kind of treatment. Things seem to change. There's a refreshing new openness in communications coupled with a higher level of cooperation and respect for what you do. Manufacturing prefers having its own "insider" whose principal concerns are productivity, quality and cost. Manufacturing seems to sub-consciously suspect any "outsiders" from HRM as having a different agenda. But with time, Manufacturing having its own HRD "insider" to help keep watch on HR, it's almost too perfect to resist.

Always remember that "direct reports" are the bricks with which vice presidents build their castles. A vice president loses all objectivity when someone tries to "steal" a brick from his castle. So don't expect a rational and logical reaction or decision when the question of changing your reporting channel is raised. For your own safety and security, never be perceived as the instigator of the question being asked. If the HR vice president ever suspects or gets the slightest hint that you were behind the question being raised, disloyalty will be suspected and you may find your "hiney in the liney" at the local unemployment office. Of special note, even if you get the opportunity to be an "insider", don't be surprised when manufacturing continues to ask HRM for management training. Once you've been stamped or labeled as a "technical trainer", how could you be expected to possess any knowledge of management skills training? The conventional wisdom still applies—you can't be a prophet in your own country!

During the good times (when productivity and profits are high), Training is often used as a reward even to the point of developing training programs and circulating training manuals. When the bad times come (decreased sales and productivity), Management's usual "knee jerk" reaction is to shut down Training. Management is notorious for shelving employee training and passing out "chairs and whips" to their supervisors and severance packages to their trainers during hard times.

A much better approach would be to maintain a constant monitoring and training strategy. Monitor associates' productivity and the quality of their performance then rotate low quality and non-producers from the manufacturing line to the training room. Train associates by simulations of how to do the Tasks of the job efficiently and effectively. Measure performance before, during and after training, transfer high quality producers back into the manufacturing line and cull the low quality and/or non-producers from the company. With this strategy in place, any downsizing forced on the organization can be done from an "informed" position. Thus, the organization can downsize its lowest quality producers rather than being indiscriminate in its terminations. The organization can theoretically come out of an economic downturn, stronger rather than weaker. The only constant in the field of HR is change! Enough HR evolution, let's explain what we'll be attempting to accomplish with this book.

Intent

This book comes at the end of what seems a short thirty-year professional career in HR. During this time a lot of changes have occurred and many HR techniques, processes and procedures have been thrown out, revamped, retired, developed, changed and/or modified. My hope is that I can share some of the processes and procedures that have been very useful when applied in field situations by me as a coach, instructor, trainer, professor, consultant and personnel researcher.

The information provided is intended to serve as a self-development tool for those of you who find yourself feeling "unarmed and alone" in a company's HR department. Those of you with subordinate co-travelers on the HR highway may find it useful as a staff-development instrument. And hopefully for students and educators, it may serve as a basic and understandable introduction to basic HR concepts and their applications in the real world. I don't presume to have found all the answers, but I have found some things that do work and I want to share them with you. Since I can't personally be with each of you, I have chosen an anecdotal approach to clarify the understanding of concepts or techniques.

Human Resources, though birthed in the behavioral sciences, is not an exact science such as mathematics where there is only one answer or statistics where there are rumored to be two, three or more answers. In HR there is never just one answer, there are just too many intervening variables (i.e., people, personalities, time, date, physical location, departmental temperature, organizational weather, changing laws, contradictory legal interpretations, public opinion, situations, etc.). Don't let indecisive action make your decisions for you. Make your decision based on all the factual information you've uncovered, a dose of good judgment and a dab of common sense. Once made, make the decision work. Therefore, since "truth is oftentimes stranger than fiction", a few war stories and "What would you have done(s)?" may be found tucked, I hope, neatly and strategically amongst and between the covers of this book. This is done to stimulate thinking and debate. My responses to the situations and the perceived consequences and ramifications are provided at the back of the book for your possible edification and/or amusement. My one true hope is that you GO FORTH, IRRIGATE, CULTIVATE AND GROW THE FIELD! Never be satisfied with your tools, constantly look for ways to hone and improve them. If this book either "ignites or energizes" at least one reader to labor in the ever-expanding HR field, I will have accomplished my objective with its writing. Now for a few words about how and why I got into the HR "seed-planting" business.

ABOUT THE AUTHOR

After high school I felt led to try my hand at Georgia Tech (GT). It was my good fortune to meet and get to know such GT legends as Bobby "The Silver Fox" Dodd and Dean of Students George Griffin. Another name comes to my mind and that was one of my most influential personal friends, Neil DeRosa, at that time the Director of Placement for GT.

As a rising senior, I was fortunate to attend his summer camp conference for corporate CEOs and rising senior Executive Roundtable students. In his camp, 8-10 seniors were assigned to a cabin with two CEOs from major American corporations during the weeklong conference. Initially, I remember feeling very unlucky and cheated to have been assigned to a cabin with Mr. DeRosa and the CEO of IBM. There went my chance to establish another CEO contact. By the end of the week I had been converted to the "I want to be like Neil" fan club.

Mr. DeRosa was the most influential and persuasive person I have ever meet. He was the "Will Rogers—I never met a man I didn't like" of the Corporate world. Mr. DeRosa once said to me, "I have the best job, selling the best products ever produced (GT graduates) to the world's 'most appreciative' customers (Corporate America). And I even get to spend five to seven weeks each year with plant trips, facility tours and chaperoning students. If a GT Graduate comes into my office neat and clean and wants to go to work, I'll put him to work!" I remember being in his office when experienced or inexperienced graduates would walk in and have Mr. DeRosa ask with whom the graduate wanted to go to work. He would then pick up the phone, call the appropriate Corporate Recruiter, tell him or her who he had in his office and ask when he or she wanted to interview his graduate. This was my first exposure to Human Resources.

To alleviate any intellectual fears you may have concerning the tools we'll be discussing, mine was an undergraduate academic life of mediocrity resulting from excessive cramming and not ever knowing how to study. Graduation requirements were finally met and I was ready to get out of there.

With Mr. DeRosa's coaching my senior year I ended up with enough plant trips to almost earn a gold card for travel mileage with the airline. At graduation I had thirteen job offers from which to choose. I walked the aisle and made my decision. After ramblin' around the Georgia Tech campus for about 13 quarters, I received a BS degree in textile management from the "North Avenue Trade School" in Atlanta, GA. In other words, I was an official card-carrying, Georgia Bulldog-hating, GT alumni. I packed my stuff and hitched up my 10-ft. U-Haul trailer to the back of my old Wreck and, with sunrise, I began ramblin' north to Virginia ready for whatever. Within a month I received word that my mentor and friend had died suddenly and unexpectedly while doing one of his favorite things, chaperoning a group of GT students on a tour of Russia.

My first few years in the wonderful post-baccalaureate world of work, I was a front-line manufacturing supervisor in a high-tech, fast-paced, highly stressful Fortune 50 chemical fiber operation. My first six weeks of employment were dedicated to "hands on" or "coverall" training. When I first heard of "coverall training" I was really impressed. They would teach me everything I needed to know in just six short weeks. Then I learned that it referred to the clothing (gray coveralls) worn by the operators. "Hands on" training was conducted by a front-line supervisor and by his 16-person crew who were spread out over five of the six operating floors of the world's largest nylon manufacturing plant.

WHAT WOULD YOU DO?—SITUATION - #01

With a whopping four weeks of job experience under your belt, your boss asks you to recommend one of your crew for promotion to first-line supervisor. You peruse your employee records and narrow it down to three operators:

Operator A— has lowest machine productivity yields on the shift, has slowest position string-up speed on the shift, has a high school diploma, has moderate quality audits, shows some initiative, shows good interpersonal skills, has lowest job seniority and has no union support.

Operator B— has highest machine productivity yields on the shift, has fastest position string-up speed on the shift, has associate's degree from a local community college, shows little initiative, shows weak interpersonal skills, has highest job seniority and is recommended and favored by the union.

Operator C— has moderate machine productivity yields on the shift, has moderate position string-up speed on the shift, has bachelor's degree in English Literature from a small local college, shows little initiative, shows weak interpersonal skills, has moderate job seniority and is recommended for consideration by the union.

The "selected" individual will be sent directly to a two-week Supervisory Training course given by the HR department. Which of the three would you recommend for supervisory training and why?

My graduate-level studies at the School of Hard Knocks began the first day of my seventh week when it was officially announced that I was promoted to front-line supervisor of the shift on which I was trained. The former supervisor was "rolled back" to operator status reporting directly to me. I was five years younger than anybody reporting to me and had the current and past union presidents as members of my crew. I also had the top three operators in seniority ranking from among 3500 union members. These guys had organized, participated and negotiated in the writing of the plant's original union contract. I had a "tiger by the tail it's plain to see" as the old song goes. During the late 60's and early 70's, I earned my graduate degree from the School of Hard Knocks.

WHAT WOULD YOU DO?—SITUATION - #02

As one of four crews on a revolving or rotating shift, you are responsible, when working the graveyard shift (12 midnight to 8 a.m.), for gathering and compiling your area's daily production figures. These figures are reviewed every morning in the plant manager's meeting with the production committee composed of all area supervisors. The operator previously assigned to gather and compile production figures had long been reputed as the plant's best "rack-up" person. Just prior to your arrival, the operator had been convicted of performing an illegal abortion on a young woman. He raised chickens as a side business and had developed a technique to drain his laying hens when they started to retain too much liquid. He had discussed his technique at a bar one night with an acquaintance who suggested it had financial potential as a possible abortion method. They decided to try it one night on a young woman in a motel room. They emerged from the motel room into a bevy of Virginia State Troopers. They were arrested, she later aborted and a conviction resulted. Both men were released on their own recognizance pending a delayed sentencing hearing.

On a Friday afternoon at the tender age of 22 and with three whopping months of job experience, your boss blind-sides you with the above story. You are blown away. The sentencing hearing had concluded that morning with the operator receiving 18 months in the county jail. Due to extenuating family circumstances (five kids), he could check out of the jail for work each day but had to return to the jail after work. In other words, since it was his first offense, the judge had decided to allow him to serve his time during his time off and on weekends. Again you are amazed. Then follows several comments from your boss about how much he and other members of upper management think of the operator. You are just fixing to add your own kudos about his work when the boss suddenly interrupts; "Well all this doesn't matter anyway. The plant manager wants your recommendation regarding the impact on the company's community image if this is or is not to be the operator's workplace. And the plant manager wants it justified in writing by Monday morning at his rack-up meeting. He's scheduled a press conference at 12:00 noon Monday to announce his final decision. I just glad I'm not making the decision! Have your recommendation in my hands by 7:00 Monday morning. Oh yeah, have a nice weekend." Nothing negative surfaced as I read through his personnel folder that night except for a continuously re-occurring respiratory infection. There seemed to be letters of commendation from everyone that the operator had ever met except maybe his kindergarten teacher. What's your recommendation and why?

WHAT WOULD YOU DO?—SITUATION - #03

The shift mechanic was such an old, cantankerous, hardheaded, stubborn, arrogant horse's hiney that you just couldn't help but like the old coot. He was two months away from retirement and was "feeling his oats" more each day. One night about 4:00 a.m., he was experiencing a "bad hair" night with one machine position. He had already had to "freeze off and thaw out" the position's drop leg five times and still hadn't had his breakfast. Freezing off a drop leg was a simple process of placing a cold wet rag on a 300°C "upside-down Y-shaped" drop leg going to one of two packs. Thaw out was a dirty, hot and slow job involving the use of a blowtorch for 15 to 20 minutes while seated between two poorly insulated positions running at 300°C. There were two drop legs per machine position on the third floor and four packs on the second floor. For a machine position to produce yarn both drop legs and all four packs had to function properly.

On an area patrol of the third floor, you happen on to him as he is thawing the drop leg for the sixth time. As you approach you observe the mechanic flagrantly violating an extremely dangerous safety rule. To properly and safely thaw out a drop leg requires moving a blowtorch continuously up and down the drop leg until it thaws. The cranky old mechanic is sitting there on his stool and behind his safety shield with his facemask on. With his asbestos-gloved hand holding the blowtorch, he is just absent-mindedly heating up one "localized" area on the drop leg. The heated area of the drop leg is glowing intensely. You immediately question what he is doing and order him to stop. He looks up all dirty, hot and sweaty and shouts, "You ain't my boss and if you open your mouth to me one more time this position can just run as waste in the floor for the rest of the shift. Now just get out of here, you act like you think I don't know what I'm doing?" You immediately head for the stairwell to track down his supervisor.

On the way down the stairs you pass the mechanic's son on his way to pick up his dad for their breakfast break. He asks if you have seen his dad and you blurt out that he is up on the third floor overheating a drop leg.

At that very instant an explosion shakes the building. The son immediately grabs you and pushing you against the wall and starts yelling, "You've killed my dad, you've killed my dad!" The next thing you remember is the son and you racing up the steps to the third floor. The first thing you both see is a "mushroom type" cloud of white monomer powder rising to the ceiling over the place where his dad had been working. You both run to the position to find his dad very shaken but all right. The safety shield had worked. The explosion had knocked him off his stool, scared the "you know what out of him" and left him temporarily deaf and bruised.

Three hours later the Spanish Inquisition begins as the safety incident accident investigation starts. You would think that Fort Knox had just been robbed. Somebody is guilty of a major safety rule violation and is about to hang! By now dad and son are together on their story. Dad had not heated one spot locally on the drop leg but had played his low degree flame up and down the drop leg. In spite of your order to specifically heat a localized spot on the drop leg and to get the position back into production more quickly, he had refused and did not violate any safety rule. Your walking quietly away to go and look for the mechanic's supervisor was your downfall. Guilt and responsibility established and enough said. What would you have done differently and why?

****

Being the rookie in engineering, I cringed as the company went through first a 15% "downsizing" of its workforce. Over the next two years the "downsizing" was followed by a 10% "reduction of force" and finally another 5% "rightsizing".

When the economic upturn finally arrived, I had survived. The staffing level of the 5 engineering units at the plant that had once stood at eleven each had been reduced to seven each. Our unit now consisted of two older white engineers (who had "birthed" the process), one Asian Indian engineer, one married white engineer and two black engineers (the only 2 at the site) with whom I shared an office.

One afternoon about three months after the layoffs ended, I was summoned to the boss's office. My boss then informed me that my job as a process engineer was being eliminated over the next six months during which time I could seek other employment. Since I had over three years experience, good performance reviews and having just "turned loose" my third trainee as the process unit's engineering trainer, I decided to question my boss's decision making. I blurted out the obvious stupid question, "The rookie I just finished training last week has only three months experience, why not him instead of me?" Having not been instructed on what to say in this situation, my boss quickly replied, "I'm sorry, but his wife's pregnant and you're the only single, white male that's left in the unit." (Even at this point, my kingdom for a tape of that conversation.)

Two weeks later I returned to the boss's office to learn I was being assigned a new black engineering trainee who would be taking my old position upon my departure. Quickly I learned a new term called "discrimination" for which my tenure was being sacrificed. Ten years later I learned an even more interesting term, "reverse discrimination".

Being on the cutting edge of technology in the chemical fiber field, I wasn't too worried about finding other employment. Resumes were typed and sent. Competitors showed enthusiastic response to my availability. Trip dates and interviews were mutually arranged and set and I informed the boss of the dates I needed to be away as a courtesy. My boss informed me that I could not be spared on those dates and would not be allowed to go to my interviews. Rather than discuss our ancestries, I headed straight to Personnel to invoke my rights.

Upon reaching Personnel I was quickly introduced to another new term, "confidentiality agreement". I was right—I could go to the interview! But under a confidentiality agreement, signed my first day on the job amongst a lot of other papers, I had signed away my right to discuss with a competitor anything about the work I had been doing there for one full year after leaving the company. With my textile career derailed, I began reminiscing about Mr. DeRosa and was determined to learn how the game was played so I'd never be blindsided like this again. Hence my interest in and later passion for Human Resources was initially ignited.

I decided I wanted to become a college placement director during my last week of employment. Figuring that I would need a Masters degree in Counseling and with all the schools ready to start without me over the next two weeks, my possibility of successfully entering a program that fall appeared minuscule on Friday my last official day of work. I formulated a plan over the weekend. Monday morning I was sitting in the Registrar's office at Georgia Tech. Amused by my perceived ignorance and the timing of my request for admission, he chuckled as he handed me the name and number of the Psychology Department's Graduate Admissions Committee Chairman. The Chairman's initial questioning revolved around when I graduated, my degree and my undergraduate grade point average. "And you plan to compete academically with the upper 5% of GT's Student Body?" he snickered. "How much Psychology have you had?" "One course." "And your grade?" "A "C" Sir." "And you want to do what?"

Number one he pointed out to me that the Department didn't even offer a Counseling degree. The closest thing they offered was Industrial/Organizational Psychology. "Besides even if you were back in school, you would have to basically take all the senior year course load as pre-requisites for graduate school." His first mistake, he had cracked the door and, baby, my foot was in.

Armed with a sage knowledge of how the GT registration system worked, within the week, I was sitting in my first senior-level psychology class. Some old contacts in my former department got me registered by signing for me to be a special post-baccalaureate student assigned to take all psychology courses. Never tell a Tech student it can't be done.

Less than six months later, I officially entered graduate school to study Industrial/Organizational Psychology at my alma mater. To my surprise I found that I was either older or had more "real-life" business experience than about half the faculty.

Concerned with this fact, I had already begun researching the faculty in hopes of identifying a possible mentor. I identified a "hot-blooded" Irishman named, W.W. Ronan. He had every credential: ubiquitously published, exceptionally well-read, national and local business consulting reputation and experience. Ronan had been a classmate of Fred Herzberg (Theory), had co-authored several books with Eric Prien (University of Tennessee), had worked with Pittsburgh Plate Glass and had been involved in the initial developmental work on flight simulators with the Strategic Air Command in WWII.

I marched quite confidently into Ronan's office and announced myself as his new graduate assistant. With a puzzled look he peered out at me over the top of his glasses and then said, "Oh no you're not, the department's already assigned me one." I quickly replied. "I'm not here to grade papers, I'm here to assist in your consulting activities." He smiled and I smiled and a deal was soon struck. A perfectly matched team of Type "A" workaholics had just been created. For the next four "lightening fast" years, Dr. Ronan saw more of me than he did of his own shadow. Days were spent in class, studying or consulting while evenings and weekends were spent at his home planning, analyzing and writing.

We seemed to always have three or four projects going. My "hands on" experience continued to increase and I was "chomping at the bit" for a shot at a "lead dog" position. I really couldn't wait to apply what I had learned.

Dr. Ronan was contracted by a former student to assist in overseeing a validation project for clerical, police and firefighter positions in a six-jurisdiction area planning and development commission. I was very fortunate to be selected the lead consultant on the validation project for firefighters. Six training chiefs were assigned to me as subject matter experts.

Our assignment was that we design and administer a set of criteria to evaluate firefighter job performance. The firefighters had previously been administered several different written examinations and the regional planning and development commission the six local jurisdictions wanted us to validate which of the exams was the best predictor of future performance on the job. I was basically given free reign to develop a test battery to evaluate firefighter performance.

Position Analysis Questionnaires

To establish the similarity between the six local jurisdictions' fire departments, we choose to use the Position Analysis Questionnaire (PAQ). The PAQ is an approximately 289-item job analysis instrument, which generates a 27-dimension profile, and a 5-overall dimension profile used primarily for job classification and compensation. I like to think of the PAQ as a measuring stick 27-job dimensions long that can be placed beside a job and used to measure its requirements. The PAQ analysis of a job produces a profile of the job's requirements. Thus we have found the PAQ to be very useful in establishing the similarity of jobs through comparisons of their job dimension profiles (See Figures 1 and 1a).

Though rather fast and clean to administer, the PAQ does present some drawbacks. The PAQ requires an experienced job analyst to assist the subject matter experts in form completion. It is relatively expensive to use and to process your data requires its shipment to the Logan, Utah Processing Center. In Figure 1a, page 13, the five jurisdictional averages, involving three subject matter experts for each jurisdiction, are plotted on the graph for comparative purposes. The results of a PAQ analysis present the data across 27 job dimensions and 5 overall job dimensions. The amount of congruence observed tends to indicate one job family across the jurisdictions. The analyst would therefore probably use the average across the five jurisdictions to represent the fire fighter's job. Often times it is very important to pay just as close attention to job dimensions which are not present as to those which are present, hence the negative as well as the positive dimensions on the graph. The higher the importance of the dimension, the higher z-score, either positively or negatively. On the other hand, there is over twenty-five years of experience and data to back up your findings and even a cursory plot of both positive and negative job dimension profiles for each job will show a profile of any relationships that may exist (See Figure 1a).

Interestingly enough the PAQ is derived from amongst 289 questions and yields to an expression of the classification of the job across a set of 32 job dimension: 27 basic dimensions and 5 overall job dimensions. The rationale behind the Task-Based Job Analysis (TBJA) is somewhat Scottish in its conception. Believing in building upon established foundations, the 33 Whole Job Requirements we collect are taken from over 30 years of research by the U.S. Department of

Labor and from its Dictionary of Occupational Titles. The Whole Job Requirements (in TBJA) represent the 33 factors on which occupations have been classified in the past. The 33 factors are presented in groupings of 10 Abilities, 10 Personal Traits and 13 Physical Abilities. Three Grand Means for these groupings are also calculated giving us a total of 36 factors on which jobs can be classified into job families. After that is done, the Key Result Areas, the Tasks and the Steps of the job process are brainstormed and then rank-ordered based their Importance to good job performance, Time Spent on performing the Tasks of the job and Frequency of performance on the job. Then the percentage of tasks to be subjected to further study is identified by the Subject Matter Experts (SMEs). Incumbents are then instructed to rate the most Important tasks on 13 factors regarding the required level of the factor to perform the task or its steps within the process. This allows the classification of job levels within a job class. The knowledge, skills and abilities necessary to perform the task are then brainstormed and rated from "essential" to "needed".

	Z-SCORES				
JOB DIMENSIONS	County A	County B	County C	County D	County E
A-01 Watching devices/materials for information	-0.966	-0.443	-0.958	0.432	-1.388
A-02 Interpreting what is heard or seen	-1.781	1.801	2.706	2.181	2.996
A-03-Using data originating with people	0.258	1.427	1.044	1.471	0.528
A-04-Watching things from a distance	0.427	0.571	0.650	1.641	0.755
A-05-Evaluating information from things	0.755	-0.043	1.180	0.863	0.709
A-06-Being aware of environmental conditions	2.783	2.414	2.026	2.535	3.510
A-07 Being aware body movement or balance	3.966	1.488	2.361	3.771	0.062
B-08-Making decisions	-0.044	0.483	-0.239	0.615	0.348
B-09-Processing information	0 361	-0.361	1.209	1.045	-0.019
C-10-Controlling machines/processes	-0.476	0.127	-0.312	0.283	-0.019
C-11-Using hands and arms to control/modify	0.750	0.994	0.670	0.983	0.654
C-12-Using feet/hands to operate equipment/vehicle	3.85	3.232	2.926	3.502	3.973
C-13-Performing activities requiring gen body move	2.955	1.918	3.203	2.176	3.821
C-14-Using hands and arms to modify/position thing	-0.969	-0.797	-0.703	-0.173	-1.497
C-15-Using fingers vs. general body movement	-0.767	-0.461	0.881	-0.490	-0.246
C-16-Performing skilled/technical activities	1.225	0.559	0.705	1.632	0.139
D-17-Communicting requirements, decisions, information	1.131	0.024	-0.567	1.641	1.130
D-18-Exchanging job-related information	1.156	2.389	3.264	1.082	0.587
D-19-Performing staff/related activities	-0.829	0.357	1.883	-0.726	1.058
D-20-Contacting supervisor or subordinate	0.075	-0.291	-0.085	0.932	0.089
D-21-Dealing with the public	1.603	1.506	0.002	3.816	3.114
E-22-Being in a hazardous, unpleasant environment	3.770	3.245	3.333	3.102	3.592
E-23-Engaging in personally demanding situations	2.441	2.049	2.668	2.251	2.699
F-24-Being in a business like work situation	-0.084	-0.061	-0.228	0.056	-0.041
F-25-Beingaleart to detail/changing conditions	1.555	0.773	1.914	1.043	2.113
F-26-Performing instructions vs. structured work	0.038	-1.271	-1.198	-1.285	-1.154
F-27-Working on a variable vs. regular schedule	-0.542	-0.127	-0.243	-0.581	-0.504
OVERALL JOB DIMENSIONS					
D 28-Having decision-making commun & social resp	1.536	1.268	1.359	1.970	1.768
D-29-Performing skilled activities	-0.220	0.086	0.001	0.754	-0.089
D-30-Being physical/related environ conditions	3.518	2.858	3.498	3.365	3.646
D-31-Operating equipment/vehicle	2.496	1.729	3.180	2.943	3.325
D-32-Processing information	1.215	0.584	2.171	1.211	0.759

Figure 1—PAQ Job Requirement Profiles

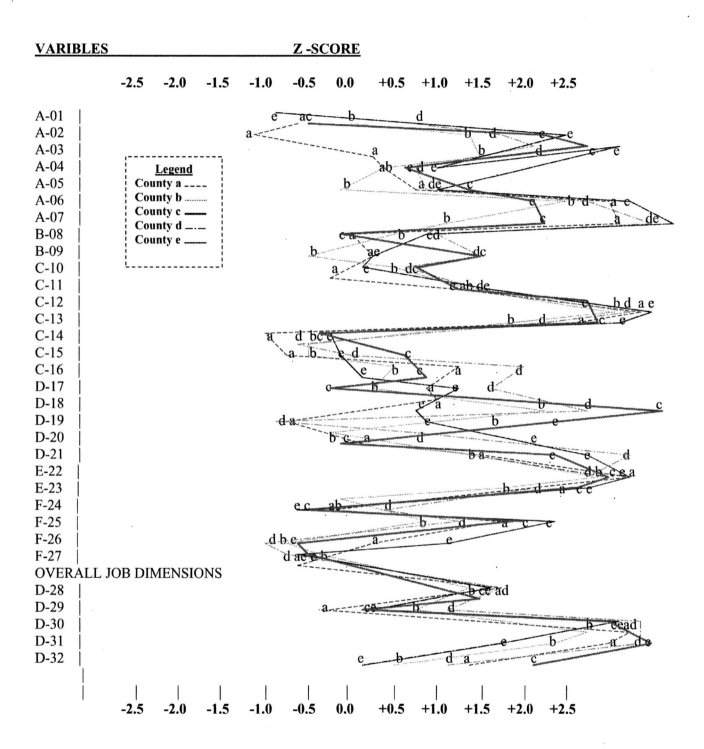

Figure 1a—Job Dimension Profile Plots

I also used the Critical Incident Technique (CIT) method of job analysis with the intent of identifying the categories involved the development of Behaviorally-Anchored Ratings Scales (BARS) for use as peer and supervisory ratings instruments. For those of you that haven't experienced CIT card sorting and characterizations, large amounts of time and space are required before sorting begins. The sorting procedure is very reparative and time-consuming. The appraisal instrument evolved as an adjective checklist containing job-specific behaviors identified as indicative of an effective firefighter. Respondents were asked whether the behavioral adjective statement was descriptive of the firefighter on a three-point scale ranging from "yes", to "no" with an option of "dk" for don't know.

The left column shown in Figure 2, and entitled Firefighter Test Battery Item contains the various examinations developed for the firefighter evaluation. The first two items were identical performance evaluations. Each of the firefighter's peers (i.e., 5 to 9 fellow firefighters) and each of the firefighter's immediate supervision (i.e., sergeant, lieutenant and captain) completed an appraisal.

If any work group should know each other's behavior, it should be firefighters. After all, they usually work together on a 24-hour per shift basis. So peer evaluations would be expected to correlate very highly with supervisor evaluations. As you have probably already surmised, by looking at the Intercorrelation Matrix in Figure 2, the supervisory-peer evaluation was a surprisingly low, 0.28. Of further interest, was the finding of an internal consistency coefficient among peer evaluations of 0.94 while the same statistic among supervisory evaluations was found to be 0.88. Therefore, both groups were extremely stable in their evaluations of a particular firefighter's performance. So you tell me, "Which set of performance evaluations should be used?"

The next set of items in the Test Battery was developed as "hands on" physical agility tests. Included in this set of tests were a knot-tying segment, a one-man 50-ft. hose lay, an apparatus (proper truck) spotting and hook up, a one-man ladder handling, a hand traverse of a ladder, a Scott Air Pac handling, a ladder climb with weight and a ladder descent with weight. These items required actual performance of a Task documented against the clock. Looking again at Figure 2, you'll notice the highest physical agility test correlation (the 50-ft. hose lay) with the supervisory rating was 0.11 (still statistically insignificant).

Next we switched to evaluation items dealing with the physical storage and inspection of equipment. At last we have a statistically significant correlation with supervisory ratings, but it's only at a 0.13 level with equipment inspection.

The next eleven items incorporated a rather unique problem-solving technique called tab tests. A simulated fire situation was actually created on paper complete with drawings, layouts, weather conditions, victims to rescue, fires to suppress, buildings to ventilate, equipment from which to choose, exposure to protect, etc. The hardest part was selling six Training Chiefs on the concept. Once they bought it, I've never seen six old men have so much fun legally. We had almost a hundred and fifty years experience to draw from in that room as we designed our test while assuring that only one possible response was correct. Often times we found ourselves working backward, continually changing and adjusting until the question supported the desired answer.

Firefighter Test Battery Item	1	2	3	4	5	6	7	8	9	10	11	12	13	14	15	16	17	18	19	20	21	22	23	24	25	n
Peer Evaluation	100																									566
Supervisor Evaluation	28*	100																								549
Knots & Ropes	4	12*	100																							535
One Man Hose Lay	11	12*	8	100																						519
Pumper Spot & Hook-up	7	2	4	12	100																					249
One Man Ladder Handling	3	4	22*	40*	13	100																				508
Hand Traverse	-3	4	5	28*	5	11	100																			524
Scott Air Pak Hardling	7	3	18*	9	1	13	16	100																		520
Ladder Climb (Weight)	0	-1	11	44*	15	41*	27*	22*	100																	514
Ladder Descent (Weight)	5	13*	4	34*	12	30*	26*	4	46*	100																503
Equipment Storage	3	1	7	-10	-16	-4	-7	3	2	-8	100															522
Equipment Inspection	13*	8	4	3	4	7	3	-1	1	4	1	100														511
Pumper Tab	-2	1	6	-2	-9	1	2	-2	16*	3	2	3	100													339
Rescue Technique	0	-1	-1	9	11	0	1	8	5	4	3	-2	0	100												580
Exposure Protection Tab	-5	1	1	8	1	-1	8	2	6	1	-2	-1	-3	12*	100											580
Rescue Equipment Tab	9	9	1	11	10	10	11	-1	12*	9	5	8	18*	10	4	100										580
Ventilation Access Tab	1	0	4	9	-5	12*	8	-2	4	3	2	2	10	9	9	17*	100									580
Order of Ventilation	-1	6	0	0	-1	-4	2	5	1	-1	3	-4	-4	6	0	6	18*	100								580
Method of Ventilation	12*	9	-7	-1	-10	-5	9	0	2	8	0	4	1	1	-4	5	20*	12*	100							580
Ventilation Equipment Tab	-3	-7	16*	0	-7	8	4	9	21*	6	1	1	15*	4	3	20*	14*	0	-2	100						578
Fire Suppression Tab	3	2	12*	3	-12	7	1	-10	3	5	-45	4	10	10	5	16*	21*	7	18*	7	100					578
Salvage & Overhaul Tab	9	1	-1	5	5	3	19*	1	4	6	-2	1	8	10	10	22*	20*	5	13*	9	13*	100				577
Air Pak Tab	5	-2	3	6	-3	12*	13*	5	16*	16*	-4	8	-1	4	8	2	18*	-1	7	20*	2	20*	100			622
Job Knowledge	20*	14*	16*	1	7	2	6	15*	1	-9	8	10	6	11	-4	10	12*	1	7	8	3	7	6	100		617
CPR	20*	15*	6	7	3	2	3	7	13*	10	-2	3	17*	5	-3	16*	4	3	4	14*	6	9	10	36*	100	

Notes:

Decimals omitted, N varies among individual Intercorrelations as reflected

* = Indicates significance at the .01 level

n = Number of firefighters examined

Figure 2—Intercorrelation Matrix For Firefighter Examination Test Battery

To understand the tab test concept you can simply go to your local fast food restaurant, get a value meal and your game card. That's right, you simply print your questions on the left of the page and your answers on the right. Add a feedback column on the right, over print the feedback column with a light coat of clear varnish and then overprint the clear varnish with a little silver nitrate and you have a tab test. One further illustrative example of a tab test question, "To rescue the seven people trapped on the third floor of the involved building requires four pieces of equipment. From the 44 pieces offered, select the four correct pieces." At this point the firefighter begins using a pencil eraser to remove the silver nitrate from the feedback response column until the four correct responses are located.

During data analysis I began to acquire an interest in the problem-solving strategy applied by the various firefighters. If there were only four erasures, the firefighter knew what he was doing. If there were 44 erasures, your firefighter was basically guessing and even then doing a poor job of that. If we had a chance to do it all again, I would ask that the firefighters number their erasures sequentially until the last correct response was located. With the possibility today of a computerized response during data collection, you could even begin to dissect the firefighter's response time in addition to the strategy (s)he employed.

Referring to Figure 2, once again, notice that only the Ventilation Tab Test showed a significant correlation but that was only at the 0.12 level with peer evaluation. The last two items were a job knowledge test and a written CPR test. Job knowledge correlated significantly with peer and supervisory ratings at the 0.20 and 0.14 levels, respectively. The written CPR test significantly correlated with both correlations at the 0.20 and 0.15 levels, respectively.

To evaluate how effectively we had assessed firefighter performance we decided to perform a factor analysis of the Intercorrelation Matrix. With a sample size of 600, we were prepared to make some pretty strong statements. The first step was to convert or transform the performance measures raw scores into standardized scores prior to performing a principal factor analysis. When the resulting Intercorrelation Matrix (Figure 2) was completed it was then factor analyzed. Following on, once the factor analysis was performed, nine factors were found. Figure 3 shows the loadings of the 25 variables across the 9 factors. The performance appraisal seemed to have loaded on a single factor. Loosely interpreted, this means that we're measuring something, but we don't know exactly what it is. We simply know it's not "actual" job performance. An unusual finding was that most of the 25 performance variables only loaded on a single factor. That means that we measured nine independent factors.

Now let's take a brief perusal of the Factor-Loading Matrix of Firefighter Performance Indices (i.e., Figure 3). Factor 1 was clearly one of strength and agility. The tests that loaded on this factor were 50-ft.hose lay, ladder handling, hand traverse, ladder climb and descent with weight. Factor 2 dealt with subjective performance evaluation. Both peer and supervisory evaluations loaded on this factor. Note once again that both evaluations of performance loaded on a separate factor from the other tests.

Factor 3 was centered on applied technical knowledge in emergency situations. The test instruments loaded on this factor include the pumper tab, the rescue tab, the ventilation tab and the written CPR test. All were measures of what to use in an emergency situation to accomplish a specific Task.

Variables	Factor	1	2	3	4	5	6	7	8	9
Peer Evaluation	1	0.02	0.52	0.01	0.04	0.03	-0.01	0.7	0.05	-0.04
Supervisor Evaluation	2	0.09	0.53	-0.03	0.04	-0.12	0.03	0.04	-0.07	0.03
Knots & Ropes	3	0.05	0.12	0.09	-0.01	0	0.47	0.21	-0.07	0.03
One Man Hose Lay	4	0.58	0.12	-0.05	0.06	0.03	0.15	0.01	0.17	0.05
Pumper Spot & Hook-up	5	0.15	0.08	-0.07	-0.16	0.05	0.02	-0.01	0.48	0.11
One Man Ladder Handling	6	0.48	0.03	0	0.03	0.09	0.49	-0.04	0.15	-0.07
Hand Traverse	7	0.38	0.03	0	0.09	0.07	-0.07	0.15	0	0.24
Scott Air Pak Handling	8	0.16	0.01	-0.04	-0.04	0.02	0.12	0.49	-0.04	0.09
Ladder Climb (Weight)	9	0.75	-0.11	0.26	-0.03	0.07	-0.03	0.19	0.4	-0.01
Ladder Descent (Weight)	10	0.62	0.12	0.05	0.01	0.07	0.07	-0.08	0	0.04
Equipment Storage	11	-0.11	0.01	0.07	0.03	-0.05	0.07	0.13	-0.15	-0.02
Equipment Inspection	12	0.02	0.21	0.04	0	0.08	0.01	-0.04	0.03	-0.01
Pumper Tab	13	0.04	-0.01	0.46	0.05	0.03	0	-0.02	-0.09	-0.03
Rescue Technique	14	0.02	-0.03	0.05	0.14	0.02	0	0.1	0.2	0.19
Exposure Protection Tab	15	0.04	-0.07	-0.02	0.05	-0.05	0.02	0.02	0.03	0.25
Rescue Equipment Tab	16	0.08	0.16	0.4	0.14	0.08	0.06	-0.1	0.13	0.3
Ventilation Access Tab	17	0.02	-0.02	0.13	0.53	0.17	0.13	-0.03	0.06	0.14
Order of Ventilation	18	0	-0.01	-0.03	0.27	-0.06	-0.03	0.08	0	0.08
Method of Ventilation	19	0.07	0.16	-0.02	0.43	0.06	-0.18	0	-0.14	-0.01
Ventilation Equipment Tab	20	0.05	-0.08	0.4	0	0.23	0.17	0.1	-0.08	0.14
Fire Suppression Tab	21	0.01	0.06	0.19	0.37	-0.02	0.14	-0.17	-0.06	0.06
Salvage & Overhaul Tab	22	0.05	0.1	0.13	0.22	0.17	-0.16	-0.03	0.09	0.36
Air Pak Tab	23	0.13	0.06	0.03	0.05	0.69	0.02	0.02	-0.03	0.15
Job Knowledge	24	-0.14	0.32	0.22	0.16	0.09	0.06	0.44	0.28	-0.11
CPR	25	0.05	0.31	0.39	0.04	0.1	0.1	0.21	0.15	-0.12

Figure 3—Nine Factors Identified Through Factor Analysis of Firefighter 25 x 25 Intercorrelation Matrix

Factor 4 was associated with firefighting techniques. The tests that loaded on this factor include ventilation access tab, method of ventilation tab and the suppression tab. All of these tests were concerned with what to do and when to do it at the scene of a fire. Factor 5 was a single item factor dealing with equipment troubleshooting. Only the Scott Air Pak tab loaded on this factor. Factor 6 was a manual dexterity and a motor coordination skill factor. The two objective performance tests loading on this factor were ladder handling and the knots and ropes exam.

General job knowledge is dealt with in Factor 7. Loaded on this factor are the job knowledge test and the objective performance measure of Scott Air Pak handling. Factor 8 was a fire apparatus operator factor. The apparatus spot and hook-up test loaded on this factor. Factor 9 dealt with situational problem solving in that salvage and overhaul tabs loaded on this factor.

Meanwhile on the academic front, the terms job analysis and needs assessment (needs analysis) were often "casually dropped" by professors in their conversations regarding the preparation of materials for either personnel or training. But "hands-on" experience was never required either inside or outside the classroom. The possible exceptions may have been as part of either thesis or dissertation research. I personally mastered two job analysis techniques while working with Dr. Ronan: the Critical Incident Technique developed by his major professor at Pittsburgh, Flanagan, and the Position Analysis Questionnaire by McCormick and Jennerette. The "how to" of job analysis or needs assessment was never academically addressed as a part of my graduate curriculum.

Please allow me to share just one more Ronan story. When I informed him that I was accepting a federally funded position in the public sector, he responded, "It'll never work, and your "fool tolerance level" is too low for the public sector. In fact it's probably too low for the private sector where they'd pay you more. You'll only be happy as a consultant. That's where their foolishness can make you rich." I could never dispute the man's logic.

Fortunately my first job after graduate school was as coordinator of a federally funded southeastern personnel research consortium. My assignment was to learn various job analysis techniques. Then I was to train state merit system personnel researchers (responsible for either pre-employment test development/validation or classification/compensation) in NC, SC, TN, GA and FL how to do and use the various job analysis techniques. We were to demonstrate competence in each job analysis technique by doing a pilot project. The job of state trooper was selected for our pilot project. In the coordinator's position, I often found myself wearing different hats, one for test development/validation, one for classification/compensation and yet another for training. Our initial objective was to identify a single job analysis technique, which would provide all requisite data during its collection for use in either test development/validation, classification/compensation and training. Going back time and time again to the same job and often to the same people to conduct additional HR analyses by each HR group had become too expensive and time-consuming.

The two most promising job analysis techniques were Functional Task Analysis (FTA) by Sidney Fine and Domain Sampling by the Minnesota State Personnel Division that deals with the concept of Knowledge, Skills and Abilities (KSA's). Each identified technique had strengths and weaknesses, but no single technique met our initial objective.

Unsuccessful in our attempt to identify a single, all-inclusive, multi-purpose job analysis technique, we decided to develop our own system by drawing on the strengths of existing techniques while trying to eliminate their identified weaknesses. This led to the development of a Technique that we dubbed Process-Based Task Analysis (PBTA) or Task-Based Job Analysis (TBJA).

Task-Based Job Analysis
Process-Based Task Analysis

Basic Definitions

A Job is made up of Processes or Duty Areas or Areas of Job Responsibility. Each Process is composed of a Cluster of related "sequenced" Tasks or Steps that for standardization must be performed the same way each time they are done. Tasks are meaningful pieces of work and refer to, "What is done on the Job". A Step is defined as how to do a meaningful piece of work or "what is done on the job." In my humble opinion, the confusion or breakdown in communications between personnel and training that has existed for years may simply be a matter of semantics. When Trainers speak of Tasks that are in a "sequenced" or "linear" form, in many cases, they should be referred to as being a set of Process Steps. Process Steps may be "flowcharted" or "mapped". Strategic (high-level) Process maps (i.e., like those done by most industrial engineers) are usually composed of Tasks (i.e., what's to be done) presented in either a linear or sequential format. A Process is composed of Steps or Tasks that describe how to do the Job. Tactical (low-level) Process maps (i.e., like those done by most trainers) are presented as Process Steps usually in a linear or sequential format describing "how to do what is done on the Job".

To perform each Task or Process Step requires certain Knowledge (K), Skills (S) and Abilities (A). (A) is defined as an innate capability to do something. (K) is defined as learned or as acquired information or as an understanding of how, when or where something is or can be done. Only when an already present basic capability of (A) exists and is augmented by (K) and followed by PRACTICE, PRACTICE, PRACTICE can a level of Skill (S) or proficiency be achieved. (K's) and (A's) may be thought of as basic qualifiers while (S's) are more quantifiable. When a (S) is identified and recorded during a KSA brainstorming session, there is no need to document the associated (K) or (A). List a (K) or (A) only when its a basic job requirement that the individual must possess but not necessarily be skilled in doing, knowing or using. (S's) can often be used to create simulations (i.e., to check one's speed and accuracy) to differentiate (e.g., spread out or separate) performance levels among applicants (e.g., pre-employment test) or associates (e.g., training—certification testing &/or job performance or performance appraisal).

Worker Traits (WT's) or Worker Characteristics (WC's) are also identified during KSA brainstorming sessions. (WC's) and (WT's) (i.e., state board certified, bonded, licensed etc.) must be possessed by job incumbents and be demonstrated by an applicant or evidenced somehow in the applicant's past.

To further clarify, we nearly all have the (A) to play the drums but only a few of us have the (K) and/or the (S) to play the drums with a symphony orchestra. So, if an applicant is applying for the drummer position with the orchestra, have the applicant demonstrate his/her (S) level by playing a similar work or the actual work for the concert in front of a panel of musicians (judges). Record the session for possible future reference. Then ask the panel to evaluate what they've heard. Simulations have inherit content validity and from a legal (attorney) and logical (applicant/plaintiff's) perspective, appear to measure what they purport to measure.

Simulations take many forms. Probably the most familiar is the simple paper-and-pencil test version of a work sample. In many jobs, reference materials (e.g., formulas, forms, conversion charts, graphs, reference numbers, etc.) are used in conjunction with doing certain aspects of the job. In the testing situation provide separate booklets for questions and for references. An optical scanner answer sheet may be used as the final piece of the testing materials.

I remember identifying a rather complicated false selvage thread-up process in a weaver's job for which I wanted to create a simulation. The corporate training director initially objected to my recommendation. When I asked why he disagreed he replied, "It's too difficult for an applicant to do. It sometimes takes six weeks to teach a trainee how to do it correctly." In a pilot administration to a randomly selected group of applicants, half of which had "zero" weaving experience, fifteen of sixteen successfully performed the complicated false selvage thread-up simulation.

Since (S) assumes the presence of (A) and (K), let's look at a TBJA example for clarification:

JOB: Car Owner.

> PROCESS or
> DUTY AREA: Car Operation Activities
> PROCESS or
> DUTY AREA: Emergency Car Care Activities
> PROCESS or
> DUTY AREA: Car Purchase Activities
> PROCESS or
> DUTY AREA: Car Servicing Activities
> PROCESS or
> DUTY AREA: Scheduled Car Maintenance Activities
>> TASK: Changes oil and oil filter every 3000 miles.
>> TASK: Rotates all four tires every 5000 miles.
>>> (Sequenced) PROCESS STEP: Gets in car and places key in ignition.
>>> KSA: (A) to get in and out of car.
>>> KSA: (A) to identify ignition key.
>>> (Sequenced) PROCESS STEP: Pulls car onto lift rack.
>>> KSA: (S) in driving a car safely.
>>> (Sequenced) PROCESS STEP: Places rack's lifting supports at chassis's lift points.
>>> KSA: (K) of safe lifting points on a car.
>>> (Sequenced) PROCESS STEP: Raises car via lift until tires reach waist level.
>>> KSA: (S) in safely operating a lift.
>>> (Sequenced) PROCESS STEP: Uses screwdriver to remove wheel cover from each tire.
>>> (Sequenced) PROCESS STEP: Places proper socket on lug wrench and removes lug nuts on each wheel.
>>> (Sequenced) PROCESS STEP: Places removed lug nuts in wheel cover and removes the tire from car.
>>> (Sequenced) PROCESS STEP: Places back tires on front of car and front tires on back of car.
>> TASK: Replaces timing belt on engine every 75,000 miles.
>> TASK: Replaces spark plugs every 30,000 miles.
>> TASK: Replaces tires every 40,000 miles or 5 years.

Not all jobs need a detailed Process Based Task analysis or Task Based Job Analysis describing the Tasks or Steps that are done on the job and KSA's required to perform them. These jobs may characteristically have low incumbency rates, be highly undesirable (e.g., septic tank inspector, horse stall cleaner, etc.), have low turnover rates, etc. Strategic or high-level Position Descriptions will suffice. But for those jobs on which detail is truly needed, prioritize the positions to determine which jobs should be analyzed first. The factors to consider when prioritizing can include such things as number of incumbents in the position, salary of position, criticality of the position, legal problems with the position, turnover in the position, etc.

Be careful with and considerate of your potential liabilities when prioritizing. An international pulp and paper company plant needed our assistance because during a plant expansion six years earlier, it created 32 positions staffed on a four-shift rotation basis. That's a total of only 128 people. When a class-action racial discrimination suit was filed six years later challenging their pre-employment testing during the expansion startup, their potential liability appeared small. However, six years later their liability stood at $38 million dollars. What made this assignment so challenging was the fact that all the subject matter experts (SMEs) were the plaintiffs and 15 to 20% of them couldn't even read or write.

Task-Based Job Analysis generally deals with only one job title at a time. A Task-Based Job Analysis does not deal with "how to do the job" but merely with what is done on the job. Process-Based Task Analysis is really just the identification and documentation in rank-order of the calculated importance indices of all the Processes or Tasks performed by a job incumbent.

Flowcharting or process mapping, when performed at a strategic or high-level, lists in sequential order each Task that is performed during the process. Process mapping, when performed at a tactical or low-level, adds the "Step-by-Step" detail of how to successfully perform each Task in its sequential order within the process. In other words, the tactical Step-by-Step detail of how to perform or accomplish each strategic Task is sandwiched in between the Tasks. Process mapping usually cuts across jobs or positions and follows the product flow through a workplace.

End-use of the data generally dictates the method used to collect the data. HRM usually picks Task analysis or "what is done on the job" as its tool of choice. The more enlightened in HRD seem currently enamored with the "when and how to perform" process mapping of the strategic Tasks and tactical Steps involved with product movement through the workplace. The fact that process map training usually cuts across jobs in the workplace facilitates an associate's comprehension and understanding of where, why and how his job fits into the overall process. From a Total Quality Management standpoint, it helps the associate to know the Processes and Tasks his Supplier is to do, the Processes or Tasks he is to perform and which Processes or Tasks his Customer is to perform. The associate soon learns what quality level to expect and accept from his Supplier as well as what quality level (Zero Defects) his Customer expects and will accept from him.

How You And Your Uncle Became So Close

What follows is my over-simplified version of Human Resource history. In the early years of Personnel and Training and before either HRM (Human Resource Management) or HRD (Human Resource Development) existed, there were few, if any, restrictions regarding how HR stuff had to be done. Some employers became greedy and ruthless to the point of taking advantage of employees. Finally employees began attempts to protect themselves by banding together into work groups called unions. Soon both groups were ready to strike their colors. Employers rallied under a flag called "Management" and Employees huddled under a banner called "Labor". Both sides soon began "to kick it up a notch". Labor began using its "strike" and "picket line" weapons. Management retaliated with "scabs" and "strike breakers" and the violence escalated.

Just when things were beginning to look hopelessly out of control, in rides our hero, later to be nicknamed "Uncle Sam", to save the nation's workplaces. Unable to negotiate a quick solution, Uncle Sam decided with his usual infinite wisdom to flex his muscle and thereby bedazzle us with his strength and power, by legislating peace. Uncle Sam whips out his trusty old gavel and pen. With a single "bang" and a simple "stroke", so "birthed" the quagmire of federal HR laws, rules and regulations we know and love today. And to think it all began with the best of bureaucratic "good intentions". This later gave rise to Uncle Sam's now famous introductory remark when sticking his nose into your business, "Hello, I'm from the federal government and I'm here to help!" Today any attempt to accurately and legally perform a set of assigned duties and responsibilities within and between the areas of human resource management and/or development requires the knowledge and skillful use of many analytical tools. Let's take a look at some tools of the trade that I have found to be useful.

My intent is to recommend and share some analytical tools that have worked for me and may benefit you and/or your staff. Always remember, we're just scratching the surface in an emerging field known as Human Resources and, therefore, from an investigative research standpoint, "Nothing's been etched in stone".

The first tool to be explored is Process-Based Task Analysis (PBTS) or Task-Based Job Analysis. Over the years I have found that even big things (e.g., like eating a chocolate elephant), once broken into manageable bit-sized chunks, can be chewed, swallowed and digested with relative ease. After teaching this job analysis technique for six years in a graduate-level course for Webster University, a nine—week course syllabus evolved and will once again have its effectiveness tested.

A consulting simulation format is employed where the trainees are treated like new junior consultants having just joined the firm. Team size for staff development can either be two, three or four junior consultants per lead consultant. The lead consultant's role is to oversee two to four projects running simultaneously and to standardize the associate's data collection and analyses regardless of the position being analyzed.

Each week the two, three or four-person team meets with its lead consultant for four hours to discuss project status and the next week's assignment. The first two hours of each session are devoted to reporting project status with each team member having 15 to 30 minutes to share and report depending on team size. Each team member is responsible for an independent project as well as advising or offering constructive criticism on the projects of other team members.

The second two hours are dedicated to learning what, where, why and how to do the assignment for the next week. The lead consultant explains what, where, why and how of the technique. Then the junior consultants get to practice their technique by rotating in and out of a mock simulation. By the time the session ends, the junior consultants are usually very comfortable with the next week's data collection and analysis assignment for their project. All the formulas necessary for analyzing the data are given during the practice sessions. I am not even opposed to the free-enterprise system, sell the developed software package to the other teams and teach them how to use it.

If any consultant becomes uncomfortable with the "how to" of his data collection or its analysis, he is not to contact the lead consultant but to first seek assistance from (network with) other team members. Team members are responsible for the care and nurture of other team members. This often creates a bonding between team members, not unlike a boot camp experience in the military, which bonding often lasts for years. If the whole team is lost, only then are they to call the lead consultant.

During the six years that I taught the course, I never received one call from my junior consultants. There were often rumors of late night calls and team meetings, but I never asked and they never confirmed it. Kind of like real life stuff, huh? During the ninth week formal presentation, when all the work is behind them, each junior consultant's sense of pride and accomplishment is obvious. "Look at what I've done!" It has been my privilege to observe the phenomena on many occasions and it still warms my heart as an educator every time I experience it. Maybe I've finally become what I have aspired to be, a real coach. I have included the syllabus in the text of this book to demonstrate the use of TBJA.

PROCESS-BASED TASK ANALYSIS
TASK-BASED JOB ANALYSIS
&
HOW TO USE IT
SYLLABUS

1.   Project Description:

Each junior consultant is expected to synthesize and integrate the learning experiences acquired in the first eight sessions and present his project at the ninth session. The project must be proposed to and approved by the lead consultant before the end of the second team meeting. Each junior consultant is responsible for advising, supporting and providing constructive criticism to other team members with regard to their respective projects.

2.   Incoming Competency of Trainee Expected by Lead Consultant:

Each junior consultant will have completed a detailed reading and review of the project syllabus and be ready to discuss his chosen project topic with the Team at the first session.

3.   Project Statement of Objectives:

The lead consultant will oversee and direct the junior consultant's project activities. The junior consultant, acting as either an internal or external consultant, is required to plan, design and implement a practical HR research project applicable to a real-life work situation. Examples of acceptable research projects include:

1.   Development of a content-valid "work simulation" selection test, its pilot administration and evaluation.

2.   Development of an integrated, content-valid performance appraisal instruments containing objective and subjective measures, its pilot administration and assessment.

Once a week the two, three or four person team will meet with the lead consultant for four hours. The first two hours will be used to discuss and share what each junior consultant experienced during completion of the week's assignment (vicarious learning). The last two hours are used to discuss, demonstrate and practice what is to be done for the next week's assignment. Any unanswered questions are cleared up at the end of the session and the junior consultants are sent out "personnel researching". "Hands-on" is the best way to internalize learning. At the team's first organizational meeting, the lead consultant should share an example of any completed projects to clarify the desired project format.

In each research project, a thorough job analysis must be performed and the developed instrument "piloted" on or administered to at least 6 people by someone other than the junior consultant. The intent here is to create a set of standardized administration instructions and procedures for the developed instrument.

26

Following the instrument's pilot administration, the junior consultant is required to analyze, evaluate and write-up recommendations based on the results of his research project. The junior consultant must then prepare and circulate a one-paragraph abstract to the lead consultant and each team member.

As a final requirement, the junior consultant presents the research project's findings to a "mock" board of directors (interested management, peers, family and guests).

The intent is for the junior consultant to leave the project having had a "hands-on" internal or external departmental consulting experience with a real-life piece of HR research.

Instructional methods include traditional lecture, discussion and role-play with coaching. Junior consultants are expected to assist in coaching their team members through the sharing of and advising on project information and procedures.

a.   The junior consultant is to be able to explain HR theories and concepts during discussions and presentations.

The junior consultant demonstrates competence in performing basic HR functions during assignments such as job analysis, work simulation test construction or performance appraisal development, data collection & analysis and project write-ups.

The junior consultant learns to lead task-oriented groups in experiential exercises, job analysis, brainstorming, and work simulation test building. The also learn to perform Task & KSA generation and identification and to develop performance appraisal groups.

4.   Schedule of required readings, meeting preparations and assignments, discussions and management presentations:

Pre-assignment: Have prepared a two-page project proposal detailing the project's experimental design or plan of attack. Have adequate copies for lead consultant and team members.

WEEK 1   INTRODUCTION and EXPECTATIONS
               (4 hours)

(First Half of First Weekly Meeting)

Topics for discussion during the first weekly meeting include: getting acquainted; bilateral expectations; establishment of the consulting firm and coverage of project objectives.

To best lower the anxiety levels and expedite the bonding process, have the team members pair up, interview each other for five minutes and then introduce each other to the other team members. Before the interviewing starts, get the team members to brainstorm for ten things they'd like to know about each other. Write the ten things on a flip chart pad and display the completed sheet at the front of the room.

Simply tell the team what you expect from them during the nine weeks and allow members to verbalize their expectations from you and the project.

Lay the foundations for establishing your consulting firm. You've basically secured a contract to analyze two to four jobs (If doing staff development, make the training both practical and pragmatic. Assign them some jobs you need to have done.) Then they will develop and pilot a battery of content-valid pre-employment tests or performance appraisals for each job within the next nine weeks. Give the team the date (9 weeks into the future) on which a management presentation of contract results has already been scheduled. As the owner of the contract, you can't meet the deadline by yourself. In the consulting business, there seems to ALWAYS be a "feast or famine" dilemma with regard to servicing current customers or soliciting for new business. Do I spend my time marketing for new business or servicing existing clients? It's always a "tight-rope walk" regardless of the path chosen. After reviewing their applicant's resumes you've determined these trainees to be the junior consultants you need to meet the deadline. Now you need their commitment. Once a junior consultant starts he can't quit or drop out. Tell them they're "honor bound" to the contract owner for the next nine weeks, you own them! Remember above all have fun creating your firm.

Junior consultants are to learn PBTA or TBJA techniques by actually performing a job analysis and then creating either a set of selection simulations or a performance appraisal instrument for it.

(Second Half of First Weekly Session)

Project Overview

Things to include in the Project Overview discussion:

- A Table of Contents must be present in the front of your Presentation notebook.
- A strategic process flow chart should be created which details the TBJA process and placed in the presentation notebook for later reference.
- A biographical data sheet on every Subject Matter Expert (SME) used in the project must be contained in the presentation notebook for possible later legal challenges.
- Be sure as a new SME enters the project that they complete a biographical information sheet. List all data (i.e., name, address, phone number, education, work history, recognition, special schools, training, credentials, certifications, licenses) and anything else that will help you sell the individual as a subject matter expert to a judge and/or jury.
- Sample size for this project requires a minimum of eight SMEs. Estimated time and SME requirements for data collection must be submitted to management long before the project commences. (Pad it and don't ever ask for less than you need in the way of support. Get all the commitment you need with regard to manpower and time allocated up front by management. Don't put yourself in the position of having to go back and ask for additional resources just to finish the project. Management's opinion of HR is in enough trouble without loading, cocking and handing them the gun. Be efficient and surprise them. Come in with a good usable result already supported by a group of their people [SMEs] and have the project finished on time and under budget! You'll be well down the road to Respectability.)

Project Estimates of Human Resources
Needed For
Management's Commitment Proposal

Task Generation & Identification—8 SMEs for 1.5-hour session. Schedule for 2.0 hours.
Task rank ordering & Duty Area rank ordering—8 SMEs for 1.5-hour data collection. Schedule for 2.0 hours.
The KSA generation session & the KSA identification session- 8 SMEs for the 1.5-hour session.
KSA-Task Linkage Rating Scale—4 SMEs for 2.0-hour data collection.
Pre-employment Simulation test development pilot administration—4 SME's for four days.
Performance appraisal development—8 SME's for four-days.
Construction and the pilot administration of the performance appraisal instrument—2 SMEs for 4 days.

- A Gantt Chart should be prepared in which a project outline is compared with the project's scheduling to visually display the project's power curve. It will help you visualize the project and quickly alerts you when you're dropping behind the power curve. In other words, a Gantt Chart will help you stay on track and on schedule. The Gantt Chart should be contained in your presentation notebook which is due at the Management Presentation.

- A daily diary should be maintained throughout the project to document things that happen. Again this becomes critical if any test or appraisal prepared from project results is ever legally challenged.

- List any identified entry requirements for the job being analyzed (i.e., bonded, certified, licensed, registered, affiliated, sworn, etc.).

In summary, the final notebook due the ninth week must contain a Table of Contents listing each part of the Project. A strategic-level process map and Gantt Chart are also expected as a piece of the final product. Eight SMEs are required for 1.5-hours for each brainstorming session (e.g., Duty Area/Task, KSA). Each data collection session, Duty Area/Task Ranking and Task-KSA linkages, requires 8 SMEs for 1.5-hours and 4 SMEs for 2.0-hours, respectively. At the beginning of every session require any new attendees to complete a biographical data sheet to document credentials for certification as an SME. Each junior consultant is required to maintain a project diary covering the nine weeks of the project. Each day that planning, researching, telephone calls, delays, obstacles, data collection, analyses, even thinking occurs, it must be documented in the project diary. Someday you may be called into a courtroom and asked why, where, when or how you did something to validate your work. You never know! All I know is that diaries have saved or protected my posterior from going down in flames on more than one occasion.

The final notebook also should contain all completed data collection sheets, a compilation of all resulting analysis and summation sheets, the final developed instrument and its pilot administration materials. In other words, every scrap of paper you generated should be in that notebook. Need you ask why? Because the notebook becomes your personnel reference manual and guide should you ever do this again. A cardboard box (banker's file box) makes an excellent final notebook, if you get my drift. Get in the habit of keeping and storing records. Some day, in your spare time, you may want to drop your Uncle Sam a "thank you" note!

The consulting proposal is presented to and discussed with the other team members. Review other projects to critique and to recommend suggested improvements.
Don't take criticism personally. It's each junior consultant's responsibility to help his other team members with their project as well as to do a personal project. Detecting and correcting the errors of others helps you learn more and best protects the consulting firm's reputation and integrity.

Brainstorm possible pieces of information to include on SME biographical data sheet.

Include qualifying information that would help convince a judge or jury that the SME is indeed an expert. Education, training, experience should be listed. List any special requirements such as certification and licensing.

Assignment for Week 2:

- "Imagineer" the total completed project. Conduct a mental "walk through" of the project. Envision, in your mind's eye, the actual performance of each step of the process.

- Make any necessary revisions to the project proposal and add a nine-week Gantt Chart. Tie events to dates to create your power curve of what has to be done and when to stay on schedule for the presentation. Be sure to specify the number of SMEs needed for each generation and data collection along the time line of the Gantt Chart.

The purpose of the Gantt Chart is to get you organized and to realize that even though the project may seem monumental, as long as you stay on schedule and mutually support the team, it's entirely doable. The Gantt Chart is not only an excellent planning tool but is also a great sales tool when talking with Management. It facilitates Management understanding and awareness of the financial and human resource commitments that must be made to the project as well as the anticipated project benefits. If management later on fails to meet its commitments, the Gantt Chart can also be used as a pretty good club too!

- Prepare a "prototype" of your SME biographical data sheet and make enough copies for distribution to the team members for review and recommendations.

The credentials of the SMEs must be documented to establish their credibility and expertise as part of the TBJA content validation and legal strategies.

- Read and re-read the "Task Brainstorming" and "Affinity Diagramming" handout. Be prepared for in-depth questioning during session.

WEEK 2   BRAINSTORMING FOR THE GENERATION OF TASKS, EDITING OF TASKS AND CLUS-
              TERING Of TASKS INTO DUTY AREAS.
              (4 hours)

(First half of the Second Weekly Meeting)

- Assure that upper management and lead consultant accepts, signs and dates the "finalized" proposal. Management and the lead consultant must be aware and knowledgeable of what has been agreed to and what the project entails. Everybody agrees to what they've heard only after it is in writing.

- Reviews SME biographical data sheets and makes necessary revisions. Include only relevant data that establish the credibility of the SME: title, education, training, years of experience, recognition received, articles published, awards received, etc.

- Conduct lectures and discussions on task-oriented groups and the qualifications and documentation of SMEs. Also discuss the relationship of Total Quality Management (TQM) and its requisite objective performance measures or Key Results Areas—(KRAs) to TBJA with its Knowledge, Skills and Abilities (KSAs) and Worker Traits (WTs)/Worker Characteristics (WCs).

When working with task-oriented groups, you must do your pre-session homework. Have management arrange for you to get together with a SME on his/her turf (work area). Introduce yourself and tell the SME exactly what you're doing and why it's being done (benefits). Next, the SME should be made aware of his/her importance to project success (i.e., credible information, accuracy, deadlines met, etc.). Explain "WIIFM" (What's In It For Me?) to the SME to assure participation is perceived as of some tangible benefit. Confess your ignorance of the job and ask SME to facilitate your knowledge and understanding of the job by show-and-tells, explanations and area tours. This should be done prior to Duty Area/Task generation session. I've been guilty in some tight scheduling situations of taking a 6:00 a.m. familiarization tour for an 8:00 a.m. generation session (not recommended) but after you've done a thousand job analyses, you can quickly pick up what you need. If you don't do the tour, both you and your SMEs will pay the price. Your session will be slower and last longer and be less productive due to communication breakdowns. You won't be perceived as being very professional and your session will not be fun for you or the SMEs.

Complete a biographical data sheet for each person participating in a session. This assures the SME's credentials are documented for inclusion in the project notebook.

If you plan to construct a performance appraisal instrument, the SMEs must identify objective performance measures. In a Total Quality Management environment, objective performance measures are called Key Results Areas (KRAs). The two major requirements of a KRA are that first it must be measurable or quantifiable in some way and second the KRA has to be under the worker's discretion or control.

KSAs are the knowledge, skills and abilities that a worker must possess in order to perform Tasks that result in quantified performance measures called KRAs. So anytime KRAs are mentioned, of paramount interest are the Tasks and KSAs required to achieve the KRAs.

Task Brainstorming Session

The lead consultant starts the Task brainstorming role-play as the session's facilitator. The junior consultants then rotate in and out of the role-play. The team assesses each facilitator's strengths and weaknesses for possible areas of improvement.

The lead consultant writes the definitions for Duty Area and Task on chart paper at the front of the room. A Duty Area is defined as a cluster of related Tasks. A Task is defined as the smallest piece of meaningful work that can be identified.

A group of eight SMEs are asked to brainstorm as the means to identify the Tasks of the job. The junior consultant's assignment is to document the Tasks of the SME's job. Brainstorming greatly reduces the pressure on the SMEs from having to individually write a detailed job description and it's quicker, easier and more fun for them to do.

A unique human trait works in the facilitator's favor during the brainstorming session. Some SMEs feel very uncomfortable when joining a group of strangers. Other SMEs feel somewhat self-conscious and do not like to open up and talk about the feelings and opinions they have. To compensate, the first two questions we usually ask when meeting people are, "What's your name?" and "What do you do?" Roughly one-third of a person's life is spent working. Most people feel much more at ease and less threatened in talking about their jobs and what they do rather than in who they are. A good facilitator taps into this fact. Most people are even flattered if you show a real interest in what they do.

Solicit an outside assistant (another junior consultant if you can get one) to help the junior consultant who's in charge, by documenting the Tasks as they are called out during the brainstorming session. The junior consultant records the Tasks on flip chart sheets as Tasks are identified by the SMEs. The junior consultant, as facilitator, tries to write the identified Tasks in a standardized form (i.e., an action verb followed by a direct object and maybe a short phrase as to why the Task is being done). The function of the assistant is to speed write all Tasks as they are identified and to prevent information from being lost during the more volatile and spirited portions of the session. The facilitator comes back to the assistant, when the identification of additional Tasks slows, to see if anything was missed during the more chaotic portion of the session. A secondary backup to prevent the loss of Tasks is to record and/or videotape the Task generation session. When editing the Task List, the tapes may be "laid back" or "reviewed" at any point for clarification.

Often a brainstorming session parallels the actions of a popcorn popper. Tasks are, at first, identified slowly. Then Task identification may suddenly accelerate with Tasks being generated over the top of each other. Then the speed of Task generation may momentarily stabilize at a steady pace only to later spike up and down randomly. Finally the Task generation slows to virtual stand still and the session is over. The junior consultant's assignment during all this chaos is to document a "rough" Task list that can be edited and cleaned up in a quieter, more peaceful, less stressful situation after the Task generation has ended.

If you enjoy high-pressure, tense and sometimes volatile situations where you have to quickly think on your feet and react swiftly while doing two things at once, you'll love brainstorming for Tasks. The mental stimulation and adrenaline rush are indescribable. I cannot overly stress the importance of pre-session preparation to allow you to visualize and, therefore, verbalize what the SME's are trying to tell you. Familiarization with and recognition of work area jargon, also adds to your credibility and success during the session.

(Second Half of Second Weekly Meeting)

Task Brainstorming Practice Session

As a practice simulation during the weekly team meeting, the lead consultant explains and demonstrates facilitating a brainstorming Task generation session. Since most junior consultants (SME's) have at least some flight experience, I suggest generating the Tasks of an airline flight attendant. This day and age most members of the team have had many hours observing attendants perform their Tasks and for this exercise would qualify as SME's for the flight attendant's job.

Following the lead consultant's demonstration, a volunteer junior consultant is picked to facilitate the practice session. Let the junior consultant start with his/her introduction and go through Task generation and documentation procedures (i.e., action verb, direct object and short phrase about why the Task is done) for four or five Tasks. Stop the generation session and have a critique of the junior consultant's performance. Urge team member evaluators to be candid and honest. Point out that suggestions for improvement are what we want. Remind team members not to take criticisms or suggestions too personally, we are just trying to help them be all they can be as a facilitator. Rotate to a new volunteer junior consultant for generation of six or seven more Tasks and then stop and critique. Remove each completed flip chart sheet and tape the sheet on the wall in full view of the SME's. Continue the rotations until all junior consultants have had the opportunity to practice and be critiqued.

Task Editing

At the conclusion of a Task generation session, the junior consultant has a couple of choices. The junior consultant can immediately start the Task editing process right then and there in the meeting room. The second option is to remove the Task listings from the meeting room walls for later Task editing. When the Task listings are removed, a sequence number should be written at the top of each sheet as it's taken down. Sheets should be folded, stacked in order and stored pending Task editing. As a rule it is best to do editing of the Task List within 24 hours of the session's ending. I'm not sure if this rule evolved from experience or old age but it's always easier working with a "warm" Task list rather than a "cold" one. In fact I have started to tape record Task brainstorming sessions just in case I may later need them to refresh my memory. I've never used the tapes in a legal defense yet, but you never know.

The lead consultant then demonstrates the Task statement editing process (i.e., action verb, direct object and short phrase about why the Task is done) at the front of the room. Allow junior consultants to practice the process by revisiting and editing the Tasks that they generated earlier. Ask for questions and clarify any misunderstandings.

Assignment for Week 3:

- Arrange for, schedule and conduct Task Generation session for the approved job.

The number of Tasks to be identified depends on the size and complexity of the job. I have seen some simplistic assembly line jobs that were comprised of as few as 32 Tasks. I've also analyzed a more complex job that had as many as 142 Tasks. I usually feel pretty comfortable that 90 to 95% of a job's Tasks have been identified when the SME's say, "That's it!" and I'm sitting on 80 to 120 Tasks already listed. I've had some Tasks identified by SME's later after the session ended, but these Tasks usually proved trivial later during the ranking process. I've rarely seen an important Task overlooked when working with at least 8 SME's in the session. If a Task is that important, one of the SME's will identify it during the session. If you should happen to identify a Task that you think has been overlooked, submit it to the SME's. It's still legal and the SME's at least get the opportunity to cull the Task.

Work with management to schedule the required SME's for the Task brainstorming session. The job situation sometimes will dictate who and how many SME's there are. If there's only one job incumbent for the position, use the immediate supervisor as a SME. The person up the process line (the supplier) and the person down the process line (the customer) can also be used as SME's in this case. Former jobholders, maintenance personnel, engineering personnel and relief personnel can be used in a pinch as SME's. In a rotating shift (7-day) situation (4 shifts/one incumbent/shift), you can do weekend sessions, but don't. It'll screw up somebody's long weekend. Minimize SME personal time-off interruption, if possible. Think it through, discuss it with management and the SME's and then decide and execute. Don't under schedule the time you'll need, because management doesn't like surprises. Remember, schedule for two hours and get prior management approval for the overtime. Always schedule and pay two hours for a Task brainstorming session even though you'll probably only need one hour or maybe a little over.

With management assistance, schedule a meeting room for a two-hour Task brainstorming session. The meeting room can be either on-site or off-site. Serve coffee and doughnuts if conducting a morning session. If performing an afternoon session, provide drinks and cookies. Make the atmosphere as relaxed and comfortable as possible. This will increase cooperation and improve productivity. Sessions can be conducted at anytime of the day or night to minimize production interruption. Sessions can be held weekdays or weekends.

• Independently edit the results of the brainstorming session to create an Exhaustive Task List.

Remember our Task editing format is action verb, direct object and, if necessary, a short phrase as to why the Task is done. Let's return to our flight attendant example. One of the attendant Tasks identified during the session might be:

Task 1: Takes orders for and serves refreshments to first class passengers to identify those passengers that are hungry and thirsty.

The above Task masks several meaningful pieces of work. Would it be of interest to know whether orders for drinks are more important, occur more frequently or require more times than orders for food? If so, the Task may be edited into two Tasks that might read:

Task 1: Takes orders for and serves drinks to passengers.
Task 2: Takes orders for and serves food to passengers.

We left off the "because they're hungry and thirsty" because it doesn't add to the meaning and/or understanding of the Task.

Would the placing of orders for alcoholic versus soft drinks be more important, occur more frequently or require more time? The answer is of course, "yes". So, now we have three Tasks.

Task 1: Takes orders for and serves alcoholic drinks to passengers.
Task 2: Takes orders for and serves soft drinks to passengers.
Task 3: Takes orders for and serves food to passengers.

Do the Significance, Time Spent or Frequency of Occurrence on the food issue of snacks versus meals really matter? Again, you bet it does, so we've gained yet another Task for our list:

Task 1: Takes orders for and serves alcoholic drinks to passengers.
Task 2: Takes orders for and serves soft drinks to passengers.
Task 3: Takes orders for and serves snacks to passengers.
Task 4: Takes orders for and serves meals to passengers.

Does it matter on the food issue, whether the passenger orders peanuts or pretzels? Not really! Are we finished yet? No, because if you're going to serve alcohol you'd better check for proof of age on younger-looking passengers. This brings us to another Task:

Task 1: Takes orders for and serves alcoholic drinks to passengers.
Task 2: Takes orders for and serves soft drinks to passengers.
Task 3: Takes orders for and serves snacks to passengers.
Task 4: Takes orders for and serves meals to passengers.
Task 5: Checks proof of age before serving alcohol to younger-looking passengers.

Now do you see what we mean by an "exhaustive" Task List? This example of editing I hope will prove informative and serve as food for thought. Please recognize that there's no absolute right or wrong in the editing process, there are only degrees of right and wrong. With experience comes inner peace and understanding. Sorry, but I've never found a short cut to get there. Upon your arrival at this knowledge plateau, it will become clear what is meant by, "Nobody does it better".

Let's take a look at another job for just a second. Down the road at the local tire store, there is a job called a tire changer. After all, the tire changer's process is linear and starts when the service manager assigns him a car and gives him a write-up paper of what the customer has purchased and wants done to his vehicle. The linear process ends when the tire changer turns in the completed write-up paper for his assigned car. What job could be simpler to document. Off the top of your head, take a guess how many Duty Areas make up this job. There may be one Duty Area, two Duty Areas at the most. Let's not jump to conclusions too fast here.

While all the guy has to do is change tires on a car, that's not really all that is involved. Let's take a little closer look. Besides removing and installing tires, we've already been given the first and last Tasks that we can add. Now we have:

1.   Receives car assignment and job write-up from service manager.
2.   Removes old tires from car.
3.   Installs new tires on car.
4.   Returns "completed" job write-up to service manager.

The next questions are, "Do any Tasks fall between Tasks 1 and 2, Tasks 2 and 3, Tasks 3 and 4?" The answer is surely yes. You can't do Task 2 without performing several additional Tasks or Steps (i.e., Finds car in the "to do" lot from information written on the customer write-up, unlocks and opens car, puts grease protectors on car seats and sits down & closes the door and starts the car, backs out of parking space and drives car to service bay area from "to do" lot, drives car onto lift rack & stops engine, climbs out of car & positions lifters under car frame, operates hydraulic lift & lifts car, removes all for hub caps & obtains pneumatic wrench, finds & installs proper socket (i.e., size, type, standard or metric) on wrench, removes lug nuts with pneumatic wrench, etc.). And there's probably some more that I've overlooked.

Remember that I'm not a certifiable SME on the tire changer job. But I have spent a few nights at Holiday Inn Express. Seriously, the more you do this, the more you catch yourself watching people as they do their jobs.

Try adding Tasks between Tasks 2 and 3 first and then secondly adding Tasks between Tasks 3 and 4 for practice. Think detail, close your eyes and try and visualize a person doing each Task or Step on the job. Always ask the question, "Does anything have to be done before a worker can perform the next Task?"

To check your understanding of Tasks and Steps, please indicate which is which in context of the suggestions offered in the above example. Once again, a Task is the smallest piece of meaningful work that can be identified while Steps are "how to do" the Tasks.

Which of the following Statements is a Task or a Step?

<u>(Draw a circle around "T" if Statement is a Task or "S" if it's a Step.)</u>

#	T	S	Statement
01.	T	S	Finds car in the "to do" lot from information written on the customer write-up.
02.	T	S	Unlocks & opens car.
03.	T	S	Puts grease protectors on car seats & sits down.
04.	T	S	Closes the door & starts the car.
05.	T	S	Backs out of parking space & drives car to service bay area from "to do" lot.
06.	T	S	Drives car onto lift rack & stops engine.
07.	T	S	Climbs out of car & positions lifters under car frame.
08.	T	S	Operates hydraulic lift & lifts car.
09.	T	S	Removes all for hub caps & obtains pneumatic wrench.
10.	T	S	Finds & installs proper socket (i.e., size, type, standard or metric) on wrench.
11.	T	S	Removes lug nuts with pneumatic wrench.

To further increase your confidence level, look at the suggestions you generated between Tasks 2 and 3 and between 3 and 4 above. Did you generate Tasks or Steps? Why all the concern about whether the statement is a Task or a Step? The reason why is because Tasks and Steps break down a job to two different levels. Tasks are at the strategic level (meaningful pieces of work) while Steps are at the tactical level (what has to be done to accomplish a Task). You simply can't mix the two without causing your SME's a lot of agony during the Task rank-ordering data collection on the Significance and Frequency variables. So, it becomes critical that you be able to distinguish between the two (Tasks or Steps) during the editing process.

Often during Task Generation, Steps are listed on the flip chart. Go ahead and write them down. But that doesn't mean that a Step has to end up on the Exhaustive Task List. The Task of which the Steps are a part may never surface during brainstorming. So you must subjectively and intellectually pick up the end of the Step's string during the editing process and trace the Step back to its Task, if possible. If you can't logically establish where it goes, ask a SME.

This may be overkill and I don't mean to be patronizing, but DO NOT LEAVE THIS SECTION UNTIL YOU UNDERSTAND AND CAN DIFFERENTIATE BETWEEN A TASK AND A STEP.

One final example is offered. You have two statements on your flip chart. The first is, "Changes car tire." The second is, "Removes tire from car's axle." Which is a Task and which is a Step? The first question that you need to ask yourself is, "Which is meaningful work?" TBJA approaches job analysis from a strategic perspective. The obvious answer when I'm looking at the job from a strategic perspective is the first one because it involves taking one tire off the car and putting one tire back on the car. Continuing to look at the job at the strategic level, other Tasks are required to accomplish the first statement (i.e., Secures new tire, Jacks/Lifts car, etc. There are also other actions (Steps) from a tactical perspective of how to get the "Changes car tire" Task completed (i.e., Removes jack from trunk, Places jack at safe lifting point, Secures lug wrench, Removes hub cap, Loosens lug nuts, Removes lug nuts, Removes tire from car's axle). That's right ladies and gentlemen; the second statement is a Step of the "Changes car tire" Task. I hope the distinction between Tasks and Steps is now clearer and that the little bulb in your head has been illuminated. (More commonly referred to as "insight" learning.)

Clustering Generated and Identified Tasks Into Duty Areas

Cluster the generated Tasks into Duty Areas. Bring the original flip chart sheets from the brainstorming session and enough copies of the Exhaustive Task List for all team members.

Clustering of Tasks into Duty Areas begins by having each junior consultant read through his/her "completed" Exhaustive Task List several times. S/he then begins searching through the List to see which, if any, Tasks are related or which deal with the same or similar things. To better understand the clustering of Tasks into Duty Areas, let's return to the earlier job example of airline flight attendant.

The lead consultant guides the team through the brainstorming identification of some potential Duty Area names (i.e., Reporting Activities, Passenger Assistance Activities, Emergency Activities, etc.). Write each suggested Duty Area name at the top of a separate page. Write any related Task on the page beneath what you believe is its appropriate Duty Area Title. Mark the Task off on the Exhaustive Task List. Continue the clustering process until all Tasks have been placed under a Duty Area.

Consolidate any Duty Areas with 3 or fewer Tasks clustered underneath. It's even acceptable to have a Duty Area called Miscellaneous. Try your best to logically separate any Duty Areas having 17 or more Tasks listed. Experience suggests anywhere from 4 to 9 Duty Areas with from 4 to 16 Tasks per Duty Area. When the number of acceptable Duty Areas with the appropriate number of Tasks clustered beneath them has been accomplished, compile your Exhaustive (clustered) Task List for the team's critiquing. Make enough copies of your list for the team.

WEEK 3   TASK/DUTY AREA DATA COLLECTION AND ANALYSIS
                      (4 hours)

-       The team reviews and edits each junior consultant's "clustered" Task List. Rank-Ordering of Tasks and Duty Areas on Significance, Time Spent and Frequency of Occurrence is discussed and practiced in mock simulations.

Pick out a junior consultant and ask the volunteer to distribute his/her Exhaustive "clustered" Task List to the team. Also have the junior consultant's original flip chart sheets from the Task brainstorming session taped across the front of the room. By this time, each team member should be well down the road to becoming an expert Task editor. The lead consultant instructs the team to critique the Task List and to challenge Tasks that are not present as well as Tasks that are not understood. Ask the team to be candid with each other in an effort to really make suggested improvements to the Task Lists. Again remind the team to try and keep their egos out of the criticisms that are heard. Continue reviewing Exhaustive Task Lists until each junior consultant's List has been critiqued.

-       Duty Area/Task rank-ordering data collection is explained along with a sample of how to calculate each statistic.

The lead consultant distributes two data collection form formats, one for Task Rank-Ordering (See Figure 4) and one for Duty Area Rank-Ordering (See Figure 5). These data collection formats are used to present the Task List clustered into Duty Areas to the SME's for the Task Rank-Ordering process. As each Task is typed into the format, the Task is assigned a four-digit identification number (i.e., 0101, 0407, 0513,etc.). These numbers are meaningless other than as a tracking mechanism. The first two digits (right justified) indicate the Duty Area and the last two digits (also right justified) identify the Task number within the Duty Area.

The first Duty Area or Process identified is assigned the identification number 0100, the second Duty Area or Process is 0200, and the third is 0300 and so on until all identified Processes or Duty Areas have an assigned number. As Tasks or Steps are clustered within the Duty Area or Process (i.e., 0400), the two digits to the right side indicate only the Task's or the Step's order of assignment (i.e., 0401, 0402, 0403, etc.) to the Duty Area or Process. Once all Tasks or Steps have been transferred onto the data collection formats, begin transferring the Duty Areas or Processes to their data collection format sheet. When all Duty Area or Process and Task or Step statements are transferred to their data collection format sheets, make enough copies of the sets for data collection. See Figure 6 for an example of how a teller rank-ordered the Tasks or Steps of her job. Figure 7 is an example of how a teller rank-ordered the Duty Areas or Processes of her job.

Data Provider _____

Data Collector _____

Task Ranking Data Collection Form

<u>Task Statement</u>

I	T	F	N E	D A	T A

Figure 4—Task Ranking Data Collection Sheet Format.

Data Provider _____
Data Collector _____

Duty Area Ranking Data Collection Form
Duty Area Statement

I	T	F	% J	D A	T A

Figure 5—Duty Area Ranking Data Collection Sheet Forma

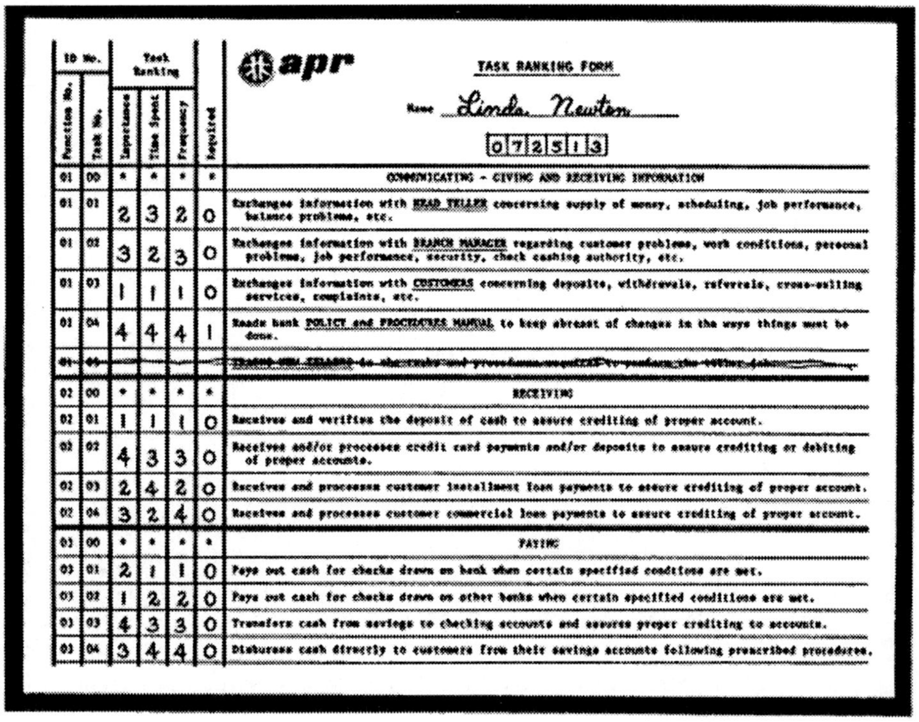

apr

TASK RANKING FORM

Name Linda Newton

0 7 2 5 1 3

Function No.	Task No.	Importance	Time Spent	Frequency	Required	
01	00	*	*	*	*	COMMUNICATING - GIVING AND RECEIVING INFORMATION
01	01	2	3	2	0	Exchanges information with HEAD TELLER concerning supply of money, scheduling, job performance, balance problems, etc.
01	02	3	2	3	0	Exchanges information with BRANCH MANAGER regarding customer problems, work conditions, personal problems, job performance, security, check cashing authority, etc.
01	03	1	1	1	0	Exchanges information with CUSTOMERS concerning deposits, withdrawals, referrals, cross-selling services, complaints, etc.
01	04	4	4	4	1	Reads bank POLICY and PROCEDURES MANUAL to keep abreast of changes in the ways things must be done.
~~01~~	~~05~~					~~[illegible]~~
02	00	*	*	*	*	RECEIVING
02	01	1	1	1	0	Receives and verifies the deposit of cash to assure crediting of proper account.
02	02	4	3	3	0	Receives and/or processes credit card payments and/or deposits to assure crediting or debiting of proper accounts.
02	03	2	4	2	0	Receives and processes customer installment loan payments to assure crediting of proper account.
02	04	3	2	4	0	Receives and processes customer commercial loan payments to assure crediting of proper account.
03	00	*	*	*	*	PAYING
03	01	2	1	1	0	Pays out cash for checks drawn on bank when certain specified conditions are met.
03	02	1	2	2	0	Pays out cash for checks drawn on other banks when certain specified conditions are met.
03	03	4	3	3	0	Transfers cash from savings to checking accounts and assures proper crediting to accounts.
03	04	3	4	4	0	Disburses cash directly to customers from their savings accounts following prescribed procedures.

Figure 6—A Completed Example of a Task or Step Rank Ordering Data Collection Sheet.

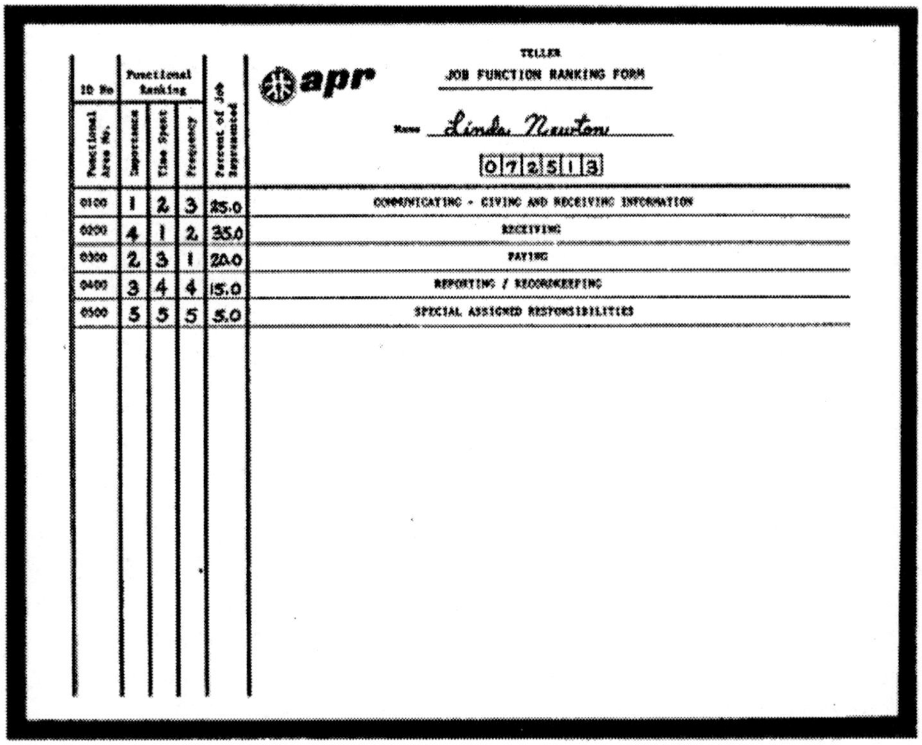

apr

TELLER

JOB FUNCTION RANKING FORM

Name Linda Newton

0 7 2 5 1 3

Functional Area No.	Importance	Time Spent	Frequency	Percent of Job Represented	
0100	1	2	3	25.0	COMMUNICATING - GIVING AND RECEIVING INFORMATION
0200	4	1	2	35.0	RECEIVING
0300	2	3	1	20.0	PAYING
0400	3	4	4	15.0	REPORTING / RECORDKEEPING
0500	5	5	5	5.0	SPECIAL ASSIGNED RESPONSIBILITIES

Figure 7—An Example of a Completed Duty Area Process Data Collection Sheet.

The Task or Step Rank-Ordering Form requires four pieces of data for each Task or Step relative to all other Tasks or Steps <u>within</u> its Duty Area Process:

1) SIGNIFICANCE The rank order of a Task or Step relative to all other Tasks or Steps <u>within</u> its Duty Area or Process.

2) TIME SPENT The rank order of a Task or Step relative to all other Tasks or Steps <u>within</u> its Duty Area or Process.

3) FREQUENCY OF OCCURRENCE The rank order of a Task relative to all other Tasks or Steps <u>within</u> its Duty Area or Process.

4) REQUIRED AT ENTRY indicates whether a Task or Step is "1"-Required or "0"-Not required to be immediately performed by a newly hired employee.

The Duty Area or Process Rank Ordering Form requires four pieces of data for each Duty Area or Process relative to all other Duty Areas or Processes <u>within</u> that Job:

1) SIGNIFICANCE The rank order of Duty Area or Process relative to all other Duty Areas or Processes <u>within</u> that Job.

2) TIME SPENT The rank order of Duty Area or Process relative to all other Duty Areas or Processes <u>within</u> that Job.

3) FREQUENCY OF OCCURRENCE or Processes <u>within</u> that Job.

4) PERCENT OF JOB REPRESENTED is an estimate of the percentage of the Job the Duty Area or Process represents relative to the other Duty Areas or Processes <u>within</u> the Job.

Task or Step Rank Ordering
On
Significance, Time Spent And Frequency

A set of Duty Area or Process and Task or Step Rank Ordering Forms is distributed to each SME by the facilitator (junior consultant) at the beginning of the data collection session. For your consideration and possible use during data collection, a copy of an Instruction Booklet for rank-ordering Tasks or Steps and Duty Areas or Processes is provided in Appendix A. If you desire to use the Instruction Booklet, please feel free to make as many copies as needed. SMEs are also given two sharpened #2 pencils with good erasers. The facilitator then instructs the SMEs to read through the entire Task or Step List and draw a line through any Task or Step that is not a part of the job or that they, as a job incumbent, don't do. The "Read-Through/Mark-Through" segment is done for two reasons:

(1) Some Tasks or Steps are performed only on one shift and need to be documented as such.

(2) No SME should be asked to rank order a Task or Step about which s/he has no knowledge.

Upon completion of the "Read-Through/Mark-Through" assignment, the SMEs are then ready to begin Task or Step rank ordering. The SMEs are instructed to start rank ordering the Tasks or Steps within the first Duty Area or Process based upon each Task's or Step's Importance or criticality to good job performance relative to all the other Tasks or Steps within the Duty Area or Process. The first thing to do is to determine the number of Tasks or Steps to be rank ordered within the first Duty Area or Process. For example, let's assume the first Duty Area or Process has 15 Tasks or Steps within it. Let's further assume 3 Tasks or Steps are dropped after the "Read-Through/Mark-Through" assignment and 12 Tasks or Steps remain to be rank ordered.

Read through the 12 remaining Tasks or Steps and decide which of the Tasks or Steps is number one in Significance to good job performance from within the first Duty Area or Process. Place a "1" in the Significance column beside the "most" Significant Task's or Step's identification number from within the first Duty Area or Process on the Task or Step rank-ordering data collection sheet. Read through the remaining 11 Tasks or Steps in the first Duty Area or Process and pick out the second "most" Significant Task or Step. The second "most" Significant Task or Step from within the first Duty Area or Process gets a "2" placed beside it in the Significance column. The procedure is reiterated until the "least important" or twelfth Task or Step is identified and labeled. Both the SME and junior consultant should carefully check back over the data collection sheets to assure that no rank order number was used for two or more Tasks or Steps within the same Duty Area or Process. Only one Task or Step per rank order number within a Duty Area or Process, please!

Although sometimes a Duty Area's Tasks or Steps appear to be simply a list of the strategic Tasks or Steps composing a linear Process, we're still concerned about which Tasks or Steps are the most important for successful completion of the job. The most time-consuming Tasks or Steps are identified and labeled as you complete the Time Spent rank ordering of the Tasks or Steps. Some Tasks or Steps require more time to do than other Tasks or Steps. When you try to rank order a linear Process on the Frequency of Occurrence variable, you may find yourself having a little trouble when rank ordering. Some Tasks or Steps, even in a linear "sequenced" Process, may have to be re-entered or redone more often than others. When dealing with the Frequency of Occurrence variable it is perfectly legitimate in PBTA for repeating or assigning more than one variable the same value. In fact, if every variable in a "sequenced" Process is rank ordered with a "1" or "2", it doesn't matter. While working on a TBJA project, where the Tasks or Steps are not sequenced, each Task or Step should be given a unique rank ordering number. Think, "Can do" rather than "Can't do" with regard to attitude when doing you're rank ordering Tasks or Steps.

Let me point out that there is no right or wrong answer in the Task or Step/Duty Area or Process rank ordering process. We're purely interested in each SME's independent opinion about the relative Significance of one Task or Step to another. If two Tasks or Steps seem of equal Significance and it becomes a real hassle to decide which Task or Step to put before the other, don't worry about it. Just go ahead on "gut feeling" and pick one or the other and don't give your decision another thought. It all works out when the Importance Indexes are calculated.

Remember, we're dealing with probably the lowest and simplest form of the job in this analysis. Is it "A" or "B"? I'm NOT asking, of measurement here, "Which one is more Significant in performing the Task" or "How much more Significant is Task A than Task B?" That's too hard for a person to measure; and besides I don't really care how much more Significant one Task is than the other!

I believe in making my research questions and answers simple and easy. The data we receive when rank ordering the Tasks are called "ordinal" data. In the wonderfully "manipulative" world of statistics, measurement doesn't get any lower or more basic than this. What makes this data so good is that statistically you can't legitimately throw ordinal data into some high-powered statistical device to manipulate the results (e.g., Change the answer). One of the two Tasks being considered for each decision has to be more Important than the other Task.

The more SMEs you have rank ordering the Tasks, the stronger your data becomes. With a minimum of eight SME's (composed of immediate supervisors and incumbents) to rank order the Tasks, the data are strong and stable. As human beings, we tend to have different opinions and perceptions. I routinely "eyeball" raw data collection forms as they are turned in just to get an idea of stability. In our previous example of 12 Tasks to rank order within a Duty Area, here's my pre-analysis prediction. Pick the first data sheet to be turned in and record SME 1's responses.

SME 1	SME 2	SME 3	SME 4	SME 5	SME 6	SME 7	SME 8
5	6	5	6	4	8	6	6
8	9	7	9	8	4	8	9
9	7	9	10	9	5	9	8
1	2	1	1	1	12	1	2
4	3	4	4	5	9	4	3
6	7	8	7	6	7	7	7
12	12	11	11	12	1	12	11
7	5	6	5	7	6	5	5
11	11	12	12	11	2	10	12
3	4	3	2	3	10	3	4
2	1	2	3	2	11	2	1
10	10	10	8	10	3	11	10

Based on a visual comparison of SME 1's data with that data provided by the other seven SMEs (e.g., 2, 3, 4, 5, 6, 7, 8), the group appears to be relatively consistent and in agreement. The responses for each SME are different but not radically different. They don't wander too far from the quadrants designated by SME 1's responses.

Now look at SME 6's data as compared to the others. Where's he coming from or what's he trying to do? I shared this with you even though I've only seen it once. Oddly enough, the data came from an older supervisor who had been passed over for promotion and decided to sabotage the company's project with us by supplying totally erroneous data from what he knew to be right. Interestingly enough he was one of eight respondents, so we analyzed the project data three different ways. But first we got another supervisor to provide us with some replacement data. One analysis was run with the old supervisor's data included, a second analysis was run with the new supervisory data and a third analysis was run without either supervisor's data. The subsequent rank orderings from most to least Calculated Importance Indices differed, but only slightly. Some Tasks only moved two to three rank ordering positions (within a quartile). When a Task's rank orders were compared across the three analyses, in other words, the final rank ordering results were remarkably stable!

In a previous illustration where we had only one job incumbent in the position, as long as he was providing his opinion or input, you had a 100% sample size on which to base your findings. My major professor in grad school once told me, there was only one thing that all statisticians agreed upon, "All other statisticians are wrong. If you don't get the answer that you want when you finish your research project, don't fret; just find yourself a good statistician. Just give him your data and the answer that you want. Given enough time, he'll figure out a way to support it!" Enough levity, let's get back to Tasks. Continue rank ordering Tasks within the rest of the Duty Areas until you have identified and labeled the "least" Frequently performed Task within the last Duty Area (The next to the last sheet in the data collection booklet).

The next step is crucial to later calculations. Go back and verify your rank orderings. It may sound nitpicking but there must be no rank order number used greater than the number of Tasks to be rank ordered. Every number between "1" and the number of Tasks to be rank ordered within the Duty Area must be used once and only once! No omissions are acceptable! Do not duplicate rank order numbers within a Duty Area!

Proceed to the second Duty Area listed on the data collection form. Apply the same steps for the rank ordering of Tasks on the relative Significance of one Task to another within the Duty Area:

    (1)   Read through the remaining Tasks in the next Duty Area after the Read-Through/Mark-Through.
    (2)   Determine the Number of Tasks in the Duty Area to be rank ordered.
    (3)   Rank Order the Tasks within the Duty Area.
    (4)   Verify the accuracy of the Task rank ordering within the Duty Area.

Continue rank ordering the remaining Tasks within each successive Duty Area until all remaining Tasks within each respective Duty Area is rank ordered from "most" Important to "least" Important on job performance. Through research and experience I've discovered that rank ordering is easier for SMEs when they're allowed to concentrate on a single variable (i.e., Significance, Time Spent or Frequency). The SMEs are more productive, quicker, less distracted, less stressed and less fatigued after working through the Task/Duty Area data collection booklet one variable at a time. It is much more productive with one variable than to be constantly switching back and forth among multiple variables.

Identification of Minimum Qualification Task

Now, there's one final piece of information I need to know about the Tasks you perform on the job. There are some Tasks on the job that require a long time to learn to perform well. Other Tasks take just a short while to master. We would like to identify those Tasks that upon arriving at the job you should be able to do and do well on the first day with minimal or no instruction as being "required" Tasks. These Tasks then become the minimum qualification requirements. It does not matter where the task was ranked "most" or "least" important. What matters now is the question, "Must an applicant be able to perform this Task before coming to the job?" If the answer is "yes", please place a "1" in the "Required" column beside the Task identification number. If the answer is "no", please place a "0" in the "Required" column beside the Task identification number. Calculate the percentage of the SMEs group indicating the Task is "needed at entry" to the job.

Process Rank Ordering
Or
Duty Area Rank Ordering
On
Significance, Time Spent And Frequency

You now have one data collection sheet left to complete in your booklet, the Process Rank Ordering or Duty Area Rank Ordering page. Read through the Process or Duty Area titles. Some Processes or Duty Areas are only performed on one shift. "Are any Processes or Duty Areas listed in which you do not perform any Tasks? If so, draw a line through the Process or Duty Area on your Process Rank Ordering or Duty Area Rank Ordering Form."

Please rank order the Processes or Duty Areas that remain on:

(1)   Significance of the Process or Duty Area and its Tasks to good job performance relative to the other Processes or Duty Areas and their Tasks.
(2)   Time Spent doing Tasks within the Process or Duty Area relative to the time spent doing work on Tasks within the other Processes or Duty Areas.
(3)   Frequency with which Tasks within the Process or Duty Area are performed relative to the Tasks within the other Processes or Duty Areas.

Upon completion of the Process or Duty Area rank ordering, ask the SME's to please review their Process or Duty Area rank orderings to assure there are no omissions or duplications of rank ordering numbers. Then tell the SMEs, "There's one more piece of information about the Processes or Duty Areas that's needed. Please estimate, to the best of your ability, what percentage of the job each Process or Duty Area represents. There are no right or wrong answers when making these estimates. Simply put what you feel or think the percentages are. In the column entitled "% of Job Represented", place your best guess or estimate beside each of the Process or Duty Area identification numbers on the data collection sheet. Then carefully add together your estimates for the Processes or Duty Areas to assure they total to 100%. If they do not add up to 100, adjust your estimates until they do equal 100. You have now completed filling out all the data collection forms. Place the forms in their proper sequence (i.e., 1,2,3,4,5, etc.) to aid in data entry and give your data collection booklet to the session facilitator. Data collection for Process/Rank Ordering or Duty Area/Task Rank Ordering is now complete."

Process
Or
Duty Area/Task
Rank Ordering Analysis
Formulas

Calculated Importance Index for each Task:

$$\text{CII (Task \#)} = 1\frac{(\Sigma \text{ Signif. (Task \#)})}{N} + 2\frac{(\Sigma \text{ Time Spent (Task \#)})}{N} + 3\frac{(\Sigma \text{ Freq (Task\#)})}{N}$$

Where:

CII (Task #) is the Calculated Importance Index for a given Task #.

$1\frac{(\Sigma \text{ Signif. (Task \#)})}{N}$ is the sum of all the Significance rank ordering values given for the Task or Step # divided by the number of rank orderings the Task or Step # received. In other words, the numerical average of the Task or Step #'s Significance rank orderings is multiplied by a weighting factor of 1.

$2\frac{(\Sigma \text{ Time Spent (Task \#)})}{N}$ is the sum of all the Time Spent rank-ordering values given for the Task # divided by the number of rankings the Task # received. In other words, the numerical average of the Task's Time Spent rank-orderings is multiplied by a weighting factor of 2.

$3\frac{(\Sigma \text{ Freq (Task\#)})}{N}$ is the sum of all the Frequency of Occurrence values given for the Task or Step # divided by the number of rankings the Task or Step # received. In other words, the numerical average of the Task's or Step's Frequency of Occurrence rank orderings is multiplied by a weighting factor of 3.

The Task or Step Ranking Calculated Importance Index formula appears on the surface to be very simplistic. The amount of thought and effort that went into the formula's development is almost inconceivable. The chief co-developers of this formula, Dr. W. Boyd LeGrand and I, spent two long years researching the literature and endlessly debating the theory and logic behind the formula.

To determine the impact of a Task or Step on a job requires a couple of operational definitions. A Step is the smallest meaningful piece of tactical-level work that can be identified. A cluster of related tactical-level Steps of the "how to" pieces of work combine to form a Task or if sequential, a linear Process. A Task is the smallest meaningful piece of strategic-level work that can be identified. A Process is a sequential or linear cluster of related Tasks or Steps. A Cluster of related but non-linear Tasks combine to form Duty Areas, Functions or Areas of Responsibility. A Job is composed of Process, Duty Areas, Functions or Areas of Responsibility.

Tasks or Steps within Duty Areas or Processes and across the Job vary on three key variables:

1)   The Importance to the job or Significance to good job performance.
2)   The Amount of Time Spent or required to perform the Tasks or Steps.
3)   The Frequency of Occurrence or how often the Tasks or Steps are performed.

Ratings across the three variables, whether using a 5-point, a 7-point or even a 9-point rating scale, usually fail to differentiate if one Task or Step is more important than another. A large group of Tasks or Steps always seem to have the same average value on any rating scale used. Therefore, we eventually settled on the Rank-Ordering of Tasks or Steps within their respective Process or Duty Area plus the Rank-Ordering of Processes or Duty Areas to help alleviate the differentiation issue. The resulting rank-ordered numbers yield an almost unique value for every Task or Step and Process or Duty Area.

Another year and a half of research with many different jobs coupled with experimentation and feedback from panel after panel of SME's was required to identify the proper relationships and subsequent weightings of the three variables. We found SME agreement with Task or Step rank-ordering results within Processes or Duty Areas were the greatest when the Significance rank-ordering received twice the weighting of the Time Spent rank-ordering and the three times the weighting of the Frequency rank-ordering. SME's supported the same weightings for Process or Duty Area rank-ordering results.

Logically all of the "most important" Tasks or Steps are not necessarily contained in the "most important" Process or Duty Area. Each Process or Duty Area contains at least one or two of the more important Tasks or Steps within the job. By multiplying the Calculated Importance Index of each Step or Task within the Process or Duty Area by the Process's or Duty Area's Calculated Importance Index, we ultimately achieved an almost unique number for each Step's or Task's Weighted Calculated Importance Index.

The Weighted Calculated Importance Index methodology allows us to spread the Tasks or Steps out along a continuum ranging from least important (highest CII (Weighted)) to most important (lowest CII (Weighted)). The relative importance of Tasks or Steps could then be compared both within the Processes or Duty Areas as well as across the job as a whole. When I say compared, I'm referring to one Task or Step being more important than another Task or Step. Be careful to notice that I'm not looking at the Task's or Step's Weighted Calculated Importance Index and saying one Task is 50% more important than another Task. Nor am I saying that a Task or Step is three times as important as another Task or Step. To put it simply, all I can say confidently is that one Task or Step is more important than another Task or Step based on the opinions of a group of subject matter experts. That's one small step for job analysis but one helleva giant leap for Human Resources.

You must be aware of a couple of important points to remember regarding Calculated Importance Indices. CII's are still ordinal data. That means you can say one Task or Step is more important than another Task or Step, but you can't say how much more important one Task or Step is than another. Also, always remember a Calculated Importance Index (whether it be a Task, a Step a Duty Area or a Weighted Calculated Importance Index) is like a golf score, the lower the number, the higher the Task's or Step's value and the greater the Task's or Step's relative importance.

Calculated Importance Index for each Process or Duty Area:

$$\text{CII (DA \#)} = \frac{1(\Sigma \text{ Signif. (DA \#))}}{N} + \frac{2(\Sigma \text{ Time Spent (DA \#))}}{N} + \frac{3(\Sigma \text{ Freq (DA \#))}}{N}$$

Where:

CII (DA #) is the Calculated Importance Index for a given Duty Area or Process #.

$\dfrac{1(\Sigma \text{ Signif (DA \#)})}{N}$ is the sum of all the Significance rank-ordering values given for the Duty Area or Process # divided by the number of Rank-orderings the Duty Area or Process # received. In other words, this is the numerical average of Significance rank-orderings for the Duty Area or Process # multiplied by a Weighting factor of 1.

$\dfrac{2(\Sigma \text{ Time Spent (DA \#)})}{N}$ is the sum of all the Time Spent rank-ordering values given for the Duty Area or Process divided by the Number of rank-orderings the Duty Area or Process # Received. In other words, the numerical average of Time Spent rank-orderings for the Duty Area or Process # multiplied by a weighting factor of 2.

$\dfrac{3(\Sigma \text{ Freq (DA \#)})}{N}$ is the sum of all the Frequency of Occurrence rank-ordering values given for the Duty Area or Process # divided by the number of rank-orderings the Duty Area or Process # received. In other words, the numerical average Frequency of Occurrence rank-orderings value for the Duty Area or Process # is multiplied by a weighting factor of 3.

Weighted Calculated Importance Index For Each Task or Step:

CII (Weighted) = CI-I (Task #) X CII (DA #)

Where:

CII (Weighted)   is a virtually unique rank-order value indicating the ordinal relationship between and amongst the Tasks or Steps as to their overall Significance to good job performance. The lower the value of the CII (Weighted), the higher the Task's or Step's or the Duty Area's or Process's Significance to good job performance.

CII (Task #)   is the Calculated Importance Index for a given Task or Step #.

CII (DA #)   is the Calculated Importance Index for the Task's Duty Area or the Step's Process #.

The CII (Weighted) allows the Calculated Importance Index of a Task's Duty Area or the Step's Process to impact the Task's or Step's rank-order position relative to all other Tasks Steps across the job. The logic and rationale of how Tasks or Steps relate with each other is also influenced by the relationship of its Duty Area's or Process's Calculated Importance Index. It is a relatively simple and straightforward concept and should be easily understood. The Calculated Importance Index, whether Weighted, Duty Area or Task, continues to be interpreted the same

Percentage of Job Make-Up Represented
by Duty Areas or Process Formula

$$\% \text{ of Job Represented (DA \#)} = \dfrac{\Sigma \text{ \% Estimates (DA \#}}{N}$$

Where:

% of Job Represented (DA #) is the Average Percentage of the Job Represented by the given Duty Area or Process #.

$\dfrac{\Sigma\ \%\ \text{Estimates (DA \#)}}{N}$ is the Sum of the Percentage Estimates Received for a given Duty Area # divided by the Number of Estimates received. In other words, it is the Percentage of the Job represented by the given Duty Area or Process #.

Percentage of Job Make-Up Represented
by Each Task or Step Formula

% of Job Represented (Task #) = $\dfrac{\text{\% of Job Represented (DA \#)}}{N}$

Where:

% of Job Represented (Task #)   is the Average Percentage of the Job Represented by the given Task or Step #.

% of Job Represented (DA #)   is the % of Job Represented by a given Duty Area Process # divided by the Number of Tasks Steps in that Duty Area or Process. In other words, it is the Percentage of the Job represented by any given Task Step # within the Duty Area Process #.

To determine the % of the Job Represented by each Task or Step within a given Duty Area or Process, divide the Percentage of the Job represented by the Duty Area or Process by the number of Tasks or Steps ranked within the Duty Area or Process. This approach provides a very conservative estimate of the percentage of job make-up a given Task or Step represents.

Assignment for Week 4:

"Where's the Beef?" Well in last week's assignment according to the old Cajun Chef, "wez maid up a tastee batch of "meat'n taters," put'em in tha ov'n an "thangs heat'd up reel fas". Furst wez gotta turnsup tha heat'n on'em "meat'n taters", ta git tha roast'n dun'n than we's gotta serv'm up nic'n cronchy far suppa." Seriously, week four is the "real meat" of the Project. You've got a lot to get done and a very short time frame in which to do it. So I've taken the liberty to <u>recap extensively</u> with each assignment for the week.

•   Make necessary revisions to "clustered" Exhaustive Task List and transfer Tasks and Duty Areas to Task/Duty Area Rank-Ordering Data Collection Forms.

After each junior consultant's "clustered" Exhaustive Task List has been reviewed, any identified helpful suggestions, criticisms and recommendations are then incorporated into the Task List. The revised Duty Areas and Tasks are then transferred to their respective Rank-Ordering data collection forms. The lead consultant provides formats for data collection forms. When transferring the Duty Areas and Tasks onto the data collection forms, we have now reached a point where tracking becomes critical.

I suggest that you assign the number "0100" to the first Duty Area you put on the data collection form. Each related Tasks clustered within that Duty Area is then listed under the Duty Area and assigned a tracking number beginning with "0101". The first two places identify the Duty Area (range 1 to 99) and the second two places identify the Task (range 1 to 99). The second Duty Area becomes "0200" and its first Task (0201). These numbers have no useful purpose other than identification and tracking.

Make enough copies of the data collection forms to create a booklet for each SME containing the Tasks to be rank-ordered within their respective Duty Areas and a sheet of Duty Areas to be rank-ordered. A minimum of eight SME's (some supervisors and some incumbents) is required. The more SME's you have, the better and stronger your information becomes. If the SME population is relatively small, say 10 to 15, I'd suggest using a universal sample size.

I have had the occasion to be asked by the SME's what they should put with regard to rank-ordering when they are faced with two Tasks which they feel are of equal rank-order on the variable on which they are working. My advice to simply assign a number by "gut feeling" to one Task the next rank-order number and continue on, giving the other Task the next number. Don't let the SMEs get hung up on which Task is first, that is why we say we just want their opinion. After all is said and done, it all straightens itself out when you start averaging the SMEs' opinions any way.

•   Collect "completed" Tasks and Duty Area Rank-Orderings from the SME's.

It takes approximately one hour to rank-order about 100 Tasks spread out over 8 Duty Areas. I suggest that the Task/Duty Area Ranking data collection session with the SMEs be scheduled for two hours. Two hours should be more than adequate to complete the Rank-Orderings data collection. Make sure that all data collection sheets are completely filled out. Turn especially to the Duty Area data collection sheet and verify the SME's total for the Percentage of the Job Represented. The percentage estimates given by each SME across the Duty Areas must equal 100 on every completed Duty Area Rank-Ordering data collection sheet.

Crunching Task/Duty Area Numbers

I recommend that three separate analyses be performed on the Task/Duty Area data. Run one analysis on just the management data, another on just the incumbent data and a third and final composite analysis on the combined data of both groups. Think for a second, "Why three separate analyses?" Could either group have an agenda? Possibly, one might. This is simply a cross validation (a sort of check and balance) of inter-rater reliability to determine if anything is going on. Don't expect the rank-orderings to be identical, but don't expect them to be that far apart either. If the project is not part of a compensation study, it's your decision and your responsibility. Remember, you're probably going to use the composite anyway.

⌨   Calculate separate numerical averages for each of the three variables (i.e., Significance, Time Spent and Frequency) for each unique Task # contained on the Task Rank-Ordering data collection forms.

Sum the SME-assigned rank-order numerical values for each of the three variables on each unique Task #. The numerical average for each of the three variables is determined when you divide each of their sums by the number of SMEs who rank-ordered that Task #.

⌨   Determine the % of SMEs indicating that each unique Task # is "Needed at Entry".

Said a different way, a new-hire must be able to perform the given Task # with minimal or no training on the first day of work. This is accomplished by simply counting the number of SME's placing a "1" in the "Needed at Entry" column beside that Task # on the Task Rank-Ordering data collection sheet.

⌨   Calculate separate numerical averages for each of the three variables (i.e., Significance, Time Spent and Frequency) for each Duty Area # contained on the Duty Area Rank-Ordering data collection form.

Sum the SME-assigned rank-order numerical values for each of the three variables on each Duty Area #. The numerical average is determined for each of the three variables, when you divide each of their sums by the number of SMEs who rank-ordered that Duty Area #.

⌨   Determine the % of Job Make-up Represented by each Duty Area.

Sum the estimates given by the SMEs' % of Make-up Represented for each Duty Area across the Job. Divide the sum of the estimates by the number of SMEs that gave estimates.

⌨   Determine the Calculated Importance Index CII (Task #) for each Task.

The next set of numbers to be crunched should be the Calculated Importance Indexes for each of the Tasks within a given Duty Area. This is done to establish the rank-ordering of the Tasks within that Duty Area from most important (lowest CII) to least important (highest CII).

⌨   Determine the CII (DA #) for each Duty Area.

Each Duty Area's numerical average is calculated for Significance, Time Spent and Frequency. Those three sums are multiplied by the appropriate weighting (i.e., 1, 2 or 3) to determine each Duty Area's CII (DA #). Here the SMEs are considering one cluster of related Tasks as opposed to all the other clusters.

⌨   Determine the Percentage Make-Up of the Job Represented by each Duty Area and by each Task within the Duty Area.

This once again is a simple matter of determining the average percentage make-up of the job a Duty Area represents by summing the SME's responses and then dividing that sum by the number of responses received. The % of the Job represented by the Duty Area is then divided by the number of Tasks within the Duty Area to determine a conservative estimate of each Task's contribution percentage wise to the job as a whole.

⌨   Determine the CII (Weighted) for each Task.

Each Task within a Duty Area has its Calculated Importance Index multiplied by its Duty Area's Calculated Importance Index. The "weighted" Calculated Importance Index that results allows the comparison of Tasks on Significance to good Job Performance across the entire job without regard to Duty Areas. The greater or closer the consensus among SMEs as to a Task's or Duty Area's rank-order, the lower the Calculated Importance Index, hence the more Significant to good Job Performance the Task or Duty Area.

⌨   Prepare a List of Tasks in Descending Order of Importance from Most to Least Importance without regard to Duty Area. Use CII (Weighted) going from smallest to largest values. Bring enough copies for the team.

Look through the "weighted" Calculated Importance Indexes for the Tasks and locate the Task with the smallest Index. Place the Task Statement, its Tracking Number, the Percentage of the Job Represented by the Task and the cumulative percentage of the Job Represented as each successive Task is added to the top of the List. Locate the Task with the next lowest Index and move that Task to the List. Continue doing this until all the Tasks are included on the List and the last Task, the one with the highest index, is at the bottom of the List. Notice how the Tasks from the most important Duty Area are distributed throughout the List. Notice where the most important Task from the least important Duty Area is located within the List. Check out the least important Task in the most important Duty Area and locate it within the List.

⌨   Prepare a List of Tasks in Descending Order of Importance from Most to Least Importance within each Duty Area. Use CII (DA #) and CII (Weighted) calculations going from smallest to largest values to construct this List. Bring enough copies for each member of the team.

Look through the Duty Area Calculated Importance Indexes. Locate the Duty Area with the lowest Index. Place the Duty Area, its CII (DA #) and the Duty Area's Tracking Number at the top of the List. Locate the Task within the Duty Area that has the lowest CII (Weighted). Place this Task, its Tracking Number, its CII (Weighted), its percent of Job Make-up Represented by the Task and the cumulative percent of Job Make-up Represented by each successive Task as each Task is added to the List immediately under its Duty Area. Find the second lowest Task CII (Weighted) and place the Task, its CII (Weighted), its percent of Job Make-up, its cumulative percent of Job Make-up and the Task Tracking Number on the List. Continue the process until all the Tasks within the Duty Area are present on the List under the Duty Area. Next, locate the second lowest CII (DA #) and place that Duty Area on the List. Locate the Task within the second most important Duty Area that has the lowest CII (Weighted) and place the Task and its associated information on the List. Continue this process until the least important Duty Area and the Tasks within the Duty Area have been added to the List.

⌨   Review handout on KSAs and objective performance measures or Key Results Areas (KRAs) related to performance appraisals. Handouts to be furnished by the lead consultant during the third session.

WEEK 4   BRAINSTORMING FOR QUANTIFIABLE KSAs AND KEY RESULT AREAS (KRAs).
(4 hours)

KSA Brainstorming

Each junior consultant's Duty Area and Task rank-ordered data are reviewed. Each junior consultant distributes his/her two Task Lists (both within "Duty Area" and "without regard to Duty Area") to their team members. This is done to allow the sharing of results as well as the gathering of feedback.

A second brainstorming session is scheduled for two hours with a group of 6 to 8 SMEs to generate and identify quantifiable KSAs.

It doesn't matter if you choose an on-site or off-site location for the brainstorming session. Again, make the meeting room as comfortable and as relaxed an environment as possible. Good food and beverages should be provided. Contrary to public opinion, a SME group is like the Army, it moves on its stomach. What really counts is that the space is quiet, with no interruptions if possible.

The SMEs are told that the purpose of the session is to list and identify the Knowledge, Skills and Abilities (KSAs) required to successfully perform the Job. Also to be identified are the Key Results Areas (KRAs) by which Job success or failure is determined. The only requirement placed upon KSA and KRA generation and identification is that they must be quantifiable or measurable in some way. Again it's a good idea to have an assistant, tape recorder or camcorder to help prevent the loss of data.

The first thing that must be done is to establish a "Cut Score" for the "most important" Tasks on the Task List.

The SMEs are shown how to use the Task List (without regard to Duty Area) to identify the transitional point at which the Significance of the Tasks to good Job Performance begins to deteriorate. The transition usually occurs somewhere between the cumulative percentages of 50% to 75%. Study each Task List and you'll begin to notice, as you're reading down the List from most to least important, that the Tasks representing the lowest 25% to 50% of the Job don't really carry much weight.

When SMEs are asked to consider the significance to overall performance on the Job of the lower 50 to 25% of Tasks, they report little if any impact. In other words, whether these Tasks are performed exceptionally well or are not performed at all, overall performance on the Job is not really affected or impacted. After using this technique for a while, you too will begin to notice this transition point in the List where Tasks seem to become more trivial. Rather than rely on my own subjective judgment, I submit the question of the existence, and if so identification, of the transition point to the SMEs.

•   The "most important" Tasks are used for stimulus/response generation and identification of measurable and/or quantifiable KSAs.

Why did we even consider the idea of a possible transition point on the Task List? By identifying the transition point, we have reduced the number of Task Stimuli, from a statistical and legal perspective, to be considered during the brainstorming session. Why brainstorm for the KSA's necessary to perform a trivial Task? Don't waste valuable time when you can legally and effectively eliminate 25% to 50% of the work to be done. Furthermore, why identify KSAs during brainstorming which are not quantifiable or measurable? If you don't see a way to measure the KSA as it is identified, immediately ask the SMEs how to quantify the KSA. If the SMEs can't tell you how to measure the KSA, don't even write it down on your chart pad. Remember always the old adage, "If you can't measure it, you can't manage it!"

For the generation and identification of measurable and/or quantifiable KSAs, an age-old psychological approach, known as stimulus-response, is used. "Let's look at the first Task on the List. What measurable or quantifiable Knowledge, Skills or Abilities are required or must be possessed in order to perform this Task?" Record the SME-identified KSAs on a flip chart pad. Do not attempt to write down linkages during the brainstorming, just write down the measurable and/or quantifiable KSAs. The assistant also stays pretty busy taking down KSAs as they are generated and identified. During lulls in the brainstorming, the assistant can share any KSAs that have been generated but not discussed and recorded. When all measurable KSAs have been recorded on the chart pad, the session is dismissed. Normally 25 to 75 KSAs are identified for a Job. The measurable aspect whittles down the number (usually to between 25 and 40) of KSAs with which you have to work.

For KSA referencing and tracking, a three-digit (right justified) identification number (i.e., 001, 003, 007) is assigned to each KSA that survives the editing process. The three digits are used for KSA identification for several reasons. It allows KSA generation beyond the 100 barrier, in fact up to the 999 barrier, if needed. Three-digit KSAs seldom get mixed or confused with four-digit Duty Area/Tasks. Three and four digits give the junior consultant more than adequate identification, storage and retrieval of project data. Edit the KSA List to assure clarity and conciseness. It's helpful if the number of KSAs is reduced to between 20 and 30. If during the editing process you discover a "missed" K, S or A, go ahead and list it, it's perfectly legal. After all the SME's can cull it during their KSA-Task Linkage session. The lead consultant provides the format for the KSA-Task Linkage data collection Form during the fourth weekly session.

•   The junior consultants are asked to role-play as facilitator in a "mock" KSA generation and brainstorming session.

During the second half of the weekly meeting, the lead consultant allows a junior consultant volunteer to conduct a KSA brainstorming. The lead consultant gives the junior consultant a list of Tasks from the flight attendant example used in session three. This list has been rank-ordered without regard to Duty Area. The volunteer practices establishing a transition cut score for the Task List. This step reduces the number of Task stimuli used in KSA generation. The junior consultant introduces the concept of a KSA being measurable or quantifiable before it's listed. A KSA provides no usable information unless it is measurable or quantifiable in some way.

"Non measurable or non-quantifiable KSA's will be culled as they are generated during the session. I just wanted you to know what I'd be doing. If I can't see how to measure a KSA, I'll ask you to tell me how we can do it and then I'll write it down. If you and I can't figure out how to measure it, maybe some of the other intellectual experts in here can give us a way to measure it!"

"Today we're only going to work with the upper 66% of the "Most Important" Tasks. We'll start at the top and work down. Now, let's take the "most important" Task. What KSA's have to be possessed to perform this Task well?"

After a couple of Tasks have been exhausted, start the rotation of junior consultant volunteers. When everyone has had an opportunity to practice KSA generation, ask for questions, answer any questions, pat them on the head and send them forth.

KRA Brainstorming

•   During this session, the concept of KRA's and the requirement that they be measurable, quantifiable and controllable are explained and discussed.

For every Job there are three, four or five areas that are essential to real success. Management has begun to refer to these as Key Results Areas or KRA's. Other companies are using a concept called Management By Objectives or MBO's. No matter what the Performance Evaluation system in use or what the KRA's are called, this 'area of responsibility' concept is the current rage.

On a personal note, the first time I was involved in using a MBO system I overheard this conversation among a group of supervisors. "Performance appraisals, I've always hated that part of the job. You know, having to figure out some creative way to say the same thing over and over every year. About this new MBO system, it ain't half bad. I just give the associate the creative writing part and when he finishes, I can just edit what he's written and slap on some 7 % improvement numbers for him to meet. When I get the typed appraisal back from our secretary, I pull him in, tell him to sign it and turn it in." I mention this because it illustrates many of my concerns in this area.

What is the purpose of a performance evaluation system? A performance evaluation system usually serves two functions. One function is as a feedback system for an associate's personal development. It's a tool used by supervisors to communicate identified deficiencies as well as management's recommendations and suggestions on how to improve performance. The second function is to document and/or justify the receipt or denial of increased compensation. Regarding personal development, the performance appraisal is also meant to serve as a motivational tool.

I have always believed that performance evaluation for personal development should be separated from compensation. This point was driven home for me one summer when I was involved in some volunteer work with a group of minority middle-school students. It was the first year of a program to provide summer employment opportunities for kids that had been identified as "at risk".

Community leaders had put together a lawn maintenance business where the city, through a federal grant, provided gasoline, lawnmowers, a telephone and a college intern for the summer to coordinate the program (to handle calls, schedule and pass out assignments, etc.). Lawn cutting services were provided for free to senior citizens over 65 years of age and living within the project's work zone. The 30 participants in the summer program were told to check in for assignments twice per day (8-9 a.m. and 12 noon to 1 p.m.). Local churches, two radio stations and a neighborhood newspaper kept our cutting appointment log pretty full. As long as the kids physically checked in twice a day, they received four hours pay whether or not they were assigned one yard, two yards or no yards. As extra motivation, the kids were told that if they averaged cutting ten yards a week for the six weeks of the project, they would also receive a new bicycle. They were allowed to request extra assignments, if needed, to obtain or maintain their cutting average of ten lawns cut per week over the six week period.

The beginning excitement of the project in the community was contagious. The first two weeks were outstanding. The second two weeks it started downhill and by the last two weeks, there was out and out dissension both among the kids and among the volunteers. Despite numerous available extra assignments and with twenty bright and shiny new bikes already in stock in our inventory, only two girls and one boy had qualified for the bikes at the program's end out of the thirty kids participating. The board of directors viewed our motivational program as a pending disaster on the self-esteem of the 27 other kids in our program. Over my strong opposition, the volunteer board overturned the motivational part of the project, raised money in the two churches for ten more bikes and gave every participant a bike.

The city later asked my assistance in evaluating the program's first year and making recommendations for improvement. I picked six program kids to give me feedback, the three kids that qualified for the bikes and three who had not. In a closed session, I posed the question, "What things did you see as wrong with the project and how could we fix them for next year?" The silence was almost deafening for about a minute and a half as I was praying that they had understood the question and were just thinking of what to say. Finally one 13-year-old girl who had qualified for a bike raised her hand. The simplicity of what she said has stayed with me ever since. She questioned me, "Why should we cut the grass when you're going to give us the bike any way?" Out of the mouths of babes come words of wisdom. In other words, every time we mistakenly compensate or reward an "undeserving" or non-productive employee, we're de-motivating our producers.

Compensation problems occur in industry as well. Let's look at an industrial example.

A company with a shortage of funds due to an economic downturn came up with what they thought was a unique public relations idea. They would call a cost-of-living adjustment a merit increase. With much hoopla the company announced that instead of a cost-of-living raise this year, The Board of Directors has decided to implement a merit pay increase program. Under the merit increase program the top producers would get a maximum increase of 3%, average producers would get around 2% and low producers would receive nothing higher than a 1% raise.

One of the largest problems the Board unknowingly faced was the lack of good objective performance system with which to differentiate producers from non-producers. Bit of a snare, huh? Panic suddenly struck and questions began to fly fast and furious. When should an employee get a raise? Is it after a certain length of time on the job? Is it after a certain amount of job knowledge is gained? My answer to their questions was, "Nope, I feel the only time a raise can be justified is when there is a productivity increase, more product or service is produced or provided for the same or less cost. Otherwise, you'll quickly find your bottom line changing from black to red."

The Board in their infinite wisdom said they already had the money in their budget and were simply changing the line item name. I was politely told thanks but no thanks for my concerns. They had a brilliant solution of their own and were going to implement it. They stuck with their original merit increase idea and of the three, two and one percent increases. But they told their supervisors in a closed meeting to give everybody the 3% increase. Suddenly my phone began to ring off the hook with questions from supervisors asking me what they should do. I could only encourage them to follow the party line as closely as possible and then to keep their heads down.

I'd finally experienced first hand exactly what my first shift supervisor, a non-high school graduate, meant after previewing the content of the first management presentation I was preparing for the regional VP and our upper plant management. He said, "No, no, no Andy, you gotta bring this stuff on down. Always remember, the higher the level of management you're presenting to, the more you have to dumb it on down so they can understand it. It ain't that they're stupid or nothing, but they don't always understand how things get done."

It took about two weeks for the full impact of the bomb's destructive blast and the subsequent turbulence it created among the ranks to be realized. For the first time the Board began to acknowledge the complexity of the interrelationships among motivation, personal development, morale, performance appraisal, selection, promotion, downsizing, training, etc. when communications are disrupted. The Board had taken the company's associates from disgruntled to the verge of a nuclear meltdown.

Not intending to belabor the point, but let's take a look at some of the situations this incident created:

- 7% of the workforce was downsized three weeks after they were given raises documenting their outstanding performance.

- Several associates were terminated for poor performance within five days of receiving a documented raise for outstanding performance.

- Poor producers who had had supervisors documenting their cases as poor performers to the left and right were suddenly told they were outstanding performers and were given the maximum raise allowed by the company.

- Outstanding producers instantly lost their motivation and desire and ultimately stopped producing.

- Morale was non-existent among associates as well as management. Employees at all levels began to speak of feeling betrayed by their leaders.

I only hope by now we have conveyed some information on why it is important to get compensation information correctly reported. What is the best way to identify a KRA? The answer seems to be in small, task-oriented groups evenly represented by associates and supervisors and led by a HR facilitator. The team serves three functions. First, the group must identify a mutually agreeable KRA. Secondly, members must reach consensus that the position being evaluated has sole possession and control of the identified KRA. Thirdly, the group must successfully negotiate how the identified KRA will be measured or quantified. There are not to be any secrets or hidden agendas in these sessions, cooperation is mandatory.

KRA Brainstorming
Practice Session

Brainstorming of acceptable KRAs is demonstrated.

The lead consultant selects a volunteer junior consultant to facilitate the team through a practice session on KRA generation. A Bank Branch Manager's job is chosen as an illustrative example for KRA generation.

For instance, management as a KRA might suggest the number of new business accounts opened. The branch managers would then argue, "That depends on where your branch is located. If you were in an economically depressed area, your goose would be cooked. If you were in an economically booming area, you could basically exceed your new business goal sitting on your butt in the office just handling walk-ins. In fact, we don't really have any control of that." The facilitator then probes, "What do you have control of in this situation?" At this point we're hopeful that things begin to germinate in the group with thoughts and ideas being shared and discussed. "We do have control of the number of presentations we make to new potential business accounts. We also control our initiative in contacting economically-depressed accounts in an attempt to come up with work out options." This is the kind of dialogue that will develop with some facilitator nursing of the two camps. Try in the measurement phase to pin your performance variable down to a percentage figure. This will make your performance numbers easier to work with on the performance appraisal and to compare between incumbents. Remember that, if a performance variable can be measured and the job incumbents do control it, it might just be the KRA for which we've been looking. And you can take that one to the bank!

Every consultant will not get to practice KRA generation in a "hands-on" situation during the session. It's simply too time consuming. Once you understand the concept and for what you are looking, it's not that difficult. In fact it's pretty stimulating and can become intoxicating to the group. I've had sessions interrupted by management saying, "Why haven't we been doing this all along? It makes more sense to do it this way". Every once in a while you can even get one of those rare, "make my day" comments like, "Why hasn't our HR shared this with us before?"

Through experience I have found it best to schedule KRA generation sessions in two-hour blocks. That's going to be about all anyone can handle should the emotions begin running too high. You can always schedule additional sessions at a later date when stress and tension levels have dropped.

Assignment for Week 5:

- Conduct a brainstorming session with the SME's to identify an Exhaustive List of measurable, testable or quantifiable KSA's.

- Individually edit the Exhaustive KSA List to make it clear and concise. Make and bring enough copies for the team.

- Conduct a KRA brainstorming session to identify measurable, quantifiable objective performance measures over which job incumbents have control. Make sure the measures are presented in percentages.

- Individually review and edit the Exhaustive KRA List to make the KRA's clear and concise. Make and bring enough copies for the team.

WEEK 5   KSA-TASK LINKAGE DATA COLLECTION and ANALYSIS
                  (4 hours)

KSA Editing

- The Team edits each consultant's KSA List.

The instructor asks for a volunteer to distribute the Exhaustive KSA List for review by the group. If any questionable KSA's are observed, with regard to measurability, ask the presenter to explain and defend their presence on the List. This is done to allow information exchange as well as to provide learning opportunities.

KSA-Task Linkage
Data Collection

• Explain and discuss KSA-Task Linkage Data collection and analysis procedures.

The lead consultant provides a KSA-Task Linkage format to facilitate data collection. This is where things begin to come together from the standpoint of Tasks and KSA's. We simply position the Exhaustive KSA List under each of the "most important" Tasks above the cut-score (transition point) on the rank-ordered Exhaustive Task List. Rather than have the consultant arbitrarily select which KSA's to submit for SME's verification, I recommend that, if possible, you submit the entire Exhaustive KSA List under each Task and let the SME's do the culling. In other words, let the SME's control the linkage completely and keep the consultant out of any conflict or prejudicial accusations.

Notice that this is the first time we have asked the SME's to use a rating scale to indicate the amount or degree of the relationship between two variables. Here we want to learn two important pieces of information about the linkage of a KSA to a Task. Does the KSA even have a linkage or relationship to the Task being performed? Secondly, if there is a relationship, does the KSA "simply make performance of the Task easier" or does the KSA absolutely have to be present for the Task to be performed? In other words, can the Task even be performed without the presence of the KSA? If not, the KSA is said to be "essential to Task performance".

Please also note that the Linkage Rating Scale is on a seven-point Likert-type rating scale. The intent is to provide as much valid differentiation as possible in terms of the relevance of a KSA to Task performance. Please point out that the rating scale values are reversed. The lower the rating scales value the higher the degree of the relationship between KSA and Task. Once again there is no right or wrong answer, we're simply asking for opinions. Be sure the SME's understand the 7-point rating scale (e.g., ranging from 1—"essential" to 7—"not related") before leaving them to their rating.

Tell them, "Whether you get 'an insight in your brain' or a 'feeling in your gut', it doesn't matter, just mark the response and continue. Don't get hung up trying to figure out exactly what to put, trust your instincts." The KSA-Task Linkage is very critical to validation but is also very time-consuming and tiring. For this reason, the minimum requirement for sample size has been reduced to four SME's and the time requirement has been extended from two hours to four hours to assure adequate time is allocated for data completion. The actual completion time for data collection usually runs just under two hours.

Get as comfortable a place as you can find for the SME's to work. Explain what you want and how you want it done, turn them loose and get out of the way. When they have completed their assignment, ask them to check over the material to be sure that nothing remains to be done. Double check data collection forms as SME's turn in their materials, thank the SME's for cooperating and dismiss them as they finish.

KSA/Task Linkage
Data Analysis

Start the analysis with the "most important" Task. Use a 7-point Likert-type rating scale. The scale values should be anchored at high end of the scale (1) with Essential, in the middle with a 4 (Useful) and at the low end of the scale with a 7 ("Not-related"). Two pieces of information are of importance for each possible KSA-Task Linkage. First, the total number of raters indicating a Task-Linkage for each KSA at a rating scale value of "4" or below (3,2,1) is recorded. And secondly, the average Task-Linkage rating scale value calculated for each KSA is recorded. The lower the value, the higher the KSA's rank-ordering.

Prepare a List of KSA-Task Linkages in descending order of importance ranging from the lowest rating scale value of 1 to the highest rating scale value of 6. List the rank-order of the KSA, the KSA, the KSA's average Task-Linkage rating scale value and the number of SME's who had rated its Task- Linkage at either a 4, 3, 2 or 1 level.

Validation Strategies

- The lead consultant explains and discusses various validation strategies and techniques.

- Let's take a look at the validation strategy employed for Task-Based Job Analysis. It is based in a Content Validation Strategy where you must establish a direct linkage between what you're doing and the job. We started with the job that was divided into Duty Areas or Areas of Responsibility. Each Duty Area was in turn composed of Tasks. Tasks were broken down in one of two ways. One method involves the introduction of Steps to be completed in order to accomplish the Task and the second method identifies the Knowledge, Skills and Abilities necessary to perform the Task. If Tests are used and their relationship to the K, S or A established via SME's, the Tests are said to be Content-Valid. Simulations of Tasks or of the Steps which make-up the Task possess a further unique characteristic which we have jokingly termed "face validity", meaning it appears to measure what it purports to measure. From a scientific or legal standpoint face validity is a meaningless term, but in real world situations, most attorneys are very hesitant to take on a test that has "face validity".

Task-Based Job Analysis can also be used in establishing criterion validity. But criterion validation is seldom used in "real world" situations because its methodology is so expensive and time-consuming as to deem the technique impractical. By its very nature, TBJA is Content Valid. TBJA has been found very useful in "predictive validity" studies where performance on a pre-employment test (best with simulations) predicts later performance on the job. In more than twelve projects I have consistently found applicant performance levels on pre-employment simulations which closely mimic the actual job to be roughly one-third of the applicant's later potential performance level after training and some experience on the job.

Assignment for Week 6:

- Make needed revisions to Exhaustive KSA List and transfer KSA's and "most important" Tasks to KSA-Task Linkage data collection form. The lead consultant provides the format for the KSA-Task Linkage data collection form.

- Collect the completed KSA-Task Linkage ratings from the SME's.

- Determine the average KSA-Task Linkage rating value for each KSA.

- Determine the number of raw data KSA-Task Linkages at a rating value of 4 or below for each KSA.

- Prepare a list of KSA's in descending order from the most to the least important. Use average KSA-Task linkage ratings ranging from the lowest number of 1 to the highest number of 7. Also list beside each KSA the number of times each respondent linked a Task to the KSA at a rating value of 4 or below. Make and bring enough copies to share your List with the team.

- Study the handouts on performance appraisals and work simulation tests. Be prepared for in-depth questioning during class.

WEEK 6   WORK SIMULATION TEST OR PERFORMANCE APPRAISAL DEVELOPMENT
              (4 hours)

•   Each consultant's KSA-Task Linkage rating data are reviewed.

The lead consultant allows a junior consultant volunteer to distribute his KSA-Task Linkage List in Descending Order of Importance. Any questionable linkages or rating scale values should be identified and discussed by the Team. Close attention should be paid to the KSA's at the top of the List. We try to make sure these KSA's are included in any testing or performance appraisal being considered. The Linkage from KSA to test item or performance appraisal variable further assures the Content Validity of whatever is constructed.

•   The concepts of work simulation testing and performance appraisal development are explained and discussed.

Now you have created a rank-ordered KSA/Task Linkage List. These Linkages contain the basic building blocks necessary to construct a legally defensible and content-valid instrument for selection, training, classification, compensation or performance evaluation for the job. Proper execution is achieved through the implementation of the following regimen:

(1).   The team is given a playbook (process maps) to study and learn.

(2).   The team trains on the playbook (process maps) in the classroom (learns process flow and how to perform its Tasks & Steps).

(3).   The team practices (process flows) on-site (allows applied hands-on experience).

(4).   The team repeats playbook (process maps) classroom training to "internalize" the process flows (Tasks & Steps).

(5).   The team returns on-site for additional hands-on practice of the process flows.

Through many literature searches on the relationship between actual performance on the job and performance appraisals, the correlation usually found is at the 0.10 level or below. Often objective performance measures are used in conjunction with subjective performance appraisals.

My contention is that management will never give up its performance appraisal. So it's our job to try and increase the inter-correlation between subjective evaluation and actual data. The trouble with most performance appraisals is that they don't incorporate any objective performance variables. Even if an evaluation instrument does contain some objective measures, they probably aren't under the direct control of the person being evaluated. Therefore, "What two criteria must be met before any correlation can be increased?" Valid performance measures must be objective and be under direct control of the person being evaluated.

Increases in the inter-correlation between objective measures and subjective performance appraisals can best be achieved by presenting each of the job's "most important" Tasks to a group of SME's. Then you can ask them how to objectively evaluate the outstanding performance of each "most important" Task. For the objective measure to be listed requires consensus SME agreement that the person being evaluated be in sole control and using his or her own initiative. Who knows the most about doing the Tasks of a job? A job incumbent does. Who best knows how to objectively evaluate performance of a Task? The job incumbent is best equipped. Who is most often asked to identify and how to quantify objective measures? The answer is usually supervision or engineering. They have different insights, supervision because it has a broader view and engineering because it designed the job. I wouldn't even object to using incumbents, supervision and engineering all together in a group to debate and argue control issues of the identified objectives. It stands to reason that debate would only make it better. Throw some brains at it. Think about the pros and cons of the measure. Could the measure be distorted or altered?

I pose this question because once as a supervisor I was evaluated on how well I kept my operators on their assignments at shift change rather than letting them stop work early. The on-coming shift was allowed to make a clean waste break within the first ten minutes of their shift. The amount of waste was used to estimate how long a windup position running at a speed of 120 miles per hour was out of production. The on-coming shift then weighed and charged me back with the waste that they had collected. Thus my performance was determined and compared with the other shifts. Some of my people worked over on the on-coming shift usually called "working a double". They reported back to me that the clean waste break was happening thirty minutes after shift change instead of ten minutes. The other shift was also reported to be throwing used metal parts in with the waste to make my weights heavier. Even though three out of four shifts were playing it straight, the measure, as a performance indicator, had to go. Finally after much accusation and heated discussion, another supposedly objective measure "bites the dust" because the person being evaluated didn't have control of the variable being measured.

The concept of pre-employment work simulation testing represents the fairest evaluation of a job applicant's potential. I have never had any questions raised about work simulation tests. Race or sex performance concerns have never been raised either. All that most people want when applying for a job is to have the opportunity to show what they can do and that's exactly what they're given.

I remember in one textile project when we were asked to prepare a pre-employment test for loom fixers. The existing SMEs told me that the job was so physically demanding that women would never be able to do it. I was told the loom fixers had to lift a 175-pound electric motor to and from its installation mounting some thirty inches above the operating floor. Upon further questioning I discovered that the loom fixers used a portable winch when handling electric motors. Thereby, bringing up another concern, never take anybody's word as "gospel", always check things out to be sure. To make my point, we successfully developed and implemented an appropriate set of simulations.

6 female incumbents took and passed the set of simulations. One female told me that after gaining more exposure to the loom fixer job during the simulations, she decided not to pursue the job any further. She said, "I did it but I didn't like it. Now I know I can do it and so does everybody else! I'm just no longer interested." What more could you want to hear from a formerly disgruntled operator who had threatened to sue for sex discrimination? Simulations also favor people who know or have had "good" experience on the job. That's a good deal for management as well as the applicant.

NO ONE EVER FAILS A WORK SIMULATION PRE-EMPLOYMENT TEST. They simply don't score high enough in the rank ordering of applicants to ever be considered for the job. As a decision-maker, you know exactly how far your new hire has to come to meet the engineering-established speed and accuracy production standards. Re-testing is allowed and is completely logical and defensible. It places the burden of proof of skill improvement squarely on the applicant's shoulders.

Have you ever been asked to ramp up a project ahead of schedule and found yourself pulling people from training programs before they've completed training? Simulations can tell you and management exactly where the trainee's strengths and weaknesses are and how much skill improvement is needed. Simulations can take the guesswork out of keeping an existing employee or replacing him with a new employee. You can know what you've got as well as what you're going to get. You can establish a specified and legally defensible time within which the trainee must be able to produce at or above an engineering-established "certified" production standard. Have you ever been able to really use the probationary period to cull a poor performer before s/he gains full employment rights or is probation just another company myth? You now have the tools to change things. Now the only thing that is holding your organization back is a lack of imagination and the intestinal fortitude to push the envelope.

Being in the staffing and training segment of the logistics and distribution business for several years gave me the opportunity to make great use of simulation testing. I found simulations to be quick to construct and there always seemed to be an abundance of potential test administrators. Applicants will tell you anything they think you want to hear during a job interview, "Yeah, I've used that forklift for ten years at another company and there's nothing I can't do with it." That's when I love to get into my act, "Well, I'm from Missouri, so why don't you come over here and show me what you can do?" Some can and some can't successfully negotiate the simulation. And the beauty of the simulation is "the applicant has to be able to put his money where his mouth is". With the help of a couple of pallets of previously damaged goods, a dozen danger cones to restrict maneuverability, some empty rack shelving and a forklift and to the applicant's surprise, you've differentiated the "can do's" from the "can't do's". You don't even have to be a forklift driver to tell if he can "walk the talk".

• Use the "most important" Tasks and the "most important" KSA's to construct appropriate work simulations or Tasks related to KRA performance identified.

The next step is to regroup two or three of the sharpest SMEs to help structure the simulations as closely as possible to the "identified" Tasks. In other words, they can assist in feasibility determinations, help with substitutions, identify equipment required, suggest locations and best times for testing and can later serve as test administrators. Get them invested and keep them involved. These resources are your ultimate keys to the success or failure of what you're trying to accomplish. Make sure to make them feel as special as they are.

When building a work simulation, be sure to build the simulation as close to the actual Task as possible. For instance, in one TBJA project we encountered several very similar clerical positions. These positions were in a clerical pool supporting nine young engineers. The "most important" Task across the clerical positions was "Prepares business correspondence to go out over the boss's signature." The "most important" KSA's were "S in preparing business correspondence" and "S in the use of dictation equipment." Part of the pre-employment test we prepared for this job involved the typing of a business letter and its mailing envelope from a cassette tape. Since there were nine possible sources from which work could come, we asked each of the nine engineers to compose a typical two-paragraph business letter and make a personal cassette of it. We then arranged for access to one of the actual vacant clerical workstations. We, therefore, were able to have applicants tested on the same hardware and software as that used on the job.

Applicants were given a business letter and envelope from which to glean the desired set-up and format. Applicants then drew three cassettes from the nine available. Each applicant was individually timed on the preparation of three business letters and their envelopes. Scoring was accomplished by taking the Total Time Required To Complete each of the three business letters and their envelopes along with the number of errors they contained. So we had the beginnings of a Content-Valid pre-employment test on which we had three Speed and Accuracy performance measures for each applicant on their typing skills.

Let's look at another practical application of pre-employment testing. In a rather bold and daring strategic move, an American textile firm had bet its future on a five-year "exclusive purchaser agreement" with a Japanese equipment manufacturer producing an air-jet weaving machine which produced cloth four times faster than traditional weaving machines (looms). The Japanese firm had already sent a four-man team over and they had trained the existing plant training team consisting of a lead trainer and her four associate trainers. Sixteen weeks of broken English interspersed with outbursts and tirades of Japanese with much head shaking and the current training staff was pronounced, "trained". To further complicate the situation, the Japanese literally did everything by hand rather than use instruments (i.e., reed hooks, scissors, tweezers, etc.). The Japanese had also employed the "Sit-By-Nellie" training technique. Before going any further, let's take look at some of the obstacles to learning present with this technique.

First you have to really be sure Nellie knows the job. Is she a good trainer? Has she ever been trained-to-train? Does she know where to position trainees for her Task demonstrations? Are trainees seeing Tasks demonstrated from the reverse angle from the way they'll have to perform them later? Is the trainee only seeing the back of Nellie's head and shoulders and not the demonstration? Does she face the trainees when she speaks to them during demonstrations or just speak back over her shoulder? Does she have any speech problems during her communications? Does she know how to focus their eyes when she's demonstrating? And this list of concerns is by no means exhaustive.

The tactical plan for the plant modernization had been to layoff all current weavers for a week and then bring some of them back (pick the cream of the crop) into a ten-week training program for the air-jet machines. Then the production ramp up would involve pulling freshly trained weavers from training to the operating floor just as each new set of air-jet machines were installed and ready to go.

The best two trainees were pulled and placed on the operating floor. Things from a production standpoint did not go well. Neither of their top two trainees could even come close to meeting the production standards rate that had been established by the Industrial Engineering department. And that was after 10 weeks of hands on, one-on-one training. Management just crossed their fingers and hoped the trainees were just having a bad day, and then later, they crossed their arms and hoped they were just having a bad week. More trainees were brought over to the operating floor from training with the same results. Frustration levels increased on both sides and then it started to happen, absenteeism, no shows, resignations and firings. Turnover began to soar to levels of 500 to 600%. We were asked by a rather desperate corporate training director to see if we could help reduce the turnover rate.

Upon completion of a TBJA using the training team and the currently best available weavers, we prepared the Duty Area/Tasks List In Descending Order Of Importance as usual. We then added a "reversed" 7-point rating scale to create a Needs Assessment that was administered to the trainers, supervisors and weavers. The Rating Scale on the Needs Assessment ranged from "Don't have a clue how to do it" on the 7 end of the scale to "Could be the master trainer on how to do it" on the 1 end of the scale. This data, when analyzed, yielded not only what percentage of the weavers felt they needed help, but also more specifically the exact assistance required. Moreover, the supervisors were asked to assess each of their employees for two reasons. First, any employees who mistakenly believe they know what they're doing were identified. Secondly, it forced supervisors to take a closer look at each employee's performance. The trainers' feedback provided a third set of perceptions. Once the problem training areas were identified and the results coordinated with the Descending Order Of Importance Task List, several Tasks were selected for use in simulation development.

One of the Tasks chosen for simulation use was the replacement of the false selvage transfer bobbin. We discovered also that this Task was critical to continuous weaving machine operation. Also in the lead trainer's opinion, six to eight weeks training was required before the bobbin string-up procedure could be consistently and correctly performed. We used the assigned SME's to identify the Steps (i.e., 18 Steps with 54 possible Total Tech Pts.) required for performance of the transfer bobbin Task. Once the Steps were documented, the performance of the Task was story boarded with a Polaroid and scripted for videotaping and 35mm photography. We created a "picture book" training manual, a videotape of the simulation, and a performance score sheet for false selvage bobbin replacement (See Figure 10).

Applicant's Name _____ SSN _____ - ____ -_____

Date _____ Test Administrator's Name _____

FALSE SELVAGE PACKAGE REPLACEMENT AND THREAD-UP SCORE SHEET

(Place a check mark beneath each statement that best describes what the Applicant did.)

1.   Shook drop wire swing handle:
        [] Successfully completed   [] Attempted   [] Did not try
2.   Opened false selvage case, removed empty cones from holding pins, took off socks and carried empty cones to supply cabinet.
        [] Successfully completed   [] Attempted   [] Did not try
3.   Obtained full cones from storage cabinet, placed socks on cones and placed cones on holding pins in case.
        [] Successfully completed   [] Attempted   [] Did not try
4.   Inserted #2 end through bottom eyelet, correctly under tension disc and through top eyelet of false selvage case.
        [] Successfully completed   [] Attempted   [] Did not try
5.   Inserted #5 end through bottom eyelet, correctly under tension disc and through top eyelet of false selvage case.
        [] Successfully completed   [] Attempted   [] Did not try
6.   Closed false selvage case covers.
        [] Successfully completed   [] Attempted   [] Did not try
7.   Threaded #2 end through eyelet in top of stop motion, through tension wire eyelet, through leno case eyelet and placed it against back of harness.
        [] Successfully completed   [] Attempted   [] Did not try
8.   Threaded #5 end through eyelet in top of stop motion, through tension wire eyelet, through leno case eyelet and placed it against back of harness.
        [] Successfully completed   [] Attempted   [] Did not try
9.   Drew #5 end through correct heddle.
        [] Successfully completed   [] Attempted   [] Did not try
10. Drew #2 end through correct heddle.
        [] Successfully completed   [] Attempted   [] Did not try
11. Placed #5 and #2 ends in square guide.
        [] Successfully completed   [] Attempted   [] Did not try
12. Drew #5 end through correct dent.
        [] Successfully completed   [] Attempted   [] Did not try
13. Drew #2 end through correct dent.
        [] Successfully completed   [] Attempted   [] Did not try
14. Drew #5 and #2 ends over temple roll and under temple cap.
        [] Successfully completed   [] Attempted   [] Did not try
15. Pulled #2 and #5 ends around plastic guide roller, tied them to false selvage take-up and clipped excess.
        [] Successfully completed   [] Attempted   [] Did not try
16. Pulled ALL ends down in false selvage case, moved tension wires from contact with detector pin on stop motion.
        [] Successfully completed   [] Attempted   [] Did not try
17. Closed false selvage case cover.
        [] Successfully completed   [] Attempted   [] Did not try
18. Pressed black start button twice.
        [] Successfully completed   [] Attempted   [] Did not try

TOTAL ____ X 3 + TOTAL ____ X 2 + TOTAL ____ X 1 = _____ TOTAL TECHNIQUE POINTS
                    (QUALITY)

TOTAL TIME REQUIRED TO COMPLETE FALSE SELVAGE PACKAGE PLACEMENT AND THREAD UP
(Please fill in) _____ MINUTES (in hundredths)
        (PRODUCTIVITY)

Figure 10—False Selvage Package Replacement And Thread-Up Score Sheet.

The 12 current weavers were tested for speed and accuracy on the simulations. Accuracy was measured on each Step of the Task with a simple 3-point scale (1—Successfully Completed, 2—Attempted, But Not Completed, 3—Omitted, Never Attempted.) See the Performance Score Sheet for false selvage bobbin replacement in Figure 10.

The false selvage bobbin presented some real access and visibility issues. Finally, it was decided to remove the bobbin assembly from the machine's interior to facilitate the videotaping of certain Steps. This approach assured that the trainee's eyes were focused where, when and exactly on what we wanted. We also knew that all trainees were trained to do a Task the same way

Please consider another suggestion about videotaping and training. Almost anybody can learn to use a videotape recorder, but not every videotape operator can learn to train. Pick one of your trainers to become your training video-tape operator. Training experience is invaluable when positioning and setting up camera shots. The lead trainer was videotaped as the demonstrator of the Task on the video and in the still photos. One word of caution here, don't short-cut on your video or audio productions for training tapes. People have become so sophisticated and over-sensitive with the video productions they see on television or at the movies. If your tapes are perceived to be homemade, the tapes will receive no respect. If locals are used for the audio of the tape, any speech differences or peculiarities from what is considered to be the norm or "of broadcast quality" can destroy the credibility of the training tape. People are not very tolerant and can be very cruel and hurtful to others. Use a "broadcast voice" and tape editing on all your video productions.

During production, the bobbin string up procedure was taped from four different angles to assure maximum clarity of the process. That night while editing the footage we had shot of the string up steps, I suddenly noticed that the second angle tape shot differed from the first angle. I queued up the third angle tape for verification as to which procedure was correct, only to see a third methodology. Number four only added a fourth set of steps. When confronted the next morning the lead trainer was incensed and proceded to demonstrate for the corporate and plant trainers and me exactly how she had performed the procedure during the taping session. As you've probably already guessed, we had number five. We then brought in the plant engineer for number six. At this point, a sit-down meeting was called and when the dust had settled, we had a "preferred" bobbin string-up procedure on videotape. Within 24 hours every trainer, weaver and trainee had seen the video and had been successfully certified on the "preferred" procedure. Overnight production yields sky rocketed from 52% to a whopping 87% and held. We had accidentally stumbled onto a production bonanza that tremendously impacted product quality and yields. Our findings seemed to confirm the old adage that "20% of the variables often control 80% of the variance".

This project was done long before the advent of the digital camera, lap top computer or flow-charting software. This approach lends itself as a valid and easy method to accomplish the requirements of current projects. You simply shoot your storyboard with your digital camera until you get exactly what you want. Then import your storyboard into your script or flow chart and voila, a "picture book" training manual even a kid could follow. Have your industrial engineer time and motion study the process you have "picture booked". In other words, "Are the Task Steps correct and how long do they require to do?" Depending on IE availability and cooperation level, you may want to save yourself some rework by involving the IE in storyboarding and photographing, or at least in a review of your materials before production. Always get IE approval before "buttoning up" your "picture book" and putting it in your arsenal for use in the battle for job enlightenment. Besides, it's good PR and you just might learn something you can use the next time. A technical trainer and an IE have the same ultimate objective, to get the job done in the most efficient and effective way.

The video tape, the "picture book" training manual" and targeted times for completion of the Tasks could be supplied to manufacturing operation teams or supervision with a note. The note could read, "When an associate can perform this Task absolutely correctly and within the targeted time, please have them report to training for validation and certification testing. Thank you."

Now let's get back to the bobbin transfer project. The simulation was administered to two different groups in one of two designated training modules. One group was handpicked by management and was composed of 4 outstanding performers, 4 average performers and 4 borderline performers. Previous performance information was withheld from researchers before and during test administration. A couple of trainers were also tested. See Figure 11 for the actual raw data from the experienced Weaver test simulation. A second group composed of job applicants was also chosen for a pilot administration to verify the simulations' performance predictability. Some of the applicants were experienced traditional weavers and some had no weaving experience.

Experienced Weaver Pilot Test Results

Simulation	Poss. Tech Pts.	Avg. Tech Pts.	Avg. Time	I1	I2	W1	W2	W3	W4	W5	W6	W7	W8	W9	W10	W11	W12
Creeling Tech Pts.	45	41.3		45	45	45	45	41	43	41	29	44	42	40	43	43	39
Creeling Time			2.23	1.4	1.39	2.81	2.31	2.86	2.51	2.19	1.98	2.48	2.52	1.5	1.9	1.72	1.94
Straight Draw	27	26.8		27	27	27	27	26	27	27	27	25	26	27	27	27	27
Straight Draw Time			1.88	1.33	1.32	2.31	1.74	2.72	1.76	2.91	1.62	1.89	2.03	1.45	1.58	1.42	1.17
Reverse Draw	21	20.9		21	21	21	21	21	21	20	21	21	21	21	21	21	21
Reverse Draw Time			1.19	0.88	0.8	1	1.08	1.29	1	1.44	1.08	1.34	1.68	0.87	1.38	0.77	1.43
Loomfixer Board	15	14.9		15	15	15	15	15	15	15	15	15	14	15	15	15	15
Loomfixer Board Time			0.65	0.43	0.41	0.69	0.42	0.72	0.51	0.49	0.39	0.54	0.82	0.62	0.65	0.59	1.36
Filling Stop	27	26.1		27	27	25	27	27	25	25	27	27	27	27	27	23	26
Filling Stop Time			0.97	0.74	0.75	0.85	0.7	1.1	1.06	0.84	1.51	0.8	1.06	0.73	1.09	0.64	1.25
Leno	54	51.1		54	54	54	50	54	52	50	52	50	51	54	51	46	49
Leno Time			2.94	2.1	2.15	2.12	2.21	2.89	2.94	3.6	3.58	2.66	3.89	2.93	2.28	2.82	3.33
False Selvage	54	52.4		54	54	54	54	54	54	52	54	50	53	52	51	50	51
False Selvage Time			6.17	4.8	4.78	4.8	5.43	5.83	7.93	6.31	5.64	4.04	9.71	3.81	6.29	5.88	8.32
Total Tech Pts.	243	234		243	243	241	239	239	237	231	225	231	234	236	235	225	228
% Total Tech Pts.		94.1		100	100	98.8	97.5	97.5	96.3	92.6	88.9	92.6	94.4	95.7	95.1	88.9	90.7
Total Time			16.03	11.7	11.6	14.6	13.9	17.4	17.7	17.8	15.8	13.8	21.7	11.9	15.2	13.8	18.8

Figure 11—Experienced Air Jet Weavers Test Results

Speed was simply measured by a stopwatch. Their individual performance scores seemed to bear out management's a priori grouping, from Fast and Accurate to Slow and Inaccurate. The performance speeds continued to show the somewhat consistent simulation characteristic of the workers' times and accuracy scores being approximately three times quicker and more accurate than those of the applicants. Again the quickest way to see if the workers would be "good" hires is to plot their times and accuracy of the "would be" associates within the four quadrants of the employment decision matrix.

The actual times and technique points of the weaver trainees are provided for your perusal in Figure 13.

Air Jet Weaver Trainee Pilot Test Results

Simulation	Poss. Tech Pts.	Avg. Tech Pts.	Avg. Time	T1	T2	T3	T4	T5	T6	T7	T8	T9	T10	T11	T12	T13	T14	T15	T16
Creeling Tech Pts.	45	37.5		38	32	40	41	39	43	29	39	41	35	45	31	32	40	38	N/A
Creeling Time			7.17	13.4	14.4	3.6	4.99	4.42	3.52	8.18	4.12	3.47	13.4	4.14	7.23	10.7	6.17	5.78	N/A
Straight Draw Tech Pts	27	25.5		27	27	24	26	27	27	23	26	27	24	27	23	23	25	26	N/A
Straight Draw Time			6.43	2.32	3.75	9.47	9.12	5.34	4.39	10.9	4.95	3.33	11.3	2.39	9.18	10.1	6.24	3.59	N/A
Reverse Draw Tech Pts	21	19.9		20	20	18	20	20	20	19	21	21	20	21	19	18	21	21	N/A
Reverse Draw Time			3.16	1.52	2.1	5.61	3.17	2.39	3	3.7	2.75	3.18	3.85	1.83	6.04	3.62	2.3	2.38	N/A
Loom fixer Board	15	14.2		15	15	15	15	15	13	15	15	15	15	15	7	14	14	15	N/A
Loom fixer Board Time			0.98	0.83	0.93	0.7	1.08	0.57	0.64	1.27	1.08	0.91	1.25	0.79	0.74	1.51	1.05	1.33	N/A
Filling Stop Tech Pts	27	23.9		25	26	26	23	25	27	17	22	27	20	27	20	23	23	27	N/A
Filling Stop Time			2.66	1.65	2.68	2.39	1.81	1.63	2.68	2.9	1.55	1.81	7.39	1.78	3.38	2.56	2.63	3.03	N/A
Leno Tech Pts	54	48.3		52	47	51	52	47	50	44	53	54	47	54	39	46	42	47	N/A
Leno Time			8.18	5.9	6.75	12.4	16.6	9.9	4.49	12	5.84	4.55	10.9	4.88	9.81	8.6	4.2	6.02	N/A
False Selvage Tech Pts	54	50.7		54	49	48	47	51	52	51	54	54	53	52	44	48	50	53	N/A
False Selvage Time			14.41	10.5	16.5	18.9	25.6	9.83	13.8	17.8	14.4	8.59	15.8	7.39	16.6	13.8	12.7	14.4	N/A
Total Tech Pts.	243	202		232	216	222	224	224	232	199	228	239	214	241	183	204	215	227	N/A
% Total Tech Pts.		85.8		93.2	83.3	87	88.3	88.3	93.2	72.8	90.7	97.5	82.1	98.8	63	75.9	82.7	90.1	N/A
Total Time			42.99	36	47.2	53	62.3	34.1	32.6	56.2	34.7	25.8	63.9	23.2	50.9	35.3	36.5		N/A

Figure 13—Raw Data Completion Times and Technique Points of Weaver Trainees.

Sixteen applicants completed an employment application and then were shown a detailed video of the simulations they would be asked to perform at a scheduled time one week later. Applicants were encouraged to stop by the training office at their convenience and review the video as many times as they liked. Each applicant was assigned a "picture book" training manual to study for the test. It detailed the simulations the applicants were to perform. Applicants were told they could mark up or make notes in these training manuals and could use them as a reference during the actual test administration if they so desired. Applicants were then scheduled at a specific time, five working days later, to report for testing. They were further told that the important aspect of the testing was to do every step in the correct order as quickly as they could without omitting any Task Steps. Again, accuracy was measured with a simple 3-point scale (1—Successfully Completed, 2—Attempted, But Not Completed, 3—Omitted, Never Attempted.) A stopwatch again measured speed. Accuracy was considered much more important than speed. Speed can always improve with practice, while accuracy seems to either be present or absent as a worker characteristic. I've coached trainees to become quicker in Task performance but I've never been able to train a person to be more accurate.

Of special note, only one applicant became frustrated and failed to complete the simulations. The best performance among applicants seems to come from those applicants having little or no experience with traditional weaving. The top applicant's scores were from a young man who had been college bound prior to his girl friend's pregnancy. He had made the commitment to marry and support his family. I questioned the corporate training director and the facility-training manager what they thought of the young man and his scores. Both men quickly responded to my surprise that although he was quick and accurate they would not offer him a job because they feared he would quickly become bored as a weaver and would leave the job. I then asked about the textile program at the local university and was assured it was top-notch. I then asked if it offered a cooperative education program. About that time their light bulbs seem to simultaneously turn on. By the next day a deal had been struck to allow the young man to enroll in a textile work-study program at the local university and their eventual regional vice-president of manufacturing, his wife, parents and in-laws were delighted.

The speed and accuracy results of the 15 applicants were plotted on the employment decision matrix.

Assignment for Week 7:

•   Prepare an administrator's manual for the work simulation test/performance appraisal instrument.

Carefully document all the information needed for someone else to administer your work simulation/performance appraisal. Prepare a detailed write-up of how to set up, administer and score your instrument to assure standardization. This write-up should include a layout map of where all necessary equipment, people and accessories are to be positioned for the administration of the instrument. Your write-up should step the administrator through the process including the use of a stopwatch; documenting of Time-To-Completes, recording of accuracy markings; and the scoring of the applicant's performance. Develop a prototype of the evaluation scoring sheets (observation of accuracy in performing the procedure) for any simulations. Make enough copies for all members of the team.

•   Prepare a work simulation test/performance appraisal instrument.

This includes preparing any required scoring sheets and instructions of how to identify and schedule suitable locations for administering the instrument. List any necessary equipment and cite the procedure for obtaining it. Any suggested notification letters to either SME's and/or their supervisors should be supplied.

WEEK 7   ADMINISTRATION OF WORK SIMULATION TEST OR PERFORMANCE APPRAISAL
            INSTRUMENT
            (4 hours)

- Each junior consultant's test/appraisal administrator's manual and instrument are reviewed by the team.

Make any changes, exceptions or suggestions for improvement that you may see. Don't hesitate; voice your expert opinions now. Each junior consultant will know where improvements may be made. By doing these projects in four person teams, each junior consultant has had the benefit of gaining experience vicariously through team member projects.

- Preparation of simulation test instrument's evaluation sheet is explained and discussed.

An evaluation sheet for your instrument must be developed. Remember this is a pilot administration of your instrument so it's still not too late to improve it. What better way than by obtaining feedback from your administrator and test subjects? Ask them what they liked and disliked about the instrument. Was instrument easy or hard to use? Were instructions clear and concise? What are their suggestions for improvement? Are questions worded clearly and concisely? What was the hardest thing to understand? What was the most difficult part? What were the good parts and the bad parts?

Get the administrator and subjects to fill out the evaluation sheet after the session and sign it as documentation to keep with the test development materials. As you have seen, the evaluation sheet can be open-ended or close-ended. I suggest some of both type questions.

- The importance of standardization of administration of instruments is explained and discussed.

The validity of a perfectly constructed instrument can be destroyed by a lack of standardization in its administration. Sometimes it almost seems as if giving the test is much more crucial than constructing the test. In order for one set of test results to be compared with others requires that the tests be tightly controlled from the aspect of test administration. Have the test instructions read out loud to subjects. It is even easier for the test administrator to have the instructions recorded by a professional "broadcast voice" and then use or distribute the tapes as needed. All the administrator has to do is follow along with the script and press the start and stop buttons. If the simulation requires positioning or the setting up of equipment so distances are the same, use a layout sheet to document where things are located. Limit the number of administrators you use and be sure you thoroughly train them while emphasizing doing things the same way every time.

- The art of writing an abstract is explained and discussed.

It is always important to be able to summarize things for people who don't have a lot of time to read like we HR types who read incessantly. If you can reduce complex issues and ideas into simple terms that anybody can understand, you have the potential for greatness in the HR field. Get in the habit of reducing the intent and results of your project to one paragraph. Place that one paragraph sheet in the front of the test development files when you store them for filing.

Assignment for Week 8:

- Junior consultants have someone administer the developed instrument to at least three (3) people.

- Administrator and three (3) people to whom the instrument were given are asked to complete an evaluation sheet regarding their perception of the instrument's validity, fairness, ease of use, strengths and weaknesses, etc.

- Review evaluations and prepare a set of conclusions and recommendations regarding how the instrument performed and how it can be improved.

- Prepare a one-paragraph abstract summarizing the project and its results.

- Begin conceptualizing what needs to be presented on Week 9 and how it should be done.

WEEK 8   PROJECT WRAP UP and PRESENTATION PREPARATION
              (4 hours)

Deadline: ABSTRACT IS DUE!

•   The Team reviews of each junior consultant's abstract.

•   Team decides how to handle the Week 9 presentation from a team and an individual perspective.

•   The Team practices the presentation format for Week 9.

Assignment for Week 9:

•   Prepare the FINAL PROJECT NOTEBOOK and DIARY.

•   Preparation and Practice for "mock" board of directors presentation.

WEEK 9   BOARD OF DIRECTORS PRESENTATION OF RESEARCH PROJECT
              (4 hours)

Deadline: FINAL NOTEBOOK, TABLE OF CONTENTS and DIARY ARE DUE!

•   Each junior consultant is given a designated amount of time to present his/her research project.

Project Requirements:

		% of grade
A.	Proposal	5
B.	Task Analysis	20
C.	Simulation, Aid, Appraisal, Survey	25
D.	Administration of Instrument	10
E.	Abstract	5
F.	Experiential exercises & help to others	10
G.	Final Notebook, Bibliography & Final Presentation	<u>25</u>
		100

Grade Breakdowns:

          A   = 95 to 100
          A- = 90 to 94
          B+ = 88 to 89
          B   = 84 to 87
          B- = 80 to 83
          C   = 70 to 79
          F   = Below 70
          I   = Incomplete

How to use TBJA Data

Let's say for instance that you have just performed a TBJA evaluation on all the secretarial positions within your law firm. Therefore, you have at your disposal all of the typical output we have just gone over so thoroughly. Unexpectedly one of your attorneys loses her secretary due to a husband's relocation. Several things need to begin. First, run a copy of the Tasks Listed in Descending Order of Importance. Present this information to the attorney having the vacant position. Have the attorney go through the Task List and mark out any Tasks that the attorney doesn't want the secretary to perform. Then ask the attorney to rank-order the remaining Tasks based on the attorney's opinion of their Importance to the job. The vacant position's supervisor then completes the Importance rank ordering of the Duty Areas. Once the vacant position's Task List has been rank-ordered, the vacant position's data is ready for evaluation.

Multiply each Task's assigned rank-order number by the rank-order number assigned to the Duty Area. Also ask the supervisor to list the equipment that has to be operated and any special requirements. Once this is done, identify the ten (10) lowest value Tasks. In the arena of recruiting, a vacancy announcement needs to be placed in the newspaper. Using the ten most important Tasks construct the necessary job ad. For an example of a newspaper advertisement, see Figure 15.

LAW OFFICE SECRETARY

To operate PC to prepare legal correspondence, reports, manuscripts, from hand copy and Lanier VIP transcriber. Resp. to one sr. partner. Skills req'd are SH, editing, proofing, billing, receive/relay calls/messages, filing, appt. scheduling. Occasional OT req'd. For appt. call 1-800 555-1234.

Figure 15—Newspaper Advertisement

Straight from your most important Tasks and their KSA Linkages comes your ad's copy. I have found this type of ad to be very productive with regard to response rates. I have even received phone calls from potential applicants who had already "self-screened" themselves but thanked me for providing them with enough information to do so. Sifting through and culling out non-qualified applicants can drive a recruiter crazy. Remember if you can get them to self-screen, it saves your time as well as their time.

As you've probably noticed from the ad copy, on some positions, I prefer telephone screening. Part of the intent of this approach is to get an insight into the applicant's "phone presence" and communication skills. An applicant call sheet should be prepared and used to differentiate the applicants. The type of things that should be included on the screening sheet are: name, phone numbers, name & number of person who can contact them, related experience, (where, for whom, how long, for how much, type of work), software used, equipment used, non-related experience. Think about some kind of rating scale that can be utilized to quantify the applicant's responses.

The next item of business involves the preparation of a job description. To get your job description simply take the top 40 or 50% of the Tasks in Descending Order of Importance Without Regard to Duty Area, then add the types and models of equipment to be operated and any special requirements or KSA's. The job description is again used for self-selection by better informing the applicant what is expected and what is important. The job description may either be read to the applicant over the phone or faxed or e-mailed. If after the phone interview both parties continue to be interested, have the applicant submit their application as quickly as possible. Don't forget e-mail and fax as an option or alternative for quick exchange of resume and/or application forms.

If after a review of the resume and application there is still an interest in the applicant, the applicant should be scheduled for an interview and testing. The interview of course will be structured. The structured interview is used for standardization of administration and to allow for differentiation between applicants based on their responses. The following is an example of how to take a top ten Task and use it as a structured interview question. See Figure 16 for an example of a structured interview questionnaire.

Structured Interview Question

Question 1: Please describe your experience with typing or keying rough drafts from recording devices. Indicate the number of different people from whose voice recordings you had to type, the types of equipment and software you had to operate, whether close proofing or editing was required, how often you had to type rough drafts and for whom and how long you did it. Specify if the voice recordings had special terminology, the number of different types of rough drafts you were asked to prepare. Estimate your words per minute typing on rough drafts, you approximate error rate, your expertise in spelling, your grammatical ability, your editing and proofreading ability.

Answer Guide: **5pts** - At least two years experience keying or typing rough drafts from a voice recordings in a company or situation exactly like yours.

3pts - At least two years experience keying rough drafts in a company or situation very different from yours.
1pts - Has typed up or keyed rough drafts from recordings of own voice.
0pts - Has never typed or keyed rough drafts from voice recordings.

Notes on applicant's response:
_____
_____
_____
_____
_____
_____
_____
_____

Figure 16—Example of Structured Interview Question.

Notice the simple "0" to "5" scoring range on which the interviewer records his/her estimate of the applicant's response. Ten to twelve structured interview questions can be developed rather quickly using the top portion of the Tasks in Descending Order of Importance listing. So the Structured Interview Questionnaire booklet can be completed with a cover sheet listing the job title of the vacant position, applicant's name, interviewer's name, interviewer's job title, date and time of interview. The purpose of the Structured Interview is as a vehicle to subjectively assess and quantify the applicant's background and experience in such a way as to allow a comparative analysis or rank ordering of applicants based upon work history.

In conjunction with this, the recruiter can administer the Structured Interview with several objective Work Simulations (i.e., the preparation of which having been previously discussed) as the means to best select the qualified applicants to present to the supervisor. Again close attention is paid to each applicant's speed and accuracy on the objective Work Simulations. I have found that presenting just the top ranked three or four applicants to the supervisor to be quite satisfactory. This would be enough to offer the supervisor a selection of candidates without cluttering the supervisor's calendar with the scheduling of applicants. The supervisor may also use the Structured Interview Questionnaire during his or her interview with the applicant to validate the recruiter's perceptions and/or as a means, from a legal perspective, to keep the interview on track. The supervisor should gain more confidence in the interview process, as his or her subjective evaluations should parallel those of the recruiter.

So the supervisor's decision becomes more one of selecting based upon their "chemistry match-up" rather than having to worry about the applicant's qualifications. Once the decision is made, use the supervisor's vacant position rank-ordering to produce a job-specific Performance Appraisal. In other words, simply type up the supervisor's Task rank ordering within Duty Areas and place a 7-point rating scale at the end of each Task. The suggested 7-point scale rating scale in Figure 17 is offered for your consideration.

Performance Appraisal Rating Scale

7 – Always Exceeds Requirements
6 – Usually Exceeds Requirements
5 – Sometimes Exceeds Requirements
4 – Meets Requirements
3 – Sometimes Meets Requirements
2 – Seldom Meets Requirements
1 – Never Meets Requirements
NA – Not Applicable

Figure 17—Suggested 7-Point Performance Rating Scale.

At the end of each Duty Area calculate the average rating for the Tasks within. List the Duty Areas and their averages on the last page along with a "blank" column for any relevant weighting factors. The Duty Area averages are then summed to subjectively determine the employee's total performance level. Any objective measures, identified during the job analysis are also used to evaluate employee performance. The supervisor can then be asked to estimate the employee's total performance level on a rating scale (i.e., Outstanding, Above Standard, Standard, Sub-Standard or Unsatisfactory). Be sure to provide a place for both supervisor and employee to sign and date that they have met and discussed the appraisal.

Give the job-specific performance appraisal to the supervisor and advise him or her to make use of the performance appraisal weekly during the probationary period to assure two-way communication of expectations and feedback to the new employee. The supervisor can acknowledge areas of outstanding performance as well as highlight areas requiring improvement. When the time arrives to make your decision regarding the granting of full status (employee benefits) to your new-hires, all the necessary performance documentation will be at your fingertips. After experiencing the process I've heard supervisors say, "It's nice to finally have HR people who understand what's going on out here!"

Job Classification

You've probably noticed by now that I have carefully avoided talking about classification of jobs using TBJA. There are reasons. Can TBJA handle classification? Not as you have been shown so far. What are we really trying to do when we classify jobs? We are looking for similarities and uniqueness, right? Simply, we're looking for the requirements jobs have in common and the requirements that make them different. I tend to call it job comparison. To compare things requires a standard of measure or what I commonly refer to as a "Yardstick". Please notice that I didn't say a ruler.

In thirty years of personnel research I was never afforded the opportunity to take part in a "dedicated" classification study. Does that mean that I haven't thought and pondered about it to the point of developing a position on the issue? Of course not, and suffice it to say, I feel privileged for the opportunity to share my opinions and perceptions on job classification with you. Notice in the paragraph above, that I used "yardstick" rather than "ruler" in my measurement comment. When doing measurement always allow yourself as many "points of measure" as possible. That's always been my rule. The more points you measure, the greater the accuracy of measurement. Hence, my constant use of seven and nine point rating scales to measure opinions. A point of concern always has and will be that clean, clear and concise (valid) points of differentiation be established and used.

The Point-Factor Approach has real merit but I feel that it stops far short of the mark on factor identification. As you're probably aware, points are assigned to a job based on the factors the organization is willing to pay. Management usually will agree to between 4 and 11 factors. I liken that to measuring each job with either a 6-factor or a 12-factor ruler. Would the job measurement be more precise with the 6-factor ruler or a 12-factor ruler? The job measurement would be more precise with a 12-factor scale. Which of the two scales would afford the most differentiation of jobs with a 6-factor scale or a 12-factor scale? This is not a trick question. With valid factors, things could possibly be spread out over twice the area of a 6-factor scale. Therefore, since nobody knows exactly how many factors there are, some group like the Society of Human Resource Management (SHRM) should coordinate the establishment of a taxonomy of factors or Whole Job Requirements.

The U.S. Department of Labor spent over thirty years identifying and experimenting with some 33 factors including 10 aptitudes, 8 personal traits and 15 physical abilities. The 10 Aptitudes include: verbal, numerical; spatial, form perception, clerical perception, motor coordination, finger dexterity, manual dexterity, eye-hand-foot coordination and color discrimination. The 8 Personal Traits are tact, ability to deal with stressful situations, effective communication, interpersonal relationships, initiative, decisiveness dependability and flexibility. The 15 Physical Abilities are finger, hand, wrist and forearm strength; upper arm strength; back and shoulder strength; leg strength; ability to perform rapid work for short periods; ability to perform rapid work for extended periods; ability to perform heavy work for short periods; ability to perform heavy work for extended periods; ability to stand for extended periods of time—indoors; ability to stand for extended periods of time—outdoors and in all kinds of weather; sharpness of vision; sharpness of hearing; sharpness of smell; sharpness of feeling; and sharpness of taste.

These 33 Labor Department factors have already been incorporated into TBJA as the Whole Job Requirements. Unlike the other measures used in TBJA, the Whole Job Requirements are rated on the job as a whole, rather than on small, meaningful individual pieces of work or Task-by-Task. These Whole Job Requirements were broken down into three factor groups, aptitudes, personal traits and physical abilities. Each factor group was transferred to one of three separate pages to create the data collection forms contained in the Whole Job Requirement Booklet. The Whole Job

Requirements data may be gathered individually or in groups. It usually takes between 15 to 30 minutes to conscientiously complete. Verbal or written instructions can be given to respondents. You choose your own procedure. Again there are no right or wrong answers; we're just interested in the incumbent and supervisory best estimates. Eight or more respondents constitute the required sampling size to assure validity of SME 's responses.

Analyzing data for the Whole Job Requirements are simple. Calculate the mean rating value for each aptitude, trait and ability. Once again, a split analysis of labor and management data may be performed if desired. Then to wrap up the analysis, calculate the grand mean for each group of factors (aptitudes, traits and abilities). You should end up with 36 means for each job after completion of the Whole Job Requirements.

Another piece of TBJA, not presented previously, as part of the Syllabus training is Task Rating data collection. Task Rating is used when trying to measure or compare jobs or to cluster jobs into groups based upon similar requirements. Often Task Rating data are gathered in conjunction with Whole Job Requirements data, just not at the same time, for they differ significantly. Whereas the 33 variables of Whole Job Requirements were rated based on their relevance to the job as a whole, the 12 variables of Task Rating were rated based upon their relevance to the previously identified "most important" Tasks which constitute the job. So, all of the Tasks of a given job are not rated, just the Tasks identified during Task Rank-Ordering by the SME's as being important to good job performance. Remember asking the SME's to identify on the Descending Order of Importance Task List the approximate place where Task completion begins to insignificantly impact job performance? All Tasks above that cut point get rated and Tasks below that point don't. A minimum of eight people is required to provide Data on Task Rating. The time normally required for data collection is one to two hours. Remember Task Rating data are collected and utilized only in classification studies or other unique cases. As with all TBJA data, Task Rating data are gathered individually or in groups. I like to have each of the "most important" Tasks resulting from the analysis of the Duty Area/Task Rank-Ordering Data, rated on 12 specific variables. These variables include: Math; Language; Reasoning; Difficulty; Time Required to Learn; Data/Information Handling; Dealing With People; Things or Objects Usage; Concept Handling; Responsibility; Impact of Poor Performance. Two additional variables (i.e., stress and physical exertion) have recently been added to Task Rating after Task Relevance evaluation. These variables were also identified and used by the U.S. Department of Labor.

Task Rating requires at least 8 respondents to supply the necessary data. A split-half analysis is again recommended as a measure of congruence. Each SME is encouraged to rate the entire Task List on a single variable prior to switching to the next variable. With this approach, less hassle is incurred by the Rater and there is less mental flip-flopping created by the switching back and forth to determine the appropriate scale value levels of each variable. Upon completion of Task Rating, the mean rating scale value for each of the 12 variables is calculated for each Task. In others words, we now know the level of 12 different variables "required to perform" each "most important" Task. The grand mean for each of the 12 variables is then calculated. This is done to establish the average level of each of the 12 variables necessary for performance of the job. These 12 variables and their 12 grand means can then be joined with the 36 means uncovered during Whole Job Requirements data collection.

Let's review what we have collected. We know the job's Duty Areas and the Tasks that compose them. We know the Steps required in performing the Task. We also know knowledge, skills and abilities required and how essential each KSA is for performance of the Task or Step. We also know the levels of some 48 Requirements associated with the Whole Job.

The TBJA approach to job analysis, we believe, makes it possible to have the information available to make better human resource decisions. The 48 Whole Job Requirements can be subjected to cluster analysis in order to identify job families or the jobs possessing similar job profiles across the 48 variables. Classification studies are often interested in creating a specified number (e.g., 32) of job grades or job levels. The analysis will group a job's profile into one of 32 job clusters. By comparing and evaluating the profiles contained within the clusters, the clusters can be rank-ordered from 1 to 32.

If constructing a simulation for pre-employment or for certification testing using TBJA data, you know what requirements (i.e., Math, Language, Reasoning, etc.) to include and at what levels (i.e., rating scale grand means) to make them when building the test instrument. If parallel forms of the tests are required, the level of difficulty for test items can be maintained.

If there is to be a lot of applicant or employee re-testing, always construct at least one or two parallel forms of the test. A parallel form is simply another alternate test that is constructed at the same standards of requirements as the original test. The tests are said to be parallel if they are constructed at the same level of difficulty and measure the same thing.

If parallel forms of a test exist, rotate the administration of forms to maintain test confidentiality. To accomplish the rotation, have the test administrator gather and report the average score made on the test each week to include the test form being used. Plot the scores each week looking for any trend upward on the scoring. If the weekly scoring average begins to steadily increase, your original form may be compromised, so switch forms. If there is a significant drop followed by a steady increase in scoring, begin construction of another couple of forms because this could indicate that your forms have been compromised. Prevent, if possible, a re-test being administered to a test taker on the same test form. Expend a little effort and energy by switching test forms for the applicant.

Allow me to offer a word on constructing parallel forms. If possible, only minimally change the question. Change the question's answer by moving a decimal point or by inserting a "not" in the question. Leave the "old correct" answer as a distracter and use an "old incorrect" answer as the "new correct" answer. If preparing a math problem, be it a word problem or numeric, always make your distracter answers "calculable" from the data supplied in the question. Then and only then is the test-taker challenged with really knowing how to do the math. Spend the time necessary in developing distracter answers. Try to make the wrong answers plausible. Poor distracters should not reduce a multiple-choice question to a merely dichotomous answer (i.e., "yes or no", "black/white", true/false question) or a give-away question (i.e., "Who's buried in Grant's tomb?"). If the test is performance-based (i.e., speed and accuracy) you naturally don't have to worry about re-testing or parallel forms. Are you beginning to see why I like simulations?

What would you do?—Consequences and Ramifications
Situation - #01

The skills required to be a good first-line supervisor are very different from the skills required to be a good production line operator. It's like taking an all-star quarterback and turning him into a head football coach. Psychologically, he must mentally adjust his thinking and self-esteem (ego) from being a touchdown maker to being a touchdown facilitator. (Ever wonder why former linemen make the best head coaches?). He has got to change to the point that he can "self-actualize" by motivating and developing his players both mentally and physically to execute the game plan with precision. Then comes the hardest part for a new and successful young coach to master and that is to step back out of the spotlight and let players have their moment of glory, honor and recognition. Always remember that an excellent supervisor needs to be a great coach or as the Bette Midler song alludes, you must be "the wind beneath their wings" to your players. You can't win unless they score!

The "supervisory" coach can accomplish his departmental goals and objectives only by the skillful and effective use of team members. Be especially careful when promoting your most outstanding production line operator. S/he may possibly lack some of the essential interpersonal supervisory skills required to perform the job successfully. In that situation you'll almost always lose twice. You'll lose not only an outstanding job performer but also gain a lousy supervisor as well. I've seen many outstanding operators resign from a company rather than face the embarrassment or humiliation of being "rolled back" from a supervisor to their previous operator's position. For that reason, I always recommend supervisory training and assessment before a promotion is given. Identify deficiencies or weakness first then see if there are any ways to correct for them. We want promotions to succeed not fail! After all, promotions are intended as a reward for hard work and dedication and not as a frustration or punishment.

In this situation, I would recommend Operator A because he does possess good interpersonal skills. Some experts used to say a supervisor is a supervisor is a supervisor. In other words, if you can supervise in one manufacturing operation, you can be a supervisor in ANY manufacturing operation. What the experts meant was that interpersonal skills were the most dominant factor in determining supervisory performance. Being a technical trainer, I take issue and totally disagree. The job knowledge portion of the equation cannot be minimized. Just ask any operator to whom they go with job-related technical questions and I'll get the names of senior co-workers, mechanics, trainers and even engineers. I'll guarantee that the last person they would contact with a technical question is their immediate supervisor. If I even suggest their supervisor as a potential source I get responses like, (i.e., Why waste my time? He doesn't have a clue! You've got to be kidding! He doesn't know his posterior from a hole in the ground!). It's the "supervisor is a supervisor" legacy and it has caused a tremendous loss of respect for supervision among those in the workforce. The so-called experts have created this mess, now how do we get out of it? There's really a pretty simple answer, make the supervisor your lead technical skills trainer. But the answer is not so easy to implement. You have to slay the great supervisory myth, "I don't have time to train my people". The truth is, "you can't afford not to train them."

My first shift supervisor, who had a sixth grade education, enlightened me, "Your job as a first-line supervisor is to work yourself out of a job. I don't care how many hours it takes you as long as you get the job done right by the time I need it. But if I see that it's taking over 45 hours a week, I'll replace you because you obviously can't handle it. Don't hog the knowledge, train your people and then delegate assignments to them. Always follow-up on what you've assigned. I don't really care who does it as long as it gets done when it's supposed to and it's done right. You don't have to do anything, but I hold you personally responsible for everything. Any questions?"

WHAT WOULD YOU DO?—CONSEQUENCES AND RAMIFICATIONS
SITUATION - #02

After much prayer and soul-searching, during the most miserable, apprehensive, guilt-ridden, tossing and turning weekend of my life, I made my fateful decision. It was to side with upholding the company and community values rather than succumb to the emotional pressure created by the potential suffering of his wife and five kids. I finally reached peace in my heart, with the Lord's help, when I realized that the operator had put his family at risk by his actions and that I should not hold myself personally responsible for what he had done. I wrote my recommendation late Sunday night trying to emphasize the operator's contributions and his good points. I tried to portray his mistake as a momentary lapse or error in judgment but one that violated the sanctity of human life in the killing of an unwanted yet unborn child. I concluded, "Therefore, in my opinion, neither my company nor my community as a whole should be seen as supporting in any way what this person has done. Based on our corporate values and his continuously re-occurring respiratory problem, I recommend that we not get involved any further with his work release program and that his employment with the company be terminated. My prayers go with him and his family as they face what's ahead." The recommendation was on his desk when the boss arrived at 6:30. He read it and said nothing to me but simply left for the rack-up meeting.

I told the operator my recommended action at 7:00, the same time as the plant manager received it. I next asked for and received his gate pass and proceeded to escort him to HR to await the final decision. At the plant manager's news conference, my recommendation was read almost verbatim. I asked for and received permission to escort him to the gate when his termination was complete and it was there that we said our good-byes. Over two years later I received a call at home one evening from the operator thanking me for my decision. He had enrolled in a computer science course under a government rehabilitation grant for ex-offenders and had just graduated from a local junior college second in his class. He was to start a job out of town the next week at two and a half times his old salary. He said he'd never have had the guts to try it if I hadn't forced him. Sometimes, it just goes to show you.

What would you do?—Consequences and Ramifications
Situation - #03

Within three months the old mechanic was retired and for being "so non-safety conscious", I was court-martialed, lost my manufacturing stripes and was exiled from operations to a place called process engineering. I guess they figured from engineering that I could only be a threat to the process and not the people. Four weeks after my transfer, results were returned from the corporate metallurgy department confirming the drop leg failure as a result of "localized over-heating". Nothing was ever said to me about the results confirming my story. I did not pursue the old mechanic on the story that he and his son had concocted. Everybody in the work area knew who was telling the truth and that the old man's retirement benefits were at stake. The transfer coupled with my not "ratting" on the mechanic elevated my status among the operators to that of almost a "folk hero". I was administratively too hot to handle, so a transfer to another work area seemed the simple solution. Besides, moving from a revolving shift to a straight-day job wasn't all that bad either. So, you want to be a process engineer?

HAVE PROJECT DESIGN & JOB ANALYSIS & WILL TRAVEL OR WHAT DO YOU WANT TO BE WHEN YOU GROW UP?

After some two months as coordinator of the southeastern regional consortium of state governments, I began to assess my situation. I found I had inadvertently set my foot squarely in the middle of a political controversy for power between two PhD Project Directors. I quietly tried to remain neutral and awaited direction because I was housed at the same physical location as one of them. One morning I walked into my office to find the Federal Grant Coordinator seated at my desk drinking a cup of coffee. I was told that no project design had been approved yet, no quarterly reports had yet been received and the project was up for consideration for renewal within the next three months. Within the next five days after a lot of stepping and fetching, we had a meeting scheduled to review and approve our project design, not to mention being current on our grant reporting requirements.

Just when I was beginning to feel that I had things under control with the feds, came a rather nasty phone call from the other PhD wanting to know what I thought I was doing. The phone call torpedoed me out of my chair. The two PhDs then went at each other. The result was a new Project Coordinator PhD to control the current consortium coordinator. The Project Coordinator had his PhD in Educational Research but knew nothing about Industrial Psychology. We became fast friends. In fact after we finished the consortium project, we collaborated on the development of Task-Based Job Analysis (TBJA). The consortium finally went the way of all good consortiums and died a quiet death. To my surprise, I received a reprimand from my Federal Grant Coordinator for bringing the project in at $100,000 under budget. After all, it was my first federal grant and I didn't understand the way you're supposed to operate non-economically and inefficiently.

As the consortium was terminated, I was set to follow suite, but seniority mandated, much to my director's chagrin, that I be absorbed into state government as a personnel researcher building pre-employment tests. My project coordinator was absorbed into the classification and compensation unit as an analyst. As my major professor had warned me at college, I grew bored and started circulating the old resume.

About eight or nine months later, just when I least expected it, my cork finally went out of sight. Hey Dude, I finally had a bite and it was in the private sector! A Fortune 500 company finally had a court date on its racial discrimination case which had been pending for six years following the plant's expansion start up. Thirty two positions across four rotating shifts and some 134 incumbents had upped the ante to around 34 million dollars in potential liabilities. The job incumbents were the plaintiffs and the sample had close to a 20% illiteracy component. The company needed someone to validate their pre-employment tests that were put together by their human resource personnel in the week before the expansion start up. Their needs and my credentials and interests were a perfect match. The interview went well and a job offer soon followed. Their offer was twice what I was making in the public sector.

But I was faced with the ethics of using or not using the Task Based Job Analysis (TBJA). I called my former boss and co-developer of TBJA to discuss our situation and his possible interest. I told him what was happening and that I thought the private company might entertain the idea of a contract rather than a job. He said he was interested if I could get their interest. I presented the contractual arrangements concept to their recruiter with a list of benefits and he took it hook, line and sinker. Days later, we signed a one-year contractual arrangement with the company's law firm

81

and that contract was in the boat and ready for mounting. Plus the state personnel department had two less people about which to worry. The TBJA system had been conceptualized but as of that point not yet computer programmed for data analysis.

The client's HR Director had only seen me in a three-piece suit as we had talked and negotiated the contract. The first day of data collecting, the sky split and the whole plant was mired in ankle-deep mud. He had just dropped by the designated data collection site to see if there were any problems. He suddenly started frantically waving his arms trying to get my attention. I immediately gave the group a coffee break and rushed to see what he needed. He just looked at me with his mouth open. He spoke, "A bit under-dressed aren't we?" I was wearing a pair of old jeans with a few tears, boots and a flannel shirt along with a baseball cap. I said, "Oh yes, the group forgot to put you on our distribution list regarding the dress code for their data collection sessions." He just smiled, shook his head and walked off. Always consider your appearance when working with job incumbents. Try to stay within the incumbent's dress codes. Don't over dress or under dress. Try to maintain as relaxed an atmosphere as possible for the data collection sessions.

So for the first year of our business, I barely stayed in the lead. I collected data from the plaintiffs, got on a plane, brought the data back and keypunched it while our systems consultants were writing the next stage of the computer analysis. An initial point of concern by the client with the Project was the literacy problem we faced with 20% of the plaintiffs. The literacy concern was readily addressed by offering any respondent/plaintiff desiring it, a private one-on-one data collection session with the "Big Guy" over lunch and at the Big Guy's expense. So I read the questions and alternatives and they chewed and responded. I carefully recorded their responses and validated each response with a final "read-through" verification of the question and their answer. Literacy had initially appeared problematic to our Project, but it really turned out to be tremendously beneficial to our cause. By contract's end we had content-validated 31 of 32 test batteries.

During the Project, I became one of the most well known members of the Company's HR Department. I had fun and received numerous nominations for the Company's "Employee of the Month". It appeared that the plaintiffs' chief concern was over not being listened to or heard by management.

Our strategy involved keeping the examinations of concern under lock and key until we had completed our job analyses. This, we would be able to testify in court. After having performed the job analyses, the issue now seemed adequately addressed in the plaintiffs' minds. Also there was a unanimous vote by the plaintiffs to drop the lawsuit. The results of the project delighted the company and placed their lawyers' minds at ease. I, on the other hand, had a working computerized TBJA system, finished products that I could show to potential clients, letters of recommendation from a Fortune 500 company and its law firm plus a reputation of bringing projects in on time and within budget.

Behavioral and Managerial Research, as we called ourselves, continued to market our services to HRM as our main concentration. Finally a major textile firm's Personnel Manager suggested that I talk with their Training Director because he had been having a lot of turnover following an extended training program. The Personnel Manager lifted his phone and then asked his Training Manager if there was any time later in the day when he could meet with me to discuss his drop out problem.

Since all of the trainees were already employees, the HRM group had dumped the problem in HRD's lap. The Training Manager picked me up at the Personnel Manager's office within two minutes. The Training Manager had been given a problem with no possibility of solution and he was exasperated at HRM. I slowly and carefully walked him through a simple TBJA job analysis and explained to him that picking people for training was closely akin to pre-employment testing. He liked what he saw. I further explained how the TBJA was used to identify the most important Task or process on the job. I told him our simulations could closely approximate the Tasks performed on the job. I explained that we could use these pre-employment simulations as a pre-test, certification and post-training exam to help him with drop outs, it would help to more quickly identify trainee trainability as well as giving the trainee a job sample to try.

Two things registered on my sales meter, first this guy was very bright and second, to say that he was excited and enthusiastic was an understatement. When I say that he wanted to try TBJA in his shop immediately, I wasn't talking next week but that very afternoon. I called my partner and relayed enough to get him started on writing a contract and spent the rest of the afternoon familiarizing myself with the Training Manager's facility. I felt just like I had just discovered a diamond buried in the ground. I had no idea how large or small it was, I only knew it glittered.

The contract was signed the next day by mid morning with no quibbling on price. He had an arbitrarily chosen 52-week training plan for his loom fixers. Trainees were "buddied" with a loom fixer for 52 weeks. At the end of the 52nd week the trainee was placed on a production line where he was alone. Trainees usually lasted maybe two or three weeks before leaving the company only to go to another textile firm in the area and work as a weaver or fixer.

The answer to his dilemma lay in the development and use of pre-employment simulations. The Training Manager seemed obsessed with seeing how everything worked. By the end of the first week, the job analysis was complete. Then the fun began. The simulations needed for validation were systematically identified by the SMEs. When it came time to do videotaping, guess whose fingers were wrapped around the camera? It was the Training Manager. The Training Manager became my shadow. Instead of process mapping the job and using that as a script, we used the trainer as both our actor in the videotape as well as the narrator of the video. We also used the trainer's walk-through before videotaping as the shooting session for 35 mm photos for the simulation training manual. To say we were operating on a shoestring budget goes without saying. Our lighting consisted of one flood lamp and after shooting the simulation there was no editing equipment to cleanup our taping errors. It was obvious we were experimenting with a concept rather than trying to create a movie masterpiece.

We asked the loom fixer trainer to serve as our actor and to just perform in front of the camera the steps of his Tasks with the audio on the camcorder shut off. Next we asked the loom fixer to sit and watch the video to check the video's accuracy. Then we turned on the camcorder's audio and the loom fixer recorded his narration for the video. This constituted the script for the video. As we soon discovered, the loom fixer could easily assist in the narration of the video but the quality of the trainer's voice was just too folksy to be an effective communicator. Trainees tended to lock in on the voice's peculiarities rather than absorb the content of what was presented. We quickly switched to a professional voice. We also discovered the obvious; if the actor is male the narrator's voice should be male and vice-versa.

We also learned that every trainer was not an actor. When the camcorder audio and/or video starts rolling some trainers freeze. So if a trainer shows any hesitation or reluctance, don't use him or her in your video. Don't hesitate to pull or to take apart certain pieces of equipment if it contributes to the clarity of your video. With either a camera or camcorder you are able to focus the trainee's eye exactly where you want it. The camcorder tends to speed up the motions of the person being photographed, so slow the action down when taping. We want the trainee to be able to do the Task Steps he sees not be impressed by how fast the Trainer can do it.

When video taping, always remember to tape two separate endings. Tape one ending for the pre-employment simulation and then tape another ending for the training and certification tapes. The pre-employment should end at the point the button is pushed to start the machine. Lock all power systems off during pre-employment testing to decrease the opportunities of accidents occurring. The certification and training segments should end with the machine running after the start button is pushed. Don't forget to get your IE involved in performing a time and motion study to determine how long the simulation should take to do.

Remember we have two concerns when a process or Task is performed. First, it must be done correctly and accurately to assure a quality product or service is provided and secondly it should be performed within a specified amount of time to assure that productivity standards are met. Always emphasize that speed is not the primary motive, quality is! Speedy production of inferior goods or services is not the goal.

Examination cut scores should be established for every pre-employment simulation but only for administrative reasons. When dealing with pre-employment testing, nobody ever fails (flunks) a pre-employment test; they simply don't score high enough to be considered for the job (e.g. we're only considering the ten highest scorers as candidates for the job!). The administrative cut score is that score on the list below which nobody has ever been considered for employment. You simply have not yet scored high enough to be considered for the job. During a pre-employment testing your scores are simply a rank ordering. Only the top scores are considered. If one does not score high enough to be considered, the applicant may take the test again to see if his score improves his chance of employment by making a higher score on percentage of correct answers or time to complete.

Re-testing is a management concern for a couple of reasons. First the equipment is tied up and second; the trainers are involved with test administration. Looking at it from a more positive note, the applicant is pro-active and is involved with trying to increase his or her skill level. There is no cause for concern on management's part about prior exposure to the test contaminating the results. So any calls about how often you will re-test is up to your discretion. You may set limits. For instance, the number of times an individual may be re-tested may be set or the number of times within a given period of time.

Points of concern about test administration must be emphasized. Show the video on a simulation-by-simulation basis. Then have the applicant perform the simulation. The applicant is allowed to use his or her training manual for whatever reference he or she needs. The more the applicant uses the manual, the slower the applicant's time. Thus the more familiar the applicant is with the steps of the process or Task, theoretically, the shorter the time for simulation completion. Hence, experience benefits both the company and the applicant.

Either of two different forms of self-improvement may be offered to the applicant. Since a copy of the training manual is given to each applicant, notes may be made in the booklet for reference during the performance of the simulation. Or you can offer either limited or unlimited screening or showing of the Task or process with or without machine access for practice. A personal observation over the years seems to hold true. Applicants generally take about three times longer to perform the simulation than an incumbent. Therefore, I like to use the term "trainability index" when referring to an applicant's "time to complete" score. I have only observed this with production figures (time to complete). I have not observed the same increase in how the simulation was completed. This is my quality indicator. It normally does not change during retesting. It does not appear that the quality portion of the equation is either a "go" or "no go" attribute.

Test results may be used for the pairing of trainees. By carefully analyzing the pre-employment test scores, you may put a slow learner with a fast learner. This can aid in team bonding. In situations with plenty of applicants, you may want to create a group of fast learners. Thus pre-employment tests scores serve to allow the grouping or team assignment. A battery of simulations serves to allow you to make an informed staff selection decision by putting your best trainees in a designated position.

My experience with simulation testing has always been a positive one. In over thirty years, I have never been legally challenged when using it. After all when a person applies for a job, all that most people want is the chance to let them show you what they can do. So simulations give both the applicant and management a very fair and effective, not to mention a "face valid" method to evaluate each other before the employment.

During another consultancy in the textile industry, I was exposed to a group of females who had expressed an interest in moving up from a weaver 's position to a loom fixer's position. Loom fixer is simply a loom mechanic's position. Management was saying that this type of job is too physically demanding to be done by females. Even the male loom fixers told me that females were not strong enough to lift into place a 250-pound electric motor on the loom.

Additional questioning uncovered that a power winch was used to do the lifting and that the Task was never done by a single person but was always done by at least a two-person team anyway. The frequency of motor replacement plus the power wench being introduced into the process does not justify using this as a pre-employment test. Always verify and validate maximum limits or standards obtained from the workforce. You may find as I did that the given requirement was exaggerated.

After covering my finding with the training manager reluctantly agreed to my experimenting on a group of females with our simulation test battery. Some even had completion times good enough to make them considerable for employment as a loom fixer. One of the females of the group tested happened to be one of the advocates for a sexual discrimination suit. She interestingly enough had one of the best sets of scores on the simulation test battery. I got permission to talk with her from the Training Manager. She indicated to me that the satisfaction she experienced from taking the pre-employment test battery had given her a taste of what the job she had wanted was like. After testing she indicated to me that she no longer was interested in becoming a loom fixer because she was not willing to push herself to do the Tasks on a daily basis. Therefore, the idea of any sexual discrimination suit was gone from her mind.

Since the court ruling that the plaintiff may not file a trivial discrimination lawsuit, there have been fewer and fewer discrimination suits. In the earlier days of discrimination litigation companies seemed to be assumed guilty until they proved themselves innocent. Rather than incur what seemed to them the somewhat staggering costs of validating their pre-employment testing programs many companies opted to drop their testing programs. As many of them later discovered, there are tremendous problems and costs associated with trying to run a business with out this valuable information. Others companies have just held on to or stayed with their testing programs. My own personal opinion is that a truly modern company espousing "world class quality" cannot afford to operate without a pre-employment and a certification-testing program. Simulation tests can easily be modified to a certification program or a promotional system. In either case it can supply valuable information with regard to your personnel decisions. Yearly certification stops problems with incumbents who have begun to loose their skill levels.

Current training seemed to be constantly indicating the success of our loom fixer pilot program. Finally one day the Training Manager asked if he could present some our data at a meeting he was scheduled to attend. I immediately inquired as to what meeting he was talking about. "The American Society of Training Development (ASTD's) Annual International Conference in Chicago. I think I ought to present something since I'm being sworn in as their International President for the next year." Picking myself up from the floor I casually responded, "Yeah that will be all right."

To make a long story short, there just happened to be a corporate training director of the fourth largest textile company in the U.S. sitting in the back of his presentation. He approached the Training Manager and asked how he could get in touch with me. I was advised of the pending call. I was a bit taken aback when I was asked, "Can the video be made to look a little bit more professional?" He wanted to use the simulation approach on a plant renovation project he had under way.

Allow me to provide a little background of what we stepped into. The textile company, as previously discussed had negotiated with a foreign loom manufacturer the exclusive rights to purchase and use a particular high-speed (4x) innovative air-jet loom. The company then went to a single plant and laid off every one of their weave room employees. All of the old looms were removed and the new looms were put in service as rapidly as possible. As quickly as a new stand of looms arrived, they were installed. Six foreign trainers had trained the company's old training staff. The training staff brought back the company's best "old" workers for training on the new loom. After approximately eight weeks of training, the weavers were put on production jobs.

This meant that they were placed on a piece rate established by the industrial engineering department. The amount of cloth the weaver had to produce was four times the amount they had to produce on the old job. The turnover had soared to125% as the production rate for the weaver's hit 50%. That meant that the weavers were only making about one-fourth of their previous salaries. They were hot!

To improve the professional look of my videos I was assigned a corporate video professional of my very own. He was a former corporate training program trainer turned cameraman. I quickly started and finished a TBJA of the weaver's position using trainers and "surviving weaver" incumbents as the SMEs. I covered all of management on the selection of simulations based upon the data. I was challenged almost immediately that I was selecting the most difficult Tasks that were performed on the job to serve as screening simulations. I won this argument with a simple maneuver, "Let's try it and if doesn't work, we won't use it."

This time we approached things very professionally. We storyboarded the job with a 35mm camera. These photographs were used for storyboarding the job and subsequently for the training manual. The video camera operator handled this duty. We also had access to a video-editing machine. One night while reviewing the day's shooting we discovered that we had forgotten to film one storyboard segment. We pieced the segment together from previous footage with the film editor and we had the trainer doing something that she had never done in front of a camera. I quickly learned that the old adage, "believe nothing that you hear and only half of what you see" was true.

Trainer Comments on Simulations

"The training video allows four trainees per trainer. Two to have in a "hands on" training session while the other two either preview or review the training video."

"The trainer's job has changed. He or she no longer trains in skills; they verify, validate or certify that skills have been mastered."

"The trainees either train themselves or each other."

"When I'm working with a trainee, I'm no longer showing him or her how to do a Task, I'm letting the trainee show me that he or she can do it."

"Quick learners help slow learners."

"Now I'm sure everybody is trained the same way. In other words, the videotape, the process flowcharts and the certification score sheets assure us that everybody has been taught to do it the same way."

"Trainees learn the necessary operator skills quicker and better."

"My training time is shorter."

"The trainee comes to me already partially trained."

"If you test your trainee every Friday you're continually ready when manufacturing asks for somebody out of your training class. You can show the manufacturing representative the trainee's progress from the hire date to the current time. Also the trainee's weaknesses are easy to spot. Manufacturing, therefore, can make a better informed decision."

Let me point out, if you want to manage the process; have your supervisors refer to a wall-sized flowchart during pre-shift meetings and have the worker's find the Process or Task Step on the flowchart which caused yesterday's production problem. Go over the Step to assure that the problem is corrected and will not occur again. If a certification program is maintained on a quarterly basis, the supervisor can use the scores in his performance appraisal of the employee. You can readily spot any drop-off in skill level. An operator may need new glasses, medical attention or possibly a transfer.

Safety must be incorporated into the training. For instance, the new loom was four times faster than the old loom. When watching the lathe beat up or push the just inserted thread line into the face of the cloth, it looks like it is being done at exactly the same speed as the older loom previously used by most experienced weavers. If you can remember, it was like in the old westerns watching the apparent slow-speed of the spokes turning in the covered wagon's wheels while the horses ran at full speed. On the old looms, to keep production and quality up, the weavers would time their hand motion to pick out a piece of lint before the lint was beat up by the lathe and woven into the cloth. This was a risky but doable feat on the old loom but impossible on the new loom. Even with our constant warning and reminding, several fingers were lost attempting to accomplish the impossible.

The Corporate Training Director was most kind in the assignment of an internal resource to the Project's training products. He also had approached his boss, the vice-president of Human Resources, with the Project's results. The Project not only had significantly improved the turnover rate from 125% to fewer than 10% but also had significantly helped the production rate by approximately 20-25% and reduced the training time by 50% to four weeks.

The Corporate Training Director had me thinking that our consulting firm had accomplished the impossible when he asked that we prepare a proposal to do what we had demonstrated already. He offered to support a scale-up of our efforts through a division of the company. His vice-president had already swallowed the bait hook, line and sinker and supported what we wanted to do. The vice-president had already asked to meet with his CEO on Monday morning to pitch the project, give him a day or two to mull it over and we should know his decision by Wednesday.

Then came the longest weekend I've ever experienced. Then came Monday and then went Monday with no word! Tuesday followed the same course. By Wednesday, I could no longer resist, I phoned. The secretary to the vice-president answered the phone. I asked to speak to the vice-president of Human Resources and was told that he was no longer with the company. I then asked for the Corporate Training Director and was then told he was no longer with the company either.

I later discovered what had happened. There had been a behind the scenes power struggle that resulted in a new CEO, which found my boys supporting the losing team. The new CEO had played golf on Saturday with the new Corporate Attorney and they had agreed to assign an attorney to each of the division's ten plants. This created a new EEOC department in the law firm and the firm was quite fortunate to have secured the services of a young attorney from the Washington office of EEOC to head up the department.

My contacts had seen the handwriting on the wall and quickly, for reasons of personal concern and security, "hit the silks!" in order to salvage their corporate careers. I was advised by my former associates to meet with the law firm's department head and present my proposal. During a brief meeting with the young attorney, I too "hit the silks!" I had never before or since experienced such an intellectual void concerning EEOC subject matter. It was hopeless!

Major disappointment affects different people in different ways. At my firm, relatively bizarre behavior began to manifest itself more and more around the office. The disappointment pushed things over the edge. I quickly learned I owned 49% of a business over which I had zero control. I had my first encounter with a manic-depressive. I prayed for direction and my prayers were soon answered.

On a snowy afternoon, with about six inches of snow on the ground, I was driving back home from a business meeting. Suddenly at about 50 mph I caught sight of an object in my left eye that was about to pass me. I looked to my left to see what it was and will never forget the horror of realizing it was my rear end. Almost instantly my life seemed to go into slow motion. I remember looking right, which was the direction of my spin and seeing an approximately 80-foot drop-off with no guardrail. I remember closing my eyes. It was just about this time that I felt the car hit something with a tremendous crash that shook the car.

With my eyes still closed I thought I had started down the side of the mountain. Eyes still closed I waited to hit again. There was nothing. So then I started to figure I had died in the first crash. I slowly opened my eyes to see where I was. To my surprise I was still sitting there in the front seat of my Z-car. The car sat at the edge of the drop-off. I must have sat there for a good five minutes checking to see if I was still alive. I finally got my wits together enough to realize that even a short prayer of thanksgiving to God for my deliverance was in order.

Having expressed my thanks, I moved from the seat and exited the car with stained clothes to inspect the damage. I shakily walked around to the passenger's side to see what I had hit. There was nothing, no dents, not even snow stacked against the wheels. One can only surmise, but I believe that the hand of God stopped me. I don't remember hearing a voice but I distinctly remember, "You've tried to do things your way and it didn't work. Now let's do it my way! I remember thinking, "You're in control."

In the next two years I was led through a corporate dissolution, avoided personal bankruptcy, saved my home and doubled my original salary. Within the next five years I met and married, Margaret, the girl of my dreams, built a brand new home in S.C., moved to Florida and went to work with a Fortune 50 company. Within the next five years I was voted Director of the N.E. Florida Chapter of ASTD, realized my dreams of teaching in a graduate school program, secured another dream job of consulting and travel in the warehousing and distribution industry and finally owning my own consulting firm. We were blessed with children David, Steven, Allison, and Andrew and now we have awesome grandchildren; Steven Ryan, Peyton Andrew and Mackenzie Athena.

Not to say that the road was always smooth or that things happened as fast as I wanted them to move or the way I wanted them to but the Lord provided every time. I received my share of terrible bosses, was involved in three reductions of force (lay-offs) but each time I landed stronger. To get me to open my own consulting firm, my faith was challenged when God encouraged me to turn down a job that provided a $500 raise just when I really needed it. It was his time that I start a consulting firm. Small contracts and sub-contracts kept things afloat until that fateful phone call from a former business associate saying that he needed me in Cleveland the next day. Two days later I started a consulting firm with a total stranger who later became my best friend. What followed far exceeded either of our wildest dreams. Everything comes in its time.

I thought the startup envelope had been pushed when I had been asked to coordinate management training (3 to 5 per location) and operator training (35 to75 employees per location) in the opening of five distribution centers in five different states in a twelve week window with a twelve week lead time. But then came the request for management and technical training in five identical distribution centers to open simultaneously in five different cities with a lead-time of four weeks.

I will never forget, walking out of a planning meeting with four weeks until startup when I had entered the meeting with seven weeks before startup. I ended up training the site managers or their assistants how to do the technical training and let them run with it. As foolhardy as this approach to the problem was, it worked. Half of the consulting business is to make a right decision and the other half is making the decision work. I am yet to figure out which is harder. Anyway, that's how things started in the consulting business. But let's switch gears.

My most successful and satisfying experience training employees was a three month phased hiring 30-person/per shift 3-shift operation. Though originally conceived as a 21-day startup of 3 shifts, management mistakes coupled with construction delays created a situation where we were given the initial 30 employees for thirty days and were told to keep them busy. We had enough time for trainees to personally validate the work process flows; the trainees also validated the computer processes and assisted in the layout, positioning and installation of equipment. The original 30 employees helped select and train the remaining 60 people.

When the warehouse was finally ready to open, the client's CEO came for an opening tour. A new and technically inexperienced plant manager took a chance on his people. The plant manager informed the CEO that he could select the facility tour guide from anybody on the 30-person shift. The CEO immediately stepped out on the operating floor and selected, to my horror, the one trainee I would have ranked number 39th among the 30 trainees. I cringed as the plant manager introduced the CEO to the trainee. To my surprise the trainee seemed to light up and proceeded to blow the client's CEO and me away with his knowledge of the how's and why's of the processes to service the client's account. The CEO couldn't believe the level of understanding he was hearing come from the operator's mouth. He walked away with a big smile, and expressed his confidence and comfort with the servicing of his products. I overheard him say to the plant manager, " I would expect you to have been able to do that, but I would never have expected an operator to have been able to carry out that tour and answer my questions. I am truly impressed."

The sales department quickly picked up on this and very quickly turned the training room into a sales theater. The operating floor remains to this day plastered with wall-sized process flow maps where the operators keep up-to-date.

Nearly a year later, I happened to be at my client's corporate headquarters on a totally unrelated matter. On the way out for lunch the International Sales Director and I were joined by two of his International Sales Personnel. The International Sales Director had been on a tour of U.S. facilities with two Bolivian companies. He said his group was bowled over by one plant they had visited. The actual operators had conducted the tour and fielded the questions. "I've never seen anything like it. You guys have got to put this one on your next touring circuit." The customer was impressed.

The training approach ties in perfectly with our management coaching philosophy. At some facilities we have been able to decrease supervisors from three to one. We kept only one salary plus benefits as a cost reduction. The other salary plus benefits we gave to the 60 shift people as long as production and quality standards were maintained. The remaining supervisor's job changed to that of a facilitator for his team leaders. The supervisor is no longer responsible for technical training. He is responsible for skill certification or for documentation of skill acquisition. In other words he is responsible for using the tools developed by Training and IE to determine the presence and level of skill possessed and demonstrated during operator assessment.

Operators are responsible for their own technical training by using the process maps, videos and digital training tools developed and provided by Training. In the event of vacation, prolonged illness or other reasons for missing long periods of work, the operator is responsible for checking the posted process map to make themselves aware of any process changes that have occurred during their absence. Process maps are dated with the effective change date. Maps are posted to the effective date to give the operators a chance to learn and practice the new steps. Then they could be personally certified with regard to the process.

Certification may be done on a monthly, quarterly, semi-annual or annual basis to assure possession and proficiency of skills required by the job. The Trainers are responsible for the necessary job analysis, digital documentation of the job, training manuals, videos, simulations, process maps and the soft skills necessary for the job.

Words From Trainees

On the last day of a five-day training session one trainee said to me in front of the group, "You haven't just taught us to work in a warehouse, you've taught us to manage a warehouse." Others have commented, "I feel confident I know what they want and buddy they'll get it." "I've never been a good mind reader, with these process maps, there's no guessing around," still others have said. "I've always wondered why management wanted us to do certain things, now I understand." "I feel more protected from management, now that they can't change their story."

The management perception of Hunan Resources is currently one of a necessary but costly part of running a modern organization. HR is viewed as worthless but tolerated. We may attribute this perception to the "good old boy" caveat portrayed by former personnel and training directors vying for prestige and power. Meanwhile, they were losing sight of other subversives as support bases for HR which were systematically being stripped. You've heard the old adage, divide and conquer. Exactly the strategy employed. Who won? That's right, HRM! Who is always the most expendable at crunch time? That's right, HRD! Academia has thus far unsuccessfully attempted to produce a Human Resource Generalist but continues to turn out basically an HRM. HRDs are somewhat undercut. Rather than intentionally, HRDs are unintentionally academically deprived not because of any oversight but because of the lack of a systematic educational approach to employ.

Even professional affiliation leads us to a sense of separation with the Society of Human Resource Management (SHRM) for HRMs and the American Society of Training and Development (ASTD) for HRDs. Not many professionals have the time to be actively involved in both. What is needed here is that a good human resource technical background to be offered by each respective organization where a Generalist is given the how and why of not only selection, compensation and benefits but training, human motivation and performance evaluation. The emphasis needs to be on co-education rather than specialization. The Generalist, in other words, needs more technical preparation while in school as well as initially on the job or at professional meetings. The Generalist needs to be perceived by management and industrial engineering as an internal Human Resource Consultant who brings much technical insight to the table and is concerned with cost and productivity. Then and only then does the Human Resource Consultant regain his value to the team.

In the past, the human resource position on the team became relegated to the affirmative action initiative where placement of a minority individual would do the least damage within the organization. Soon mistresses, girlfriends and former secretaries found their way into boardrooms. In most organizations this became akin to the fox being hired to guard the chicken coop as barriers beneath the boardroom began to fall drastically and as the once male dominated positions began to shift. But the now infamous glass ceiling remained firmly in place. Within the organization, the human resource department was the first to turn into a female bastion. The educational level of human resources began to change about this time with a greater disparity of education. Academia quickly picked up on this void and soon undergraduate as well as graduate level human resource programs began to fill course catalogues.

It's now time for the HRM/HRD bickering and finger-pointing to stop and for personnel researchers to begin joint cooperation to improve the capabilities of human resources thus moving the field into it's rightful place of prominence. Let's take an example of a warehouseman to express our concept. A taxonomy of warehouse Processes (i.e., receiving, put-away, picking, packing, shipping, etc.) may be brainstormed by SMEs Then possible Tasks performed within the Processes are brainstormed by SMEs. Next, the Steps of each linear Process or the how to perform each Task is identified by SMEs. Next, the Knowledge and Abilities necessary to develop into Skills with continued practice are brainstormed by SMEs.

Finally the levels of certain specified variables and Whole Job Requirements required in Task performance such as Math, Language, Reasoning, etc. are rated by SMEs. HRD, HRM, Industrial Engineering or Manufacturing maps the processes. Process maps offer insight learning, rather than traditional learning theory. Process maps acknowledge the applicant's preference over the original types of training formats and materials. Finally the Process Steps are written down on paper reducing arguments and confusion and increasing the quality of production and product reliability. The mentality and training of Applicants is already structured towards the current best approach thus implying that change is forthcoming.

The Industrial Engineer may verify the accuracy and thoroughness of the Processes and Tasks as well for their performance times. Simulations, Training Materials and Score Sheets of the most important Processes and Tasks can be constructed by HRM or HRD. HRM establishes minimum qualifications for the job using job analysis results. HRM may then classify the job using cluster analysis based on the specified variables and Whole Job Requirements. HRM assures that each applicant meets minimum qualification standards. HRM shows simulations to applicants and schedules simulation testing for the up-coming week. Applicants practice necessary performance Skills.

HRM or HRD administers the content-valid simulations to applicants and completes Score Sheets to document their strengths and weaknesses. Next the applicants are Rank-ordered based on Score Sheets from the best, most economical applicant to train, to the poorest, least economical applicant to train. HRM or HRD presents simulation results or the applicant's trainability index to Manufacturing and schedules applicant's interviews for hiring decisions. HRM sends out job analysis results as part of a Wage and Salary Survey to determine compensation to be offered. HRM submits salary recommendation to Manufacturing. Manufacturing makes hiring decisions and job offers. Applicants are offered positions that are accepted as New Hires. Trainees report to the appropriate HRD Training Session to further hone their performance Skills. Trainees can be grouped as faster learner paired with a slower learner or fast-to-fast learner or slow-to-slow learner. At the end of week one of training HRD can administer Simulations to Trainees and document their Trainee performance levels. Manufacturing and HRD meet to evaluate Trainees performance levels and performance improvements. This is done each week until the trainee's performance level reaches the Industrial Engineer-determined production levels. HRD documents performance levels and over time determines an acceptable training course length.

With testing, if Manufacturing decides it needs to pull an employee from training it knows exactly who it's getting, where his strengths and weaknesses are and when and where further training is appropriate or necessary. With testing, HRD and Manufacturing know when a trainee is ready for transfer from training to production. The use of simulations would also allow for the establishment of a certification program to ensure continued production levels are capable of being maintained by employees. Manufacturing may post process maps. Manufacturing may reference yesterday's production problems on posted process maps at the morning production meeting. A Pay-for-Knowledge or Pay-for-Performance program may be set up with the timed simulations serving as the check and program balance. New Processes or Process Changes will only be implemented following thorough documentation and training.

The most under-explored area within HR, but possessing the most potential, is the field of human motivation. Much research has been done in this area but with results that have thus far been very disappointing. Many theories abound but none of note have been substantiated by research. The most promising theory yet proposed is by a consultant from Charlestown, South Carolina, a Mr. Jack Henley. It is known as the Barrier-Facilitator Theory of Motivation. In his theory man is purported to seek facilitators and to find ways around barriers. Under his theory man is motivated not by satisfaction but by dissatisfaction. When man becomes enough dissatisfied with his situation, he gets motivated to the point that he seeks a way to change his situation. Perceived satisfiers do not at all times motivate a person. It depends on the situation! For example, apple pie would appear to be a motivating factor to a person who had just been trapped in the desert for three days, but not after five hamburgers had just been consumed by the person. In fact, the apple pie might even, at times, be knocked out of the offering hand in disgust by the satiated person. What a way for a perceived satisfier to come to it's end!

With dissatisfiers as motivators, one must understand that the dissatisfiers are on a continuum. They are not static; the continuum runs from basic needs to self-actualization needs. With all human beings dissatisfiers are constantly changing. As one dissatisfier is met another one takes over. This is easily understood when addressing the teenage mentality of "What have you done for me lately?" The thing to remember is "What is important to me, NOW? The level of importance of the dissatisfier becomes the key. When the level of importance of the dissatisfiers is measured, the next dissatisfier along the continuum can be often predicted. And this becomes a highly important factor. Imagine, being able to accurately predict what will motivate a group of people six months in the future.

This requires that two measures on each variable be identified. These are satisfaction-dissatisfaction and importance. Just imagine if political surveys were correctly applied at the beginning of a campaign to properly identify the voters' issues before establishing the party's platform. Then you could survey your potential candidates to determine the correct candidate to place in the election. This doesn't require a degree in rocket surgery! Politicians continue to insist in trying to do the process backwards. That is, choosing their candidate first followed by their platform and then matching the two. No wonder we keep seeing examples of "hoof in mouth" disease because in this day and time, it's hard to renege on a publicly documented position or to deny a statement from the past.

So determine the dissatisfaction variables followed by how important the variable is to the rater. Let's take an example, am dissatisfied with world hunger but you don't see me selling all that I have and giving it to the poor overseas. I am dissatisfied with it but it is not important enough to me to spur me to action. On the other hand, if this were important to me then I would have acted to change things.

Trainers must remember that "perception is reality" among humans especially among those with lower educational levels. It is important to understand that the next most important dissatisfier takes precedent immediately upon removal of the previous dissatisfier. This is termed "locking into the drive cycle." If we can maintain a successive list of dissatisfiers on which the human can become focused, we are locked in a drive cycle where we are constantly motivated to remove the new barriers as they appear. One should always remain aware that those with a low education level in this country tended not to like high school or the curriculum in high school and there is no reason to think that because they have grown a little older that their perceptions have changed. What didn't work then probably won't work now! But we as trainers have persisted in trying to enforce the classroom style of learning. Assign lots to read in the training manual, read aloud in the classroom and have trainees' follow along, class discussion and test for retention. Exactly what we did in high school. What's the trainee's reaction? You guessed it, boredom and resistance to learning, or a half—baked attempt at retention! We learned our lessons well. Remember the old saying "those who fail to learn from history are doomed to repeat it." Always remember, the best type of learning is called "insight learning" and causes the highest rate of retention. So, go for something new and different. Try process mapping.

And Then There Was Training!

I will always be enthralled by a challenge, as evidenced by the resume I had forwarded to a rather intriguing blind ad in the newspaper. Looking back, I was probably "easy pickings" for the plant manager for a Fortune Top 50 corporation, who called me about 10 o'clock one night. Our conversation began with an exchange of bio data including the talent and skills for which he was looking. Quickly our biggest obstacle to friendship and communication surfaced. We had to overcome it before we could continue. You would have to be either a Georgia Tech alumni or Georgia dropout to understand the bitter and intense rivalry between the two schools. To make matters even more interesting, we were the same age, putting us in school at the same time.

Then came the big question, "Would you even consider coming to work for a Bulldog?" By that time, we had both discovered there was a kindred spirit but with a different allegiance. I suggested that, "This has to be one of the most difficult phone calls that you've ever had to make. You know, calling a Yellow Jacket and admitting you need help." He quickly responded, "Yeah, that's why I've put off making this call for three days!" We discussed his assigned responsibility, to manufacture the world's first disposable contact lens, and what had to be accomplished until almost one o'clock in the morning.

A plant visit was arranged to check my chemistry with that of his existing staff. My day on-site began in HR with a battery of pre-employment tests (i.e., placing a pencil dot inside the "o" in a page full of "o's" as many as one could without touching the line and within a ninety second window.) During the day all went well from supervisors, engineers, and superintendents to the Vice president of Manufacturing. The Vice president of Manufacturing asked me one "loaded" question, "What do you, think of our pre-employment test battery we give our employees?" I decided not to share that my dots in circles had lasted for three minutes because the test administrator had been distracted with a phone call and forgot to stop me at 90 seconds. She simply rectified the problem by doubling my time and dividing my score by two. Instead, I simply stated the obvious. "The test battery appears to have a lack of face validity and therefore, it would be hard to defend in court!"

The plant manager had arranged a final "courtesy interview" for me with the company's Vice president of Human Resources for I would be working with him but not for him. The Vice president arrived thirty minutes late for the interview. I respectfully stood and extended my hand when he entered the room and closed the door. He brushed by me without an introduction or a pardon for his tardiness. Before either of our fannies could come into contact with a chair, he attacked. "After reviewing your resume, the question I have is what the hell are you doing applying for a plant job rather than a teaching job?" I explained my interest in the applications of research to "real world" problems instead of pure academic research. The Vice president of HR responded, "You don't belong here and I'll do everything in my power to prevent it. Just send your trip expenses and receipts to this address," as he handed me his card. He then opened the door, walked over to his secretary's desk and said, "See that he gets to the airport." The Vice president then walked straight down the hall, out the front door and never looked back.

Suddenly, my rather high-flying emotional roller coaster had suddenly jumped the track. Upon my arrival home, I quickly completed and submitted my expenses for reimbursement. Needless to say, I didn't include a letter thanking the Vice president for his consideration. Five days later, an envelope with just my expense check arrived. For four weeks I heard nothing. Then one night the plant manager called and asked, "Do you still want to come to work for me?" My response was, "Oh, so you won the war?" He said, "That's pretty perceptive! How did you know that we were fighting over the position?" I then shared what had happened with the Vice president of HR. He apologized for my treatment and said the Vice president of HR was a former "bean counter" with an associate's degree who had no idea of what he was doing. He was probably worried that I might expose him. The plant manager assured me that the position was a direct Manufacturing report and posed his question of my interest, again. He said his team really needed me; and with that I had been hooked, played, landed, filleted and fried. The plant manager had to only stick his fork in me, for I was done.

Three weeks after my arrival, the company decided to add a second shift so I quickly found myself with 750 trainees across the two shifts. The next six to nine months were exciting times as the shifts doubled in size again to over 1500. Believe me when I say that the number of people to be trained was almost an insignificant concern when compared with other concerns. With some 250 engineers pooling their research and development talents on the plastic injection-molding manufacturing process for contact lens, nothing was stable for very long. The manufacturing line was shut down every Saturday for sanitization (complete sterilization of the manufacturing production and supply lines) and process upgrades. The manufacturing process was, in reality, an ever-changing research and development process. The only constant that I had with the process was change. My boss used to ask R&D every morning during the daily rack-up meeting, "Do we have a process yet?"

For the first six months we never ran the process the same way more than two days in a row. Talk about an agile and flexible workforce. We were blessed with the best "core groups" of operators with which it has ever been my pleasure to work. I was responsible for maintaining the "process diary." I would "pencil in" the process and continue to erase and re-write the changes until the final process steps were "pinned down." Later at a Fortune 50 Quality Training program I learned a very appropriate term for Tasks in a volatile process such as this. The trainer referred to these Process Tasks as CBAs (i.e., Current Best Approach). As the name "CBA" implies, in a continually improving process, the process map is only temporary and is therefore, ever changing. That puts the burden of responsibility squarely on everyone's shoulders to constantly look for new and better ways to improve the process.

HRM & HRD worked very closely in the selection and training of "core group" associates for the plant start-up. I learned very quickly, as training manager, that I had a lot at stake during the selection of new employees. The old computer adage still holds today, "garbage in, garbage out". Share control; if possible, or at least attempt to gain strong influence in HRM's selection process. Volunteer to develop and supply HRM with pre-employment simulations of your technical training for their selection process. Sure it's more work for you initially but it's your success that you're trying to guarantee. Think of it, after all, as the faucet through which your future trainees must flow. They get to demonstrate their potential trainability for you before they are hired.

When I'm in a HRD position (trainer), I try to prevent others (i.e., personnel managers) from controlling my fate (e.g., training success) whenever possible. Always try to put yourself in a position where you can master or strongly influence your own destiny or outcomes. Never knowingly put yourself into a position of having to "make a silk purse out of a sow's ear." It's virtually impossible to accomplish. You alone control your boss's perceptions of you as procrastinating and lazy or energetic and successful.

Process or Task Documentation

Before training can take place, the process must be documented. This can be accomplished during a Task- Based Job Analysis or by an alternative device known as "process mapping." Tasks as well as processes are the smallest "meaning-ful" pieces of work done on a job. Both are composed of steps. A set of sequenced process steps is used to describe in detail the "what is done" and the "how it is done". Process mapping can be done at two different levels (i.e., high or low). High level is used for overviews and for process orientation of management and labor. Low level is used for the technical training of those who actually perform the job.

The low level is often referred to as to as at the "keystroke" level. An example of what this actually means is that if the operator interfaces with an accounting process. The process map would walk the operator step-by-step through the data entry process. This would include which key to push, what would appear on the computer screen if the right key is pressed, what the operator should do if the right screen does not appear and what's the next step if the data input is correct. High level mapping on the other hand would suffice if you were only concerned with the fact that data are entered into the computer as part of an overview of the process and not with the specifics of how the data are entered.

The best way I have to flowchart a process is by management's formation of a team composed of an equal number of supervisory and operating personnel (i.e., 2-4 people) and one process engineer and the flow charter. The flow charter meets with the team and explains the project's purpose, the team's mission and project definitions. The team then brain-storms to identify key critical processes of the job and the most knowledgeable individuals responsible for process documentation as well as for the scheduling of sessions and reviews required for timely project completion.

Along with identifying the process, I ask the team to also help me document the process's initial and final steps. The flow charter works with one operator and/or one supervisor to document the assigned process. The function of the flow charter is to facilitate the process documentation by use of probing and leading questions. The function of the process engineer is to assure that no critical process steps are overlooked and for arbitration. To begin, the initial step is written on the flip chart pad located at the front of the room. The facilitator simply asks, "What's the next step?" Simply record the next step that is suggested. Write the step on the flip chart exactly as it's identified. The step's wording can be edit-ed for grammatical correctness later after the session.

This format convention is different than the one used for writing a Task statement. Here, I'm following the product or service as it is being prepared for delivery to the external customer. The format convention for writing a step is to first list the job title of the individual doing the step, followed by an action verb (what happened?) and then with a direct object (on what the action was performed and what happened as a result of that action?).

Example: Picker (P) enters "picked" ITEM CODE into the "high-lighted" seven boxes on the computer screen and presses "enter" key and blinking cursor moves to ITEM NAME.

The usual convention for flow-charting for an action or Task performed on the job is the use of a rectangular-shaped box surrounding the written Task verbiage. The supervisor is in the group to assure that no critical process steps are overlooked or disputed following arbitration by the process engineer. The technical trainer responsible for training material development can do flow-charting or it can be delegated. I prefer to do it myself simply for process familiarity for subsequent training purposes. There are also many commercially available computer software programs for documenting or mapping the process.

Process documentation must be a cooperative effort between Labor and Management. Any communication breakdown between the two groups must be resolved before any training can begin. Ask your Industrial Engineer to perform a time & motion analysis of the process steps as well as to measure the process's quality standards. Assure that the decision is quantitative.

The criteria for process adoption or implementation should be to choose the method or procedure requiring the least amount of time to accomplish and/or causing the least number of quality problems or concerns. Always have Management "sign off" on any process maps that are developed during documentation. This assures later Management support of all developed documentation. Have Labor "sign off" on the maps also. Now that the training materials are ready, let's concentrate on how these materials are used in the selection process.

SELECTING NEW HIRES

An HRM manager with no specialized training in test construction was able to utilize his TBJA data to produce a valid pre-employment device for use by a nationwide temporary services employment company. The author was Mr. George Russell as he served in the position of Human Resource Manager for a company in Jacksonville, Florida. At this time, Mr. Russell was serving as the state President of the Society of Human Resource Management (SHRM).

His employer at that time was the largest third-party warehouser and distributor in the country and one of its contracts was about to take over the operations of five identical regional distribution centers for one of its clients. In other words, individuals were to be hired and trained to seamlessly take over the client's five distribution centers in five different cities within a 12-week period.

Explain and administer the Forklift Flow Chart Examination (see Appendix G). Have the associates write their names and the date at the top of the exam. Give the group approximately fifteen minutes to complete the exam. Make sure adequate time is allowed for all to finish. Then and only then have the group put down their pencils. Have the group exchange papers. Walk the group through each question and review the correct answers with the group before collecting the exam papers for scoring. Record the scores for each associate in his personnel file.

This particular situation is intriguing in that in it verified safety knowledge as well as the operating knowledge of a forklift but it measured the employee's ability to read and understand a flowchart (a tool with which the person was to be trained). Used in conjunction with a driving, picking and put away simulation and it had a content valid standardized method of picking the best available future warehouse operators in each location.

Training by Process Map

Divide the trainees into pairs or groups. Pairs if you wish the "buddy system" or a "fast learner matched up with a slow learner." One trainee will sort of push the other one along or pull the other along. We're trying to motivate the trainees to get them to figure it out rather than telling them the answer and asking that they simply repeat it back to the trainer. This is taking advantage of several concepts. One, it provides feedback or information to the trainee about what management wants and expects on the job or in the process. Second, it is presenting manageable bit-sized pieces of the job or process. Third, it allows the trainee the means to figure out the next step followed by immediate reinforcement or corrective feedback. Four, it provides the necessary assistance, other than the trainer, to provide corrective feedback and guide the process. Five, it provides the trainee more effective visual cues and more touchy-feely things than other learning strategies.

Phase 1a Give the group one copy of the process map with the "yellow-brick road" printed on it (all symbols filled in) and to be "highlighted" in "yellow." Give each group a yellow highlighter. This map will have all the steps listed. The group will be responsible for "highlighting in yellow" the shortest critical path through the map. The group will work together to find the most logical path through the map. Results will be compared with the trainer's master map. The fastest group to reach a solution will choose a spokesperson that in turns presents the group's solution to the entire session. This map study session should take approximately two hours.

Phase 1b Immediately allow the group at least four hours of "hands on" process practice training. Allow as much access to the video training tapes, maps and training manuals as possible to assure standardization of training. Encourage them to write notes in their manuals. Post-it notes work very well in the "hands-on" practice session and gets trainees used to writing down the steps. This process practice session should take approximately two hours followed by a break. Then give the group a short break before beginning Phase 2a of the training.

Phase 2a Give the group one copy of the process map with the "odd" symbols left "blank." Give each group a deck of cards with the "odd" steps printed out on the cards of the deck. Working together the group should fill in the "odd" map empty symbols on the handout map using the correct terminology or step. The results should be compared with the "yellow brick road" map to assure the accuracy of the solution. All steps must be filled in. The first group to finish with a solution chooses a spokesperson that then presents the solution to the other groups in the session.

Phase2b Immediately allow the group at least four hours of "hands on" process practice training. Allow as much access to the video training tapes, maps and training manuals as possible to assure standardization of training. Encourage them to write notes in their manuals. Post-it notes work very well in the "hands-on" practice session and gets them used to writing down the steps. This process practice session should take approximately two hours followed by a break. Then give the group a short break before beginning Phase 3a of the training.

Phase 3a Give each group one copy of the process map with the "even" symbols left "blank." Give each group a deck of cards containing the "even" steps of the process listed on the cards within the deck. Working together the group should fill in on their handout map the "even" symbols using the correct terminology or step. The results should be compared with the "yellow brick road" map to assure the accuracy of the solution. The first group to finish with a solution chooses a spokesperson that then presents the solution to the session.

Phase 3b Immediately allow the group at least four hours of "hands on" process practice training. Allow as much access to the video training tapes, maps and training manuals as possible to assure standardization of training. Encourage them to write notes in their manuals. Post-it notes work very well in the "hands-on" practice session and gets them use to writing down the steps. This process practice session should take approximately two hours followed by a break. Then give the group a short break before beginning Phase 4a of the training.

Phase 4a Give each group one copy of the process map with the "all" symbols left "blank." Give each group a deck of cards containing "all" steps of the process listed on the cards in the deck. The group working together should fill in "all" the symbols using the correct terminology or step. The results should be compared with the "yellow brick road" map to assure the accuracy of the solution. The first group to finish with a solution chooses a spokesperson that then presents the solution to the session.

Phase 4b Immediately allow the group at least four hours of "hands on" process practice training. Allow as much access to the video training tapes, maps and training manuals as possible to assure standardization of training. Encourage them to write notes in their manuals. Post-it notes work very well in the "hands-on" practice session and gets them use to writing down the steps. This process practice session should take approximately two hours followed by a break. Then give the group a short break.

By now each member of the group is beginning to "own" the steps of the process. In the "hands on" process practice that follows (repeat process practice Phases 2b, 3b and 4b), members of the groups will spend less time referring to their process maps because they will have at least partially internalized the maps. Any reference to the process maps should be quicker and more accurate simply because of familiarity. When you discover something for yourself you remember it better and stronger. That is the basis of insight learning. This allows for cross training of incumbents on different jobs and for those who are staying at the same level, for changes in the current job as well as for promotional training before the actual promotion becomes effective and someone who is incompetent or unable to perform is not promoted. The training technique does not change; only the program content is altered to meet the needs of trainees. Only those individuals who meet or are below the performance times that have been set are trained. A Pay-for-Knowledge or Pay-for-Performance System may be installed with this training technique and it will thus support whichever one is implemented. With the time for performance determined by the Industrial Engineering Department, the company can promote, certify, or sanction the trainees.

NEW HIRING CONCEPTS

A couple of new hiring concepts have emerged from some companies with a small head count in their HRM departments. For the start up of the five facilities in twelve weeks, all site managers reported to then initial training and site startup. The purpose was to leave behind some of the Site managers to help out and gain insight into startup problems that their facility may face. They were later pulled out of the situation and thrown into their own startup. Instead of hiring new employees and placing them on a 90-day probationary period, a contract is negotiated and written for a period of time (for 4-weeks, 6-weeks. 8-weeks, 90-days or one year) with a temporary personnel service provider. Before negotiating, calculate your "loaded" (i.e., FICA, insurance, vacation, workman's compensation, etc.) personnel cost. Any loaded cost that the temp agency is not going to pay the worker can be considered as part of the agency's fee.

First, for Temp-To-Perm (4-weeks to 90-days), your personnel costs should be stabilized for the first year or so of employment with employees receiving benefits as they come on board or at some set time after hiring. The temp agency agrees to provide workers for a given negotiated period and price. It then becomes the company's option to hire the worker as a full time employee thus severing his/her relationship with the temp agency. This gives the company an opportunity to observe the worker doing the job before investing heavily in an individual. You can better tell what you're buying. That's sort of like seeing a horse run a race on the track before having to bet on it, much yet buy it.

Second, for Employee Leasing (annual renewal), workers are employees of the leasing company but are leased to you to do work for you. The leasing company's employees work for you and at your discretion. They can be replaced by a simple phone call to the leasing company. Your company has a smaller HRD department that works with the supervisory management team. Workers never become your company's employees but report to your supervisors. This allows you simply to pay all your human resources expenses with just one check.

Regardless of the approach chosen to operate your company, work simulations can and should be utilized in selecting and assigning new hires. Only this time, you supply the selection instruments to the leasing or temp company and after you train them how to use the instruments, the leasing or temp company administers and acts upon the results in making their initial assignments of personnel to your jobs.

Technical training materials still have to be prepared and administered by your company. Any time technical training is employed either in the conventional situation to your employees or to leasing or temp employees, I recommend it be done by your first line supervisors. Why, you ask? Because modern management theorists have been wrong in advocating a supervisor is a supervisor is a supervisor and that the technical part of the job doesn't matter. So, with this new management theory, we have young people coming directly from the college classroom to a position as front-line supervisor of a manufacturing line. Do they know the process? They probably don't know the process unless they have an excessive abundance of initiative, because nobody makes them. Thus we have planted the seed in the minds of the operator that management doesn't know the process. "How could they possibly know, they've never had to do it like we have."

With management's careful nurturing (the elimination of all superfluous expenditures on wasteful technical training for our supervisors), we have successfully implemented our own self-fulfilling prophecy; at least in the minds of operators, that has stripped the technical credibility from our first-line supervisors. We all have heard employees say, "Management has no idea of what I do on the job" or "Why ask him? The supervisor is a nice guy but he doesn't know his "posterior" from a hole in the ground about the process." So there's one trainer's take on the situation.

At the same time that we're banging operators and supervisors over the head for low production levels and high quality problems, we're eliminating "hard skill" (technical training) and "soft skill" (teambuilding, communication and quality training) as a knee-jerk cost-saving step. This is not just a simple example of shooting yourself in the foot; it's an example of blowing away both legs as well as your own rear-end in one shot. I advocate that dollar for dollar your best long-term investment is in your people. Unlike equipment that only depreciates over time, people can appreciate over time with good care and training. By appreciate, I mean several different things (i.e., in knowledge, in production, in quality, in commitment, in attitude). I have discovered over time that the best methodology is to work on perceptions and relationships.

After my first few start-ups as a professional technical trainer, I left the project with a tremendous sense of accomplishment and adoration from my trainees. Sort of felt like a dad proudly watching his kids as they graduated, got a good job and moved out on their own. I also felt a deep sense of sorrow (like a mother hen) as I left my chicks in the care of their supervisor. Each time I would return to their work area, it was like a reunion or dad coming home with all of the gossip about who has done what to whom, interspersed with process questions. Anyway it sure made me feel special. Also my phone would ring endlessly with technical questions from earlier trainees. Once I had two or three or more projects completed these questions became more irritating than ego flattering. Time to investigate! Was my training methodology that bad? What had I not done or done wrong to cause all these technical questions?

As my investigation soon revealed, I had done nothing wrong. The trainees and I had simply "bonded" so that I was perceived as their sole source of technical information. Management had allowed the supervisor to be process trained but only with the trainees. Trainees perceived their supervisors as being technically weak, and viewed their credibility as a source of technical expertise to be a negative number. That position had been reserved for their technical trainer, and that's exactly what I didn't want to happen.

So with the next project I presented management with my findings and they bought in on my approach. I trained just the supervisors on the technical portion of the program and taught them how to use the technical training materials as well as how to measure and manage the process on the job. When training started, I trained supervisors and trainees on the soft skills of teambuilding, communication and quality and the supervisors trained the group in the technical part of the job. This time the desired perception was created and the desired bonding was accomplished.

PLOWING THE FIELD—PARADIGM SHIFT

Before any change should be attempted within an organization the employees need to be properly prepared or armed. Any change usually involves some kind of paradigm shift. A paradigm is a broad framework or conceptual structure within which something is viewed or perceived. A paradigm shift is the breaking down and subsequently the reconstruction of the conceptual framework within which something is usually perceived or associated. This "thinking outside of the box" may be accomplished by applying the materials contained and explained in the appendices. It involves helping incumbents increase their creativity and productivity concerning the potential uses of a plastic cup.

Breaking the Ice

Very rarely is a Task-oriented work group, much less a group of trainees, composed of family members who are intimately familiar and are comfortable with each other. Rather the groups are usually composed of total strangers who have never seen each other before or at best co-workers or acquaintances that barely recognize each other's faces. No matter what the group's composition, there's always a high anxiety level present.

I would hesitate to initially refer to the people in the group as "members," because some of the people are not sure whether they want to be a part of the group or not, much less a "functioning" member. Where do you begin? First, be aware that people will sit with people that they know or with people that they perceive to have some commonality (race, sex, age, long hair, etc.). So get them on their feet, paired up and re-seated with a stranger. Have each couple interview each other using 10 standardized questions (i.e., spouse or significant other's name, age, children's names and ages, favorite NFL team, movie last seen, favorite color, etc.).

Each individual is given five minutes to interview and five minutes to be interviewed. The level of sound in the room always increases as the people begin to discover some commonalties between themselves. Each pair is then asked to introduce each other to the group. Thereby, uncovering more things in common among the group's individuals. People are more likely to join a group with which they have something in common. And, that's just what you've done, is facilitate the identification of commonalties. Now that you've got the group warmed up, what's next?

A follow-up icebreaker can be "You Can't Judge A Book By It's Cover". Pass out the Book Cover Sheet to all individuals in the group. Get the group to generate one additional question to fill in the blank section on the form. Ask each associate to fill out the form completely. Allow each associate five minutes to interview his or her partner. Have each associate stand and read his or her answers aloud in front of the group. The management team should lead out in this exercise to relax the group and reduce the anxiety.

Breaks for the first two days should be organizationally provided. This serves two functions. One, it makes the individuals feel special and two; it also allows you to control the time of the restart of training. Not to mention, the first two days the group usually doesn't pair up for lunch, there is more time for bonding.

Orientation

And you thought you were just a trainer? Not by a long shot because a trainer must be above all, a salesman. First, you must sell new employees on the company. Your new group of trainees may have thought they were interested in the job

101

when they applied but it's extremely important for you to excite them about the company. How do you do it? Simply by presenting your company's standard sales presentation and then passing out some of your company's standard promotional "giveaways" to your employees. Remember, the reason the sales presentation was originally constructed to excite the customer about your company, so isn't it even more important to first excite your troops?

Obtain a commitment from the highest-ranking member of the management team possible to give the sales presentation to the new employees. This impresses the new employees and can lock in their loyalty and commitment to the company when upper management gives the perception that they are interested enough in their people to get involved with their initial training and orientation. I personally met with the CEO of a hospital in Florida who personally conducts or has the hospital's president present the initial orientation to every single employee.

I personally like to invoke a spring football practice motif. During spring practice positions are pretty much up for grabs. In other words, there are no guarantees. The coaching staff or management is on constant watch for meaningful performance and quality indicators as a means of selecting individuals who would start at various positions as well as for position back-ups.

The new employees are exposed to the company's mission statement, operational diversity, growth plans and current as well as potential customers. Employees usually get very excited and begin competing for the existing positions. Each person wants to become a player on the company's team. If the employee does not get excited and start to compete, it is better to cull the person here and now rather than later. Some trainees upon learning what is expected tend to "de-select" from the training program, which is once again good for both the individual and the company. Now is the time to present your outside customer. This is the primary user of your products or services outside the company and to which in the supply chain you are a supplier.

Obtain a commitment from your biggest customer to explain to your trainees his company's needs and requirements regarding your products or services. Also ask them to explain their company's position and reason for being in the marketplace. This approach to orientation has many positive attributes. First, it makes points with your customer when his company is perceived as important enough to have direct access to your people to list his needs and requirements. Second, it allows the trainees to hear the needs and requirements directly from the customer's lips. Now, isn't that more powerful and better remembered than hearing it secondhand out of some supervisor's mouth?

Learning Readiness

Surprisingly enough, most high school dropouts do not like or perform well in classroom training situations. They lack the ability to see the correlation between classroom instruction and the real-life applications of the subject matter being presented to them. So the trainer must create or establish the trainee's "learning readiness." To do this requires the "WIIFM (What's In It For Me) Strategy". Moreover, it's simply getting the trainee to comprehend and understand that what they will be taught will make their job easier to perform, will get the boss "off their back" or whatever motivates them. In other words, you have to assure them some potential gain for their patience, attention and cooperation. Try to create a feeling of the training being really special for them. It has been shown that different people learn in different ways. And there is no "best" way! To maximize the opportunity of reaching the most people the best method is to utilize as many different learning approaches as possible during training presentations. Most trainee light bulbs go "on" the third time they hear the same information.

THE SECRET OF SUCCESSFUL TRAINING

What is the real secret to successful technical training? It lies in communication. The "What", "When", "How", "Why", "Where" and "Who" given in the training are all very critical aspects for success. Most people arrive on their job and are not shown "How" to do, "What" is expected, much less have "What" is expected outlined or fully explained. The employees are often left to their own devices not only to determine "What" to do, but "When" and "How" to do it. Meanwhile management sits perplexed and pondering, "Why are my products or services viewed by potential customers as having such poor quality that they buy from my chief competitor?"

Especially in startup situations, trainees are often told that initial starting assignments are only temporary and that individuals may get moved around as the manufacturing or service process begins to stabilize. I always tell trainees, "Don't be too concerned if you don't like your assigned startup position, you or it will probably change." I say that for many reasons, some of which include: jobs are usually evolving at startup and rarely end up as they are anticipated at the start; people are being asked to perform new job skills which may be awkward and will become easier to do only over time and with practice. At any rate, management is usually attempting to match employee strengths with job requirements to create a win/win situation anyway. A technical trainer must be constantly attuned to the training audience. I'm not insinuating that a trainer has necessarily to be performer or an entertainer, though a bit of that never hurts. But, rather I am saying that the trainer be aware of the likes and dislikes of the training audience. Most often the rule seems to be, the lower the education level, the greater the challenge to keep training sessions interesting.

Don't ever underestimate your audience's intellectual level or what they can and cannot understand. I personally like to incorporate some of the videos by Joel Barker in part because he is considered a premier futurist, which is a predictor of future trends in the business community. Several videos have been prepared by him to help explain some of the concepts he uses. One concept, a paradigm shift, is defined as a framework within which a person perceives things in his environment. He also refers to paradigm pioneers or the people who first recognize future trends and champion the new paradigm. Paradigm shifters are, in turn, the people involved in shifting their paradigms. I have found that showing a couple of his videos helps trainees to better understand and utilize Barker's concepts. That being, "you have to think outside the box."

For what it is worth. "Thinking outside the box" can be dangerous to your professional career. If your boss is your intellectual inferior, your boss may possibly misconstrue your suggestion for improvement as a personal threat. If this happens to you don't sit around pouting about it. You are better off circulating your resume than trying to work things out. Once you are considered a turncoat, either rightly or wrongly, it's hard to change perceptions. If your boss is small in stature, you may possibly face what is called the "Napoleon Complex." That is a situation where the boss may compensate for his perception that his height is being challenged by exerting his position's power over you. This most commonly occurs in situations where the subordinate is superior both in height and intellect to his boss.

Joel Barker's video "The New Business of Paradigms "may be purchased from www.starthrower.com Or by calling 1-800 Paradigm and is filmed in 2002. The underlying message in the video, however, remains eternal. You must have a vision of the future in order to see the trends in business. You must be able to convey your vision to others or sell your ideas. First you must bring every member of the group to the same plateau or level with regard to soft skills or communication. Construct a "detailed" Soft-Skills Training or an agenda incorporating Soft-Skills as well as Technical-Skills Training. Dedicate at least 2.5 to 3.0 Days (20-24 hrs) in Training Time to educate the Associates in Communication,

Teambuilding & Total Quality. Prepare a "detailed" Teambuilding Training Agenda to include (at a minimum) the following Topic: "What is a team according to Webster?"

Distribute the Team Building and Total Quality Management handouts (Appendix B) to each associate. Ask the associate to open his folder and remove the Team Building definition handout for use in the session.

Provide the Associates with the following: **Definition of Team—A Group of selected Individuals who must work "interdependently" in order to attain their established Individual & Organizational Objective.** Have each member of the group take a clean sheet of paper and a sharpened pencil. Inform them that the objective is to count the number of "e's present in the paragraph" for the definition of the word "team". Have each individual work independently. Then present an overhead with the above "team" definition to the group for five seconds using an overhead projector. Have each individual record the count on his sheet of paper.

Next have the group divide itself into teams of three to five. Have each team select a team leader. The team leader then coordinates the development and implementation of his or her team's strategy in determining the number of "e's present in the paragraph" for the definition of the word "team."

Present the overhead once again to the various teams for 5 seconds. Allow teams five minutes to reach their primary decision. Record each team's preliminary decision. Give each team leader the opportunity to change their number and thus submit a final count.

There are thirteen (13) e's in the paragraph and two e's in the title. Congratulate the teams and have them compare which way was more accurate and more fun. This approach was taken for two reasons. First, this approach serves to introduce the trainees to the team definition and secondly, to subliminally introduce team concepts to the group at the same time.

Emphasize group/team dynamics. Discuss the four (4) stages of team development:

Stage 1: FORMING—Membership—Joining the group. Membership cautiously explores the boundaries of acceptable group behavior. The team accomplishes little.
Feelings: excitement, anticipation, optimism, pride, attachment, suspicion, fear and anxiety.
Behaviors: Define task, how to accomplish, determine acceptable behavior; how to deal with problems; what info to gather; discussions of lofty, abstract concepts/issues; symptoms or problems not relevant to task; complaints against organization; task barriers.
Stage 2: STORMING—Members jump in deep water, start to drown, thrash about. Realize task is different and more difficult than imagined. Members get testy, blameful and overzealous but begin to understand one another.
Feelings: Resistance; attitude fluctuations, pessimism.
Behaviors: Arguments, defensiveness, competition, factious, questioning owner's wisdom, setting unrealistic goals, concern over workload, pecking order, disunity, tension, and jealousy.
Stage 3—NORMING—Members reconcile competing loyalties and responsibilities. Accepts team norms, codes and member individuality. Conflict is reduced and cooperation improves. They help each other stay afloat. Progress begins.
Feelings: Constructive criticism, acceptance and relief.
Behaviors: Achieve harmony, avoid conflict, friendly, confiding sharing, cohesion, common goals and spirit establishing and maintaining norms.
Stage 4: PERFORMING—Members have settled relationships and expectations. Involves diagramming and solving problems; choosing and implementing changes. Accepts individual strengths and weaknesses. Swim together, effective and cohesion. Get the work done.
Feelings: Satisfaction, understanding and insightful.
Behaviors: Constructive self-change, prevent or work through group problems, close attachment.

Characteristics of An Effective Team

Have each person write down three things that are characteristic of optimally performing teams. Divide the group into four person teams. Have teams of four (4) Associates independently brainstorm to identify and write down on a flip chart sheet what their perceptions are of the characteristics of an effective optimal team following the selection of a team leader. Have each group's team leader present the team's findings to the entire Training Group. This is done to trainees to have the individual group members begin to think about what they need to do and the ways they need to change. This exercise should take approximately 30 minutes to complete.

Characteristics of an effective team:

Establishes clear goals and objectives that are accepted by team members.

Establishes high standards of performance for itself.

Allows members to disagree has an effective way to resolve problems and conflicts.

Resolves past actions to plan for improvements.

Has a sense of unity.

Members listen to each other and provide useful feedback.

Recognizes individuals for contributions.

Attaches a high value in creative approaches to problems.

Members influence one another and the Team Leader.

Compare and contrast findings with the above list and explain that the group has just performed its first brainstorming.

Identifying and prioritizing critical start-up factors

(This should take approximately 30 minutes to administer.)

Have each associate write down at least three (3) things that must happen, occur or be done for the facility start-up to be successful. Divide the associates into teams of five to ten people. Have each team identify a scribe and spokesperson. Have the scribe document on a flip chart each unique critical start-up factor identified by members of the team. Once all factors are listed have the spokesman facilitate using the Nominal Group Technique (described below). The team will reach a consensus on the rank ordering of start-up factors from the most important to least important. The spokesperson for each team then presents the results to the entire group.

Demonstrate the Nominal Group Technique—The facilitator may allow short, but timed, group discussion of each factor before overall voting begins. When voting begins, each tem member is then asked to silently pick and write down three (3) start-up factors he believes are the most critical to the start-up's success. The facilitator next asks each team member to share his choices that are then recorded using "hatch marks" on the flip chart sheet beside each start-up factor. The factor with the most votes gets ranked #1, the factor with the second most votes gets ranked #2 and so on. Whenever there is a tie, simply ask each team member to re-cast his vote between the factors that were tied. If re-voting results in a second tie, then and only then does the facilitator cast the deciding vote. Very rarely will the facilitator be asked to cast the deciding vote. This method is a quick and easy way to reach consensus without arguing and lengthy debate.

Barriers to Teamwork

Have teams of four to six Associates independently brainstorm to identify and then, after the selection of a team leader, to present the "Barriers to Teamwork" to the entire Training Group. This is to get the group to begin to think of things which they should watch for and avoid, if possible. If you know certain things to avoid or not to do, a lot of unpleasantness can be avoided.

Have each individual, including supervisors, determine and share his or her communication style. This can be done using a short (approximately 20 Questions) Communication Style Questionnaire. I personally like a simple questionnaire. (See Appendix C for an example of the questionnaire.) There are no right or wrong answers. Respondents are asked to indicate the answer which best describes how they really feel. Responses are then transferred to the scoring sheet. Point out that each of the four columns must be totaled. The column having the highest number of incidents on the questionnaire is the respondent's dominant communication style. Read the interpretation sheet. Explain the there is no right or wrong style. Styles are determined to convey the dominant style of the person doing the talking and that of the person who is listening to the communication. Certain styles facilitate good communication and understanding and other styles impede communication. It is good for you to know which style both parties have in order to facilitate and insure good communication. If both styles are known, you can always rest assured that what was said rather than how it was said gets through to the receiver. We must be aware of our dominant style and how it might effect our communication with others.

Communication Tendencies of Associates.

A Score Sheet groups the Associate Trainees based on their Responses to the Communication Style Questionnaire. A Descriptive Sheet explaining the general Tendencies of Individuals possessing a particular Communication Style is created with a minimum of four (4) Styles.

> Key Principles of effective communication
1. Be more descriptive than evaluative.
2. Use specifics rather than generalities.
3. Listen attentively.
4. Maintain the self-esteem of the other person.

How To Listen
How many of you are good listeners? Let's try a test. Read the following list of numbers out loud ask the group to only listen. After you finish, have them write down what they heard.
5, 22, 11, 3, 15, 17, 12, 7, 13
Ask the group: What was the first number? What is the last number? What is the one in the middle?
Listening Skills
1. Remain Neutral.
Don't give advice, agree or disagree, criticize or interrupt.
2. Give Your Complete Attention.
Let them know you're listening. Nod your head. Say, "Uh, huh, I see what you mean."
3. Ask About His or Her Statements.
Dig Out Information Invite Them To Tell You More. Say, "In addition to that, is there anything else?"
4. Restate The Main Points
Let them hear their words restated by you. This prompts them to stick to the facts.
5.Get Agreement
Summarize what you have both said. Ask the other person for their opinion on what the next step should be. Develop a course of action.
Communication Skill Practice (See Appendix C)
A Review
An Action Plan

Think for a minute about your previous job. Please write down five (5) things (BARRIERS TO QUALITY PERFORMANCE) that prevented you from doing a quality job (doing the right things right).

Divide the group into four (4) teams. Have each team select a leader. The leader should then write down the unique Quality Barriers on a flip chart. He should then facilitate the team in reaching a consensus (using the Nominal Group Technique) to rank-order the barriers preventing quality performance from the largest to the smallest. Each leader then presents his team's findings before the entire group. Compare and contrast the findings of each group.

EXPLANATION OF CORPORATE VISION & MISSION. Present and discuss the company's vision and mission statement.

Introduce the concept of Total Quality Management

The "Heartless Card Factory"—A Simulation of the Authoritarian Style of Management is demonstrated.

Prepare a record-keeping sheet to monitor defects (number of hearts) in each hand. Also prepare a graph to track defects per production run (every time three hands are produced). As the Owner of "Heartless Hands" explain that the idea of selling a winning (Heartless) card hand was conceived while playing with a "free" deck of cards on a plane flight to Baltimore. Later market research showed that people would buy an eight (8)-card hand that is void in hearts.

This simulation was chosen over Deming's box of red and white marbles due to the comparisons of start-up costs. Have fun with it. Celebrate their victories and scold the shortages. I have even had a fellow in a Texas training session to get so caught up in the simulation as to take a swing at me. So stay alert! How do I start the business? First, talk to friends at city hall and have them condemn the front table and four chairs. Proceed to inform the associates seated there that they are being evicted so you can open your business. Place the table in the front of the room with three chairs on one side and one on the opposite side. Proceed to hire yourself a human resource (HR) manager. Explain that his duties are to help you hire a quality work force to produce "heartless" hands.

Have HR hire an administrative assistant (AA) to keep your production records. Explain the job as keeping records on each production run. Have HR hire a Quality Director (QD). The Quality Director (QD) gives the production run information to the Administrative Assistant (AA). His job is first to work with HR and hire two Quality Assurance Inspectors (QA's). The QA's are to count the number of hearts in each 8-card hand produced. They then report the number of hearts produced by each associate to the QD who the reports it to the AA. Have HR hire a Production Manager (PM) who then works with HR to hire three (3) production associates (PA's) to draw 8-card "heartless" hands. He also hires a supply clerk (SC) to shuffle the deck and provide the cards face down for the PA's to draw. Have HR hire a Training Manager (TM) whose job it is to make sure everybody on the production line knows what to do.

Start the process and transfer, hire, fire and replace people as performance dictates. The TM is the first to go, closely followed by the Production assistants (PA's). The PA's are soon followed by the replacement of their supply clerk (SC). The QA's, QD, PM and HR are replaced in an attempt to solve production problems you face. Do not, under any circumstances, allow anyone to change how you want the business run. After nine (9) hands are produced, count how many "heartless" hands you have that you can sell. Declare bankruptcy. Point out that the process works because some good hands are produced. In the owner's mind the problem is obviously poor employee attitude and performance.

Have the group suggest what they see as better ways to operate the company. Point out that middle management is caught in the middle between upper management and the associates. They are helpless but to do what they are told.

EXPLAIN PROCESS MANAGEMENT—HOW TO SET IT UP IN AN ORGANIZATION.

Introduce the concept of process management. Talk briefly about how it is implemented. Show Video: "Stuck On Quality"; www.videomedia.net/catalogquality html, Implementing a continuous improvement philosophy. List the key component. Customer focused. Shared responsibility.

Talk about regional owners and steering committees and identification of regional critical success factors. Talk about facility steering committee and its identification of facility's critical success factors (getting the most bang for the buck).

UNDERSTANDING PROCESSES AND THE NEEDS & REQUIREMENTS OF INTERNAL & EXTERNAL CUSTOMERS.

Introduce the concept of INPUT—TASK—OUTPUT. Also explain the concept of internal & external customers. Discuss identifying customer needs, requirements and expectations. Show Video: "The Customer is Always Dwight."

ww.videomedia.net/catalogquality.html. How did SUPERMARVELEX define quality? How did GISCO define quality? How did the WORLD NUT COMPANY define quality?

Assignment:

Create an Action Plan to identify the needs and requirements of an internal customer. Create an Action Plan to identify your needs and requirements to an internal supplier.

Exercises for teaching associates how to perform other quality assurance skills. Flow charting or placing a call on a pay phone.

Tell the group that they will be responsible for maintaining the "Current Best Approach" (CBA) flow charts for each old process after initial start-up training is completed. Associates will also flow chart any new processes that are developed. Therefore, each associate needs to understand how to create a functional flow chart. To illustrate how a flow is done, first have the group work together to flow chart the process of "placing a call on a pay phone." Emphasize that the process starts when the phone booth is entered and ends when the party answers the phone. Define and demonstrate the "Action or Task Box" and the "decision" or "diamond box." Show how a "Yes" and a "No" arrow becomes complex as the group provides the lead from each decision diamond. Make the flow chart as simple or as complex as the group provides the lead. After all questions are answered, ask the group to individually flow out his or her "getting up and getting out of the house" process that they perform each morning.

Getting up and getting out of the house—Ask each person in the group to flow the steps they go through every morning from the time the alarm goes off until they walk out the door headed for work. Have the coaches walk around the room and observe and help associates as they flow chart the "getting up" process. Allow at least 15 minutes for associates to accomplish this activity. When the flow-charting is complete, ask for three or four associates to volunteer to share with the group what they put down on the flow chart. Compare and contrast the various levels of flow-charts from MACRO to MICRO. The MACRO level contains few steps and provides only a cursory overview while the MICRO level contains many steps and is highly detailed.

PROCESS SIMPLIFICATION

Show boss's record of arrival times at work. Identify the process owner, the process itself (Getting To Work On Time), the start, the end and the time to accomplish. Pass out the flow chart that was developed. Unitize the flow chart into its components (Getting out of bed, bathroom activities, kitchen activities, dressings, locking up and leaving.) Add up the total time to accomplish the process, as it is flow-charted. Then record totals for each unit until you have reached the bottom of the flow chart. Have the group review each step of the flow chart and decide whether it should be retained or eliminated. "X" out the process steps that can be eliminated. Then total the times of steps that remain and see if it is within the acceptable amount of time to get to work.

PRACTICAL FORKLIFT/ORDER PICKER DRIVING SKILLS SIMULATIONS

Set up standardized simulations and/or obstacle courses on which floor associates can demonstrate their skill in handling order pickers and forklifts, etc.

FORK LIFT—Have the associate drive through the obstacle course. Then have the associate remove a pallet of finished goods from a designated storage rack using a forklift. Have the associate drive back through the obstacle course and set the pallet down. The associate's skill level is determined by the speed (timed with stop watch) and accuracy (number of pallets knocked over) with which the simulation is accomplished. Reverse the process and have the associate put the pallet back in its proper storage location. This gives a second time and accuracy measure.

ORDER PICKER—Have associate drive an order picker through a course lined with pallets standing on their edges. Have the associate properly secure himself with the order picker's safety belt and then use the order picker to remove an item from the top shelf of a storage rack. Then have the associate return through the obstacle course. The associate's skill level is determined by the speed (timed with stop watch) and accuracy (number of pallets knocked over) with which the simulation is accomplished. Reverse the procedure and have the associate replace the item back in its proper storage location. This gives a second time and accuracy measure.

PROBLEM-SOLVING & BRAINSTORMING

Discuss the concept of brainstorming and explain the rules of brainstorming: Encourage everyone to freewheel; don't hold back on any ideas even if they seem silly at the time; the more ideas the better. No discussion during the brainstorming. That will come later. No judgment. No one is allowed to criticize another's ideas, not even with a groan or grimace! Let people hitchhike—build upon the ideas generated by others in the group. Write all ideas on a flip chart so the whole group can easily scan them. Draw a fish bone on a flip chart. Pick a problem like "picking errors". Have the group brainstorm for causes of picking errors and record them in the appropriate place. Divide the group into three or four teams and have them use the problem solving procedure on "shipping errors". Have each team select a facilitator to run the team. Have each team present the results of its analysis.

MEASUREMENT

Prepare a data collection form on which respondents can record their data. Prepare a pareto chart on which to document the collected data. Pass out small bags of peanut M&Ms. Then talk about the process of making a bag of peanut M&M's. How many different colors are present in a bag of peanut M&M's? How are colors placed in the bag? How is the number of pieces a bag contains determined? Show five (5) storage bins with gates at the bottom and weighing belt running underneath them. Ask the group to estimate the number of pieces in each bag. Write their guesses on the flip chart. Have the group open their bags and dump them in a small dish. Proceed to count the number of pieces of each color and the total number of pieces. Have each person come to the flip chart and record his or her data. Look at the data while some one calculates the average for each color and the average pieces per bag. Have the group come back to the second flip chart and place an "X" on the pareto chart indicating the number of pieces contained in their bags. (If the average number of pieces per bag should be 22, does the weighing belt speed need to be adjusted (faster/slower)?) If so, which way? If the average number of pieces is 22 and there are 5 colors, how many pieces (4) of each color should be present in each bag? Do any of the gate(s) need to be adjusted (opened/closed)? If so, which ones and which way? Let the data tell you what to do to adjust the process!

AFFINITY DIAGRAMING

A technique known as "affinity diagramming" is used to cluster Tasks into areas of job responsibility. Simply stated, this means grouping together things that appear to have something in common. SMEs find it very easy to do. Prior to reassembling the SMEs, write each Task legibly on a separate 2"x 2" Post-It note. Number each Post-It note sequentially (i.e., 1, 2, etc.) Spread the numbered Post-It notes on the meeting room table. Hang at least eight (8) sheets of blank flip chart paper on the meeting room wall. Most jobs have from 4 to 10 Duty Areas, hence, the eight separate chart papers. More sheets may be hung during the session, if needed. Instruct the SMEs to study the Tasks on the table and look for common areas of job responsibility. When similarities are seen, SMEs "STICK" the Task on the same sheet of chart paper hanging on the wall. All "related" Tasks end up on the same single piece of chart paper. Most Duty Areas contain 6 to 20 Tasks.

Note: SMEs MUST ACCOMPLISH THE "CLUSTERING" ASSIGNMENT WITHOUT SPEAKING.

When all Tasks are taped on the wall, a consensus has been reached. Ask the SMEs to brainstorm for Duty Area titles. Duty Areas titles end with the word "Activities". When a consensus is reached, the best titles are then written on the tops of the hanging charts. After the session when everyone's thanked, assign an identification number (i.e., 0100, 0200, 0300, etc.) to each Duty Area. The first two numbers identify the Duty Area. The last two numbers identify the Task within each Duty Area (i.e., 0101, 0103, 0104, etc.). The Task List is then typed using the format shown in Appendix A

System, System, Got to Have A System!

In the modern world, both suppliers and customers seem greatly concerned with quality issues of products used and services delivered. Customers will no longer tolerate poor quality in either the products or services they purchase in the marketplace. As a result, most suppliers have been forced to this quality realization by their economic concern. Purchasers are now demanding quality for their hard-earned dollars. In order to assure total quality, and especially for world-class total quality certification, a company must institute and adhere to one standardized systematic process or method of producing its product or delivering its service. As a result of this process standardization, a company's human resource department needs to adopt a uniform and consistent method of hiring, training, evaluating and promoting its people. Therefore, any human resource data generated by one department should be useable by all other departments within the company. This is an entirely logical argument from a Total Quality point-of-view. Even more, it is also economically sound in that it affords the best and cheapest way to operate. Once a pathway to a total quality process has been established, every stepping stone must be touched or used every time the process is initiated.

A modern competitive company cannot financially afford to "inspect in" the quality of its product or service. It's simply economic suicide. An inspection line is an unaffordable dinosaur. Your money is already invested in the product or service and your choices of what to do are limited to remanufacture, redo or toss it. In most cases the cost to remanufacture or redo outweighs the cost to toss it. With a total quality approach, quality is built into the product or service as it is manufactured or delivered, therefore eliminating the need for the post inspection step in the process.

One of the basic tenets of the total quality philosophy entails the concept of product and/or service repeatability through process standardization, whether the company be a manufacturer or a service provider. Even more importantly you need to be able to measure how well process steps are being done. There has to be standardization before any process measurements can be meaningful. Comparisons cannot be done if things aren't done the same way. Without a uniform set of standards, all measurements become meaningless. You don't know if performance adherence to process steps is getting better or worse. And remember the old saying, "If you can't measure it, you can't manage it." How can you improve a process, when you have no idea what steps you're currently doing? You can't even begin to experiment to find the best practice or procedure because process steps may become so inconsistent as to performance, that certain processes are almost never done the same way twice.

In the area of total quality, both national and international certification bodies have taken the world-class total quality position to have companies document their processes as a means of assuring through a series of on-site audits that the employees of are performing their jobs as prescribed in the company's process maps. A word of advice, most certification groups will tolerate and attempt to work with two sets of process maps, one describing the actual processes and one outlining the training processes. Most users tend to do the manufacturing and service process maps at a strategic or high level because when personnel audits are performed on your employees using your process maps, the auditors expect every "i" to be dotted and every "t" to be crossed as per your product or service process maps. So "don't write yourself into a box" when doing your strategic process maps.

I would like to share some insights gleaned over the past thirty years in my experience with human resources research. The Task-based Job Analysis (TBJA) approach seems to be more useful at the strategic level and in the area of human resource management (HRM). The Tasks of TBJA deals with the "who", "what", "when" and "where" of the things to be done on the job. The flow chart approach has been more useful at the tactical level and in the area of human resource development (HRD). Task or Process Steps contained in tactical flow charts or process maps deal with the "how" to do things on the job. In other words, this is where process standardization is achieved. The more detail provided during the process mapping for training, the greater the process repeatability that can be achieved through training. Strategic level flow charts or process maps convey a strategy and are more typically geared to the management or engineering level and deal with the "who", "what", "when" and "where" of the things to be done on the job.

It's a good idea to use only one SME when doing strategic level process maps. It's also good that the SME be a member of the management team to do this because of his or her more global perspective and because he or she has a better understanding of the map's intended use. A word of wisdom, at this point in time, too many cooks can spoil the broth. I don't mean to infer that one person makes the final decision regarding the process. What I'm referring to is in the process generation phase. In the editing and revision stage you can put as many sets of eyes (both labor and management) on a process map as you choose. In the initial generation phase, multiple personalities will often times cloud and confuse the issue. Always constantly remind yourself, that initially your mission is strive for creation of a paper target at which to shoot.

I like to think of tactical flow-charting or process mapping as the "tactile", "touching" or "the laying on of hands" of "how" things get done or how our strategies are implemented. When performing tactical process mapping for training purposes, the use of only one SME is also recommended but this time choose an incumbent. Who but an incumbent would possess a better knowledge of "how the job is really done"? Also, working independently with an incumbent SME, the incumbent might be more likely to share his or her concerns or points of contention with the job.

The incumbent's supervisor should be available in a back-up mode to assure that no critical or disputed Steps are overlooked during the process review. The process engineer is available to settle or arbitrate any disputes that arise. The supervisor then spends his time reviewing what the flow charter and SME have documented. Once the supervisor has reviewed the process map, he or she signs off on the process's acceptability. Another SME incumbent should be designated as responsible for validating the processes as they are documented and signed off. I don't care if the designated SME delegates the actual process performance validation to other non-incumbents as long as the non-incumbent is overseen by the SME during the validation's administration. Having a non-incumbent follow the process map is done to further verify the process map as correct.

Remember the process engineer is to aid/assist the Team also. In start-up situations, the supervisor and the process engineer will often combine their experiences and expertise to document new processes. The process engineer or industrial engineer can offer multi-faceted assistance. They can help in setting production standards, doing time & motion studies and establishing cut scores for the certification of trainees. Always stay on friendly terms with the engineers for they can make life much easier for you. Engineers tend to be primarily concerned with the design and layout of an efficient and economical workstation as well as with the ergometric impacts of the job on employees.

Once again, at this point, we are more concerned with the generation phase of process mapping. The editing and review portion of the procedure generally takes care of itself. Again, scrutiny of process maps by multiple people from both labor and management is encouraged.

In the past I have noticed that strategic or high-level process maps usually wind up collecting dust on a manager's shelf or in his bookcase except during certification audits each year. The tactical or low-level (training) process maps rarely, if ever, get done. So once a year the strategic process maps are removed from the shelf, get dusted off and get reintroduced to the workforce. During this anniversary review period each year, the workforce should be reminded that everyone in the company is responsible for total quality all of the time.

Once an error occurs in the process and is not corrected, the product or service is flawed and no additional routine process steps will make it right or cause it to go away nor will they correct it. Every job incumbent in the process has the responsibility not to accept or produce anything less than a "quality pass" of either a service or product. In other words, if you receive a substandard product or service from a fellow employee, don't accept it, reject it and send it back to be redone. The same goes for you. Don't put out or forward a substandard product or service because it's going to come back.

You must no longer avoid confrontation about quality with fellow employees. Some people had rather fix problems themselves than run the risk of upsetting someone by sending something back in the process to be reworked. How will a fellow worker ever know that he is producing inferior work and needs to adjust his process if he isn't told? If you don't tell him, don't expect things to change. It's a lose-lose proposition. You will forever spend your time doing work you are not being paid to do and at the same time be negatively affecting your own productivity and job security. If your fellow employee does not care to produce a quality product or service, why are you letting him or her threaten your job security? Those individuals are not, because of their bad attitude, contributing members of the Team and should be terminated.

I have debated long and hard with associates complaining about too much detail in my flow charts. I have never had a single operator to complain about too much detail. Do you reckon that it's more than management wants to know about the process? Hopefully not, but they may fear too many restrictions to their processes. Quality may still be misunderstood by some managers and may not be embraced as a good thing as such, in effect tying the hands of the more production-oriented.

From a quality standpoint, once the process steps have been identified and validated, always document, at whatever level of detail is required to assure absolute compliance, that the required process steps are performed each time a product is produced or a service is provided. Once documented, the process may undergo controlled experimentation for improvement. This is truly the only way to know for sure the degree of positive or negative impact an added or deleted Step actually has on the process. The process change can then be systematically introduced without the scheduling of training sessions. By simply posting the process change, providing any necessary training aids (videos, process maps, diagrams, etc.) and holding everybody responsible for his or her own training, the trainer can in, full confidence, rest assured of implementation at the specified location, date and time.

I've found that even below average IQ individuals can handle the detailed maps when they are embedded on 4-person teams with other employees. Those employees with average IQs get the opportunity to shine and provide mentoring for slower employees. Also I have observed that they appreciate the detail after years of being put down by management for not doing what they've never been taught or told how to do. I've been told many times by operators that it was good to finally know what management really wanted. Most employees will do exactly what they are trained to do.

Most employees want to please their supervisor. With the supervisor's expectations listed on the process map, the employee knows what is expected of him. If the written expectations are realistic, the ball is in the employee's court. Most employees prefer having supervisors off their backs when management's expectations can be met. It is important to point out that in terms of the supervision of quality and teambuilding, you can't really manage employees; you can only measure and manage the processes that employees work on. To reiterate, you can't manage what you can't measure.

Behavioral Science variables are sometimes difficult to measure and this makes progress with regard to certification very slow. Up to the present time, the efforts to put a real Systems Approach to human performance measurement with regard to HRM and HRD has not, to my knowledge, been carefully explored by many researchers. I advocate the construction of a paper target for the personnel researchers in HRM and HRD departments to either prove or disprove. What I'm suggesting is a target. If a true Systems Approach is developed and adopted then all of HRM's efforts at data collection will benefit HRD and vice versa. Let's first begin with the functions performed by human resource management HRM, HRD, IE & QC.Standardized Job Analysis System

If a standardized Job Analysis System is adopted, each and every time a Job Analysis is performed, the same methodology is used to collect human resources data regardless of the department responsible for initiating the action. For an illustrative example, let's look at TBJA. There will always be a brainstorming session conducted using 4-8 job incumbents and their direct supervisors to identify the Duty Areas and Tasks of the job. Usual duration of the sessions is 1-4 hours. The results of the Brainstorming session are edited and transferred onto a form to be rank-ordered by a group composed of from 6 to 8 incumbents and supervisors. Respondents can be either incumbents or former job personnel. Supplier or customer SMEs may be used but must be currently on the job. Supervisory personnel must be current and must provide direct supervision. Data are collected either on-site or off-site with written instructions provided.

A Calculated Importance Index (CII) is calculated for each Task and its associated Duty Area. These virtually unique values, in conjunction, allow a Task to be rank-ordered based on the premise that the lower the Task's $CII_{(Task)}$, the higher the Task's Importance to good job performance. Always remember that a Calculated Importance Index is derived from an ordinal database and thus values are relevant only to that one set of data. Therefore, the $CII_{(Task)}$ serves as a ranking tool that can only be said to be larger or smaller when compared to another $CII_{(Task)}$ within the data set.

The group of SMEs is then asked to determine the $CII_{(Task)}$ cut-score or the transitional point within the Task List when Task performance becomes trivial to job performance. This determines the cumulative percentage of the job that is further analyzed for Rating and KSA Brainstorming data. The upper percentage of the Task List is then submitted in the Rating format to 6-8 incumbents and supervisors to Rate on12 seven-point Scales. The same percentage of the Task List is used in two stimulus-response type Brainstorming sessions. The first is to identify measurable and measurable Knowledge, Skills and Abilities (KSAs) and the second session is to identify measurable Key Result Areas (KRAs) and the ways to obtain the numbers. The identified KSA List is then submitted under each retained Task on the List to a group of four to six incumbents and supervisors. They are asked to indicate the required need for the K, S or A during performance of the Task. All KSA-Task Relationship averages ranging from (4.0) needed to (7.0) essential are identified.

Once the initial TBJA is completed, all the work on that particular job is done. Most job analyses used to be the subject of review every three to five years even if there hadn't been any activity. With the advent of computerization, jobs are constantly changing, so much so that the review process for job analysis has been shortened from three to six months. The advantage of adopting a system's approach is the size and speed with which jobs may later be validated. The job description must only be read by one job incumbent one immediate supervisor and then signed by the two to assure the job description Task Statements as being validated. Also, human resource data may be shared departmentally (HRM to IE, HRM to HRD, HRN to QC, vice versa etc.). The level of departmental expertise of backup personnel allows their interchangeable substitution as they become available. TBJA Task Statements serve to provide the strategic flow charter with basic Processes (who, what. when & where), which in turn leads the tactical flow charter to the Process Steps (how to do the process).

All new supervisors in their initial training should be trained in the systems approach. This includes the TBJA phase as well as the process-mapping phase of the system. This can serve as a dull-edged sword in the quality wars on the production floor. First, you can enlist the additional person power and second, it creates better cooperation and understanding among managers. For a new supervisor in operations, it can be a godsend. One of the main tasks of any new supervisor is to learn what is going on within his operating area and beyond. If, for instance, the new supervisor were assigned to perform a TBJA or a process map on one of the jobs he will be supervising just think how beneficial this would be. If an incumbent SME, which he will be supervising, was assigned to the project, just think of the opportunity for bonding as well as increasing the supervisor's job knowledge. If jobs within the new assignment have been previously "TBJAed" or process mapped, the new supervisor can quickly peruse the results to familiarize him with the tasks of the positions.

I'm not advocating TBJA over process mapping. But in fact, the most pragmatic tool for operations and any subsequent training where cost is concerned is process mapping or the "how to do" the tasks. Remember the old "80-20 rule", that 20% of the people do 80% of the work. The same rule tends to hold when Key Result Areas (KRAs) over which the employee has control are applied to the operations process. Since we are talking about process mapping and hence operations managing to the process, there are usually KRAs which must be identified, documented and measured for each job's most important 20% of its processes. These are the processes which usually account for over 80% of the productivity of an operation. Once these KRAs are identified, documented and measured, the employee is held accountable. Next the tasks or "what is done" in the KRA processes and steps or "how to do these tasks" must be identified. The rating of tasks gleaned from the process steps can serve as job performance standard requirements to the employee by supervisory personnel. The process steps data serve to help supervisory cross training from section to section as well as for vacation relief within sections.

Job Termination—HRM System Approach Alternatives

When HRM & HRD personnel hear the words job termination, many different images might be conjured up in their minds. Whether those images are positive or negative depends on how and who prepared the HRM or HRD personnel for the job. I come from a Manufacturing background where my boss espoused the philosophy that if an employee was terminated, it was the supervisor's failure for not finding a way to reach the employee. The boss had explained to me that if I'd spent as much time and effort trying to save the employee as I did case building to get rid of him, I would have saved his twelve years of experience.

During my next performance review, I remember very well, at the tender young age of 22, thinking that maybe my boss was right. If I had just been able to get my hands on him, he and I would have "reached an understanding." As a brief background, I had just rounded the corner of his machine with my boss on an area tour when I observed the employee, in a fit of rage with his first floor associate, purposely cut back or sabotage 12 units. When I confronted him with what I had witnessed, he threw an 18-inch wrench at me followed by his employee ID badge and a comment, "Here, you've been after this ever since you got here!" If my boss had not physically restrained me, the operator and I would have been embracing on the operating floor. Instead we were sent to separate rooms to cool down. Later I walked him to the gate, but his ID badge was mine!

You see my philosophy is that I don't owe anybody a job. In the workplace, it's HR's job to provide capable, competent, trained people to manufacturing to produce quality products for the least amount of dollars. Management interviews the people that HR sends them but manufacturing makes the ultimate employment decision and job offer.

HRM is sometimes responsible for terminating employees but usually HRM is asked to bless management's justification and back-up documentation for an employee's termination. To put it simply, it's management's call and responsibility for the termination. HRM often serves as an advisor should an Employment Security Commission representative decide to challenge the manufacturing supervisor's employment decision and subsequent actions. Remind management of the need to constantly follow-up on supervisory personnel as they implement the company's termination or grievance policies. Assure that policies have been followed correctly and have been properly documented in each employee's case file. The secret behind successful applications of termination policy is documentation, documentation, and documentation.

Be careful not to set unwanted precedents during employment decision-making. Never make a decision based on expediency of the selection process that can't be lived with later. From a job analysis standpoint, (TBJA Tasks or Process Map), the job learning curves for any individual can be tracked from selection, through each week of training as well as later culminating in a trainee's certification to probationary status and subsequent promotion to full-benefit status on the job. Any minimum job performance levels should be established by IE and published to the masses at this point.

Always assure that the three steps (informal oral warning, formal oral warning and formal written warning) leading to termination have been taken and documented in files and that everyone that is worth saving is saved, through training interventions. My personal opinion is that if the proper selection techniques are utilized, we reach a win-win situation with the employee. Not everybody is able, capable and willing to perform the Tasks of the job. Some people can't perform but want to perform, while other people can perform, but won't perform.

Job Vacancy Announcements— HRM System Approach Alternatives

The most Important Tasks and requisite KSAs are always identified during the TBJA. This human resource information can be utilized for job postings or job vacancy announcements and conveys more information about the job to potential candidates. If sufficient information is supplied in the job vacancy announcement to potential job seekers, the probability increases that some of the less-motivated candidates will self-screen during the selection process. Don't be afraid to list the requirements of the job, even if they seem distasteful. Applicants should always be made aware of employer expectations as well as the undesirable aspects of the job. The last thing either party wants is to be surprised by unanticipated job expectations being expressed after employment begins.

Standardization of a system would allow HRM to cluster analyze TBJA Rating Data and place the Job within the organization's existing Job Classification or Grade System. Cluster analysis is a statistical methodology, which allows for the grouping of jobs into a specified number of job families, which have similar requirements across multiple variables. This would allow HRM to establish the Job's appropriate grade level. A subsequent Wage and Salary Survey can then be conducted to establish the correct compatible Compensation Level. The job opening or job vacancy could then be posted or publicized for selection. A Scoring Methodology with which to rank-order applicant training and experience based on information contained on submitted Resumes could be developed. Cut Scores to cull the Applicant pool could be established with help from IE to give HRM more administrative control. A Cut Score, under this scenario, is not a "pass or fail" score, but simply a score below which an applicant will not be "considerable" or "be reachable" (not positioned among the top three candidates, etc.) as far as administrative policy is concerned. The beautiful aspect of this simulation approach is that the applicant can choose to further educate himself or practice on his own initiative and then request a retest. Therefore, the applicant's motivation is established. This basically allows an experienced applicant to go in with an advantage. HRM then rank-orders submitted resumes based on the candidate's training & experience (T&E). A phone list can then be prepared of the highest-ranking candidates from T&E data contained on resumes (needed versus possessed KSA's). HRM should construct a set of structured interview questionnaires and an evaluation scale for scoring an applicant's T&E after phone and/or face-to-face interviews. Every stone must be turned to assure that every applicant jumps the same hurdles (answers the same questions). HRM can then telephone down the rank-ordered candidate list and cull the applicants based on verified past T&E data as well as their phone presence. HRM should call past employers to verify the candidate's previous employment dates. Most employers will readily supply this information. Try to contact the candidate's immediate supervisor and sometimes unknowingly he or she may reveal additional information. It never hurts to ask.

Pre-Employment Hybrid Paper & Pencil/Simulation Test Battery Construction System Alternatives

HRM can build simulations of job processes or Tasks. To do test construction, HRM generates or receives and reviews TBJA Task ranking, KRA/Duty Area ranking, Task rating and KSA/Task linkages. HRM can supplement this with additional information from strategic and/or tactical sets of process maps, scripts and videos supplied by HRD or IE. HRM and its SMEs can study all of this human resource data and determine what set of hybrid paper and pencil tests/simulations best measure skill acquisition on the job. As a job applicant, most people simply want the opportunity to demonstrate their expertise while HRM desires a measurement of the job candidate's capabilities. In other words this approach is a win-win situation for the two parties, HRD and applicant.

HRM can then identify any outside hybrid-references and/or resources (i.e., charts, graphs, files, formulas, forms, etc.) used in performing the KRA's Tasks and/or Process Steps. HRM next collects a set of hybrid-utilized materials and clarifies what, how, when & where materials are used.

HRM can then study and determine which of the Materials need to be included in a Test Reference Manual. Next, the group can prepare a hybrid reference manual to supplement the hybrid test booklet containing actual Task and Process Step simulations of composites (i.e., calculations, formulas, forms completion, data entry, data analysis & reading, interpreting, comparing, transposing data, etc.). As the final step, HRM should construct hybrid (objective performance/paper and pencil) test questions to reflect as closely as possible the actual work (tasks or steps) done on the job.

The HRM department can then compare, link and document hybrid test items with job linkages (i.e., KRA-task's ranking data, process steps and KSA-task linkages) to establish the job-relatedness (content validity) of each test question. HRM can then compare and document test items to task rating averages to assure that hybrid test items are written at the appropriate task rating levels (i.e., math, language, reasoning, etc.).

Pre-Employment Hybrid Paper & Pencil/Simulation Test Battery Validation for System Alternatives

HRM personnel can build hybrid test items and assure requisite reference page numbers are cross-referenced to hybrid test and reference booklets. The test builder must choose whether to construct a speed or a power test. A speed test measures the amount of information the test taker can accurately provide within a specified time. While a power test measures the amount of information the test taker can accurately provide without regard to time. HRM develops any required hybrid scoring methodology appropriate for the situation (i.e., time-to-complete, items completed, items attempted, items omitted for some tests while others tests may be multiple-choice, etc.). To prevent the test from being compromised, HRM can construct parallel or alternate forms (at least two: Form A and Form B) of all testing materials for periodic rotation into the testing system.

Monitor test administration, either daily or weekly, for the average score. These scores must be plotted to watch for and determine any trends. If, after a period of time (7 days or weeks), a consistent upward trend is observed, then the test may have been compromised. As a security measure, switch from Form A to Form B and immediately begin monitoring the daily or weekly average test scores once again. If after seven plots, a consistent upward trend is once again observed, switch back to Form A.

HRM can then randomly select 12 applicants to test on the hybrid test battery. This should be accomplished by having management select 12 job incumbents (i.e., 4 above-average performers, 4 average performers & 4 below-average performers) to blindly be administered the hybrid test battery. HRM can then administer and validate the hybrid test battery of simulations to test the skill acquisition level as well as to determine the applicant's potential for skill improvement. HRM together with IE researchers can then determine average performance scores and cut scores for both incumbents and applicants. This number is usually 85% of the theoretical yield. It has been my experience that when simulations are used, the applicant time to complete and technique score averages are usually three times below the incumbent's averages. Thus training of applicants can lead to a three "X" improvement in performance.

Pre-Employment Simulation Test Battery Construction System Alternatives

HRM can schedule and conduct sets of face-to-face structured interview questions (looking for chemistry in the form of personality matches) from among the top ten phone candidates. HRM, under a systematic approach, can obtain strategic and tactical level process maps and scripts from HRD or IE. The HRM can also request High-Level Task & Low-Level Steps sets of digitized Process Photos & Video-tapes from HRD or IE. HRM and its SMEs can review received job data and select 8-10 representative KRA processes to simulate. HRM can utilize chosen digitized process photos and scripts to create an instructional (picture book) training manual for pre-employment simulation tests. HRM can edit the chosen process videotape and script to create instructional pre-employment testing videotapes. HRM can build a content-valid battery (8-10) of KRA process step simulations to test the applicant's present level of skill (i.e., time-to-complete, technique score as well as their potential for skill acquisition and improvement etc.).

Pre-Employment Simulation Test Battery Pilot Validation System Alternatives

HRM can request that management randomly select 12 applicants to test on the pre-employment test battery. Management selects 12 job incumbents (i.e., 4 above-average performers, 4 average performers and 4 below-average per-formers) to blindly be administered the simulations battery. In other words, the HRM personnel tests the incumbents without knowing who is who performance wise. HRM and Management can also select 12 applicants, based upon a review of resumes, to administer and validate a Battery of KRA-process step simulations to test the applicant's skill acquisition level. IE, HRM and its SMEs can together determine the applicant's average performance scores and cut scores (both for incumbents and applicants).

Applicant Pre-Employment Test Battery Pilot Administration & Evaluation System Alternatives

Once HRM has selected the top ranked applicants for the pilot testing, they are scheduled for testing. HRM can give the applicant an instructional (picture book) training manual for study and note taking. HRM can then show the pre-employment test videotape to applicant and schedule the pre-employment test administration for one week later. HRM can tell the applicant that test video tape may be seen as many times as wanted during the next week at HR. A week later HRM shows the videotape of the simulation being performed and administers the pre-employment test. HRM allows the applicant to perform the simulation with an open training manual. HRM can record the applicant's time-to-complete (in seconds) and his total technique score (3 points for correct step performed in proper order, 2 points attempted and 1 point omitted) for each Step in the simulation. HRM can schedule and coordinate top simulation per-formers for face-to-face structured interview with Management. HRM can then present rank-ordered top performers and their performance results to Management (chemistry check) for final hiring decision.

Employment Decision System Alternative

Management can make a formal Job Offer, negotiate & finalize the offer. HRM then can enroll the new hires. Enrollment can then be done during the first day of training or (if preferred) the day before.

Performance Appraisal System Alternative

HRM and its SMEs review TBJA Data related to KRA's to identify which ways the KRA's are measurable or quantifi-able. HRM and its SMEs can then assure that the methodology used to measure or quantify the KRA is controlled sole-ly by the incumbent. HRM can identify the Duty Area, Tasks, Process Steps and KSA's associated with each KRA. If the KRA is not being satisfactorily accomplished, Management and the incumbent can be provided the Tasks or Process Steps which are not being performed correctly to discuss as well as providing an improvement plan with which to high-light the KSA's that need work. HRM can incorporate measurable, quantifiable and controllable KRA's into the com-pany's performance appraisal format listing beneath each KRA its associated and requisite Tasks, Process Steps & KSA's for employee feedback on how to improve performance.

Job Classification System Alternatives

HRM can review TBJA data average levels for Whole Job requirements and Task rating averages for the job under consideration for classification. HRM can subject the job's required averages along with any relevant weighting developed and the number of grades the company's grading system utilizes to a cluster analysis statistical package. HRM can then evaluate the resulting clusters to discover in which job family within the company's pay grade system a job should be classified. HRM then assigns a grade to the job based on cluster analysis results.

JOB COMPENSATION

HRM can then send the TBJA-based job description containing rank-ordered tasks and KSA'S to other companies' HR departments within the area and request a return of wage and salary survey feedback regarding what a comparable job is paid within their company (wage and salary survey information is shared). HRM can compare wage and salary feedback. The company must decide at this point whether it wants to pay the highest, the average or the lowest salary for the job in the community. In other words, does the company wish to be an industry leader or a follower with regard to pay? Does the company want to compete for the top recruits or settle for second best? Once Management makes its decision, HRM can then establish an average, a maximum and a minimum for the job.

Point of Clarification

I am not advocating that everything be done on every job. This would be tremendously wasteful not only in terms of the finances involved but the person power that would be required. I am saying, however, one-way of doing the job analysis should be adopted and subsequently adhered to every time a job analysis is applied. Therefore, any previous effort and energy expended are useable and are not wasted.

Much sound logic and commonsense are used to determine if and when to apply parts and pieces of the selected system. Policy needs to be established and not deviated from. The size or criticality of the job family needs to be carefully considered before any action is taken. Only those jobs having a high enough incumbency or operational criticality to warrant it, evoke either a full-blown or partial job analysis. If simulations and supporting videos are done for training purposes by HRD, minor editing of videotapes by HRM are necessary for their use in the selection process.

Let's say for instance that a HRD training video is edited for selection and is subsequently used and challenged, would you be comfortable defending it? First of all let me point out that only a tactical flow chart had been done by HRD. No full-blown or partial TBJA exists. Could you explain and defend use of the simulation for selection to an incumbent or his attorney? I hope that by now you are feeling confident and competent enough with the system to go to battle armed with it. You are using the same videos that those who are later hired will be trained with. You plan to hire those who achieve the highest performance on the simulations because you'll have to spend less time and money training them. Why were these simulations chosen? SME incumbents choose these simulations to support the identified KRAs of the job. There you have it. Always remember, an attorney is supposed to be logical and rational and so should the system data you have chosen as your defense.

HRD System Alternatives

Job Analysis System Alternatives

HRD can perform a Task-Based Job Analysis (TBJA) project on any specified job. TBJA is not HRD's primary responsibility, but usually HRD serves in a back up role. HRD receives Task-Based Job Analysis (TBJA) Data from HRM & IE and HRD uses it to supplement its tactical flow chart mapping. HRD flowcharts and cross-validates selected low-level process steps to create maps. HRD can then submit sets of High & Low-Level Process Maps to Industrial Engineer (IE) and HRM on any jobs on which they do job analysis.

Digital Image Documentation System Alternatives

HRD can digitally photograph and videotape performance of chosen high-level process tasks for overviews. HRD can also photograph performance of low-level process steps for testing and training with a digital camera. HRD can also videotape performance of low-level process steps for testing and training with VHS video camcorder. HRD can then submit digital photographs and videotapes of high-level process tasks and low-level process steps to HRM and IE.

Heliograms As A Training Vehicle

HRD can also make use of a relatively experimental methodology known as the heliogram. It is a methodology based on projecting the assembly/disassembly of a piece of equipment or product. This projection can be followed step-by-step as a method of training employees in how to do the steps of the process. This approach, while holding much promise is at present prohibitively expensive until technology is drastically improved.

Needs Assessment System Alternatives

HRD can use TBJA data and a level of comfort when performing task scale to develop and can construct a needs assessment survey. HRD can then administer the survey to the workforce and can analyze the needs assessment survey to determine the actual training needs.

Certification Test Battery Building & Job Incumbent Validation System Alternatives

HRD can receive high-level task and low-level steps sets of process maps and scripts from HRM or IE. HRD also can receive high-level task and low-level steps sets of digitized process photos and videotapes from HRM or IE. HRD and their SMEs can then review received job analysis data and select 8-10 KRA processes and from the data to construct process simulations. HRD can then utilize the chosen digitized process photos and scripts to create an instructional (picture book) training manual for certification testing of skill acquisition. HRD can edit selected training videotapes and scripts and make the changes necessary to create instructional certification testing videotapes. HRD can then build a content-valid battery (8-10) of KRA process step simulations with which HRD can test the employee's current skill level (i.e., time-to-complete, technique score, as well as any need for improvement). HRD can have Management select 12 job incumbents (i.e., 4 above-average performers, 4 average performers and 4 below-average performers) to blindly be administered the certification battery. HRD can then administer and validate a battery of KRA process step simulations to test trainee's or employee's present skill level as well as any need for skill improvement.

Trainee Certification System Alternatives

HRD can schedule trainees (each Friday) for skill certification testing. HRD can show the certification test videotape to the employee, give the trainee an instructional (picture book) training manual to study for a week and to take any necessary note-taking and can schedule time one week later for certification test administration. HRD can administer a certification test battery and show a videotape of the simulation being performed and allow the employee to perform the simulation with an open training manual. HRD can record the trainee's time-to-complete (in seconds) and the total technique score (3 points for correct step performed in order, 2 points attempted and 1 point omitted) for each step in the simulation. HRD can then calculate the simulation averages and plot the averages and the individual performance data (completion times and technique scores) for tracking and for comparative purposes (i.e., improving, declining, holding). HRD can then present trainee performance data to its Management team for them to make the HR decision to (i.e., continue training, certify and transfer to production, reassign or terminate).

Trainees are always being prematurely pulled from their training classes and placed in a production role. As pertaining to the employee, in most cases no documentation has existed in the past regarding the skills that have been mastered and those which remained to be mastered. The training certification program can represent a solution to those concerns. The latest test results can be used to select the appropriate person to be placed into the production line. Further application of an employee certification program or a trainee certification re-test can tell management if the employee's "hands on" experience has allowed the acquisition of needed skills.

Employee Certification System Alternative

HRD can then schedule incumbents (once each quarter or semi-annually) for the skill certification testing. HRD can show the certification test videotape to the employee, give the employee an instructional (picture book) training manual for study and note taking and can schedule the certification test. HRD can then administer certification test battery and show a videotape of the simulation as it is being performed and allow the employee to perform the simulation with an open training manual. HRD can then record the employee's time-to-complete (in seconds) and the total technique score (3 points for correct step performed in order, 2 points attempted & 1 point omitted) for each step in the simulation. HRD can calculate the simulation averages and plot the averages and the individual performance data (completion times and technique scores for tracking) and use for comparative purposes (i.e., improving, declining, holding). This could be the answer to questions of health or age concerns. HRD can then present the employee performance data to Management for the HR decision (i.e., re-test, certify, re-certify, de-certify, re-train, continue training, re-assign or dismiss.)

Years ago I found when using TBJA that I often times identified what I thought was a cluster of tasks, only it turned out to be a sequenced list of process steps. It was virtually impossible for SME's to rank-order since every task statement appeared to carry the same weight. What I had thought was a duty area had turned out to be a meaningful piece of work (a task) with a set of "How to" sequential or linear process steps necessary to perform the task successfully (efficiently and economically)

PROCESS MAPPING

Before we begin discussion of process mapping, let's begin a review of TBJA definitions. Tasks are meaningful pieces of work and are referred to as, "WHAT IS DONE on the Job". A Process is composed of Steps that describe how to do the Job. A Process Step is defined as "HOW TO DO" a meaningful piece of work.

When doing a process map always keep in mind the reading level of trainees. Only use simple symbols. In Allclear 3.5 the punctuation at the end of a statement determines the shape of the box within which it is typed (i.e., a period will yield a rectangle or parallelogram; a question mark will yield a diamond with a "yes" and a "no" branch statement; a colon will yield a hexagon with three choice branch statements; a semi-colon yields an oval with an inside loop statement and an exclamation point yields an unattached parallelogram.) The thing I like about AllClear as a flow charting software package is that AllClear is transportable to and from Microsoft Word. AllClear also converts the script as it is typed from narrative to flow chart. Thus AllClear makes changes to flow charts automatically as changes are typed in the script.

Since I am most familiar with the distribution process, I'll use it as an example. In most warehouses you have some sort of Pre-Receiving activities. Prior to the actual shipment of any product, the supplier or manufacturer optically scans each package's Universal Product Code (UPC) label to produce a Bill of Lading (BOL) listing the product load's content and then either e-mails or faxes the BOL to the warehouse. This is referred to as an Advanced Shipping Notice (ASN). If a TBJA has been performed, the most important tasks have already been identified. Now I want to describe the process steps that must be performed to accomplish this task.

Before even beginning with process mapping the job, have management identify a subject matter expert (SME) from among the work force to do two important things. Number one, conduct a plant tour of the job site. Specifically allocate time for yourself for job observation of the SME and familiarization with both the SME's production techniques and equipment. This must be done before starting. As your exposure to different manufacturing processes and companies increases, you may be surprised as you learn that the same type of equipment may be used to manufacture anything from nylon to soap to candy depending on the company with which you're working.

To begin process mapping go to ALL3 folder and open it. Double click the icon A3W and the Open File screen appears. Single click the "New" button and the "Please Select The Diagram Type" screen appears. Single click the Process Chart and the Diagram/Script split-screen appears. Single click the word Script and only the Script screen appears. Place the cursor within the word <Title> and single click. Type in the Name of the process you are mapping and then press the Enter Key and then type in the Date. The Date is used for tracking purposes. Any time the process map is updated, changed or modified, the new Date is entered here. Place the cursor within the words <First Statement> and then single click the left Mouse button. Always identify the first, initial, beginning, starting Process Step. Type this opening process step in the <First Statement> block. Place the cursor within the words <Last Statement> and then single click the left mouse button. Identify the last, final, climactic, finishing, ending process step. Type the closing process step in the <Last Statement>block.

Now that the first and the last Process Steps have been recorded, move to identify and document the remaining linear or sequential steps between them. Ask your SME, "What do you do next to accomplish or complete the process?" As the SME begins to describe next step of the process, I suggest that you just take a moment and close your eyes. Look into your mind's eye and try to visualize yourself performing this step.

Would the information you have just received and recorded from the SME allow you to perform the next step or is more information required? Don't hesitate to ask for additional information to clarify the step. The first time that process mapping is used; you will not have much experience on which to rely. As time goes on, your experience will increase. It will help if you adopt the convention of beginning each process step statement with the job title that performs the step. This helps clarify who does what or who is the customer and who is the supplier as the process is worked through. "What" and "Why" are always allies and will serve to stimulate input from the SME. Operator SMEs tend to process map at a tactical level. Supervisor SMEs tend to process map at the strategic level.

Back to the warehouse, the first strategic-level pre-receiving and Unloading probably ends with the unloading of rail cars, trailers or containers and the staging of the product for receiving. The second strategic part of the process deals with receiving the product. This is the formal comparison of the paper work (BOL) with what has actually been received (product loaded in the container, trailer, rail car, etc.) and the entry of that information into the Warehouse Management System (WMS) computer. After formal receipt of the product, it moves through the third strategic part of the process known as Put Away. This part of the process deals with placing the product in a physical documented storage location within the warehouse. The fourth strategic part of the process involves the picking or retrieval of product from its storage location within the warehouse as per a Purchase Order (PO). This part is initiated by the Customer and generates a Pick Ticket (PT). The fifth strategic part of the process involves packing or packaging the product. This usually involves the gathering or assembly of all products on the PO and its preparation for the sixth and final strategic part of the process called Shipping. Shipping should include all the shipping paper work preparation and the loading of the product thru pull away. This process map would serve you well for a quality audit but is not detailed enough for training an operator how to perform his part of the process. This calls for a more tactical process map detailing the process steps necessary to successfully accomplish performance of the process.

CONCLUSION

My intent has been to share in this book what I've been able to glean from my experience, especially technical things that have worked. Having been in academia as well as the public and private sectors I have noted a dearth of technical information (how to perform). I have tried to supply the HR community with tools for a beginning technical knowledge (process-based and task-based job analysis data collection forms, process mapping examples and products, etc.). I have tried to tie experience (the written word) together with the latest technology to create pragmatic tools for use and for experimentation. Individuals, staffs and classes can benefit from this approach. I also advocate the collaboration of HRM and HRD. I hope you find something useful in this tool kit for your growth in the profession.

Appendix A

DUTY AREA AND TASK RANKING INSTRUCTIONS

PURPOSE OF THIS PROJECT

Your organization is undertaking a systematic study of its jobs. The basic purpose of this project is to obtain critical information that can be used to improve the personnel policies, practices and procedures of your organization. The results and benefits of the project will be of interest and value to you.

YOU ARE ESSENTIAL TO THIS PROJECT AND YOUR SUPPORT AND COOPERATION ARE VERY IMPORTANT. *Your information and insights are required to assure the success of this project. Please cooperate in providing the requested information as completely and accurately as you can.*

Simple questionnaires will be used as the basic method for gathering data during this project. These questionnaires are NOT tests! THERE ARE NO RIGHT OR WRONG ANSWERS *to the questions which are asked! In fact, your individual responses will not be calculated.*

You are urged to work alone when completing the questionnaires. ONLY YOUR PERCEPTIONS AND OPINIONS ARE IMPORTANT. *Do not indicate what you think the organization wants to hear, indicate what you really think and feel.* PLEASE GIVE YOUR OWN HONEST AND INDEPENDENT OPINIONS AND PERCEPTIONS.

The project will be broken into TWO phases:

The first phase will obtain information about parts and sub-parts of your job. These parts are called Duty Areas and the sub-parts are called Tasks. In this phase you will be asked, using your own PERCEPTION and/or OPINION to RANK-ORDER the Tasks and Duty Areas on three important factors.

In the second phase, you will be asked about the more important Tasks of your job. You will be asked to RATE the most important Tasks on the level of certain factors required to adequately perform them.

None of the things you will be asked to do will be hard. Your answers can be given easily and quickly. PLEASE READ ALL THE EXPLANATIONS AND INSTRUCTIONS VERY CAREFULLY BEFORE GIVING YOUR ANSWERS. *Some thought and a little of your time is all that is required.*

Your help and cooperation in making this project a success will be greatly appreciated.

This phase of the project deals with the rank-ordering of Tasks and the Duty Areas of the job in which they fall. You will be asked to rank-order your Tasks and to identify Tasks which represent minimum requirements for entry into the job. You will also be asked to rank-order your Duty Areas and to indicate the percent of the job each Duty Area represents. Please turn to the next page and read the instructions regarding how to prepare for Task Ranking.

PREPARATIONS FOR TASK RANKING

A job exists when there are things to be done. These things to be done can be thought of as Tasks. Tasks are the smallest meaningful pieces of work that can be identified and "PICKED OUT" from the job. Task Statements are clear and accurate descriptions of these pieces of work. Tasks Statements may be grouped or clustered into Areas of Job Responsibility or Duty Areas.

A group of your fellow employees and team leaders have together identified the Functional Areas of Job Responsibility or Duty Areas that they feel make up your job. They have also listed under each Duty Area heading the Tasks, which they believe you may perform.

You are the expert on how your job is done. You know far better than anyone else which Tasks you do and do not perform. Some Tasks that you do not perform may be contained in the list.

Tasks that you do not perform must be eliminated from the list of Task Statements before you begin rank-ordering the Tasks of your job.

FIRST IMPORTANT STEP
Please read the entire list of Task Statements.
Draw a line through the Task Statement and through its
ranking spaces all the way across the Task Ranking form if:
1. You do not perform the Task
2. The Task is not part of your job.
RANK ONLY THE TASKS WHICH YOU PERFORM!

IDENTIFYING MINIMUM REQUIREMENT TASKS

Every job has some Tasks that are so basic and simple to perform that even people new to the job should be able to do them immediately. It is important that you and your fellow employees identify these "REQUIRED" Tasks.

You are the expert on how your job is done. You know far better than anyone else what should be required of someone when he starts the job. Please consider each Task Statement separately and independently before giving your opinion.

STEPS FOR REACHING YOUR DECISION
1. Read the Task Statement Carefully.
2. Decide whether a new employee is expected to perform the task when he first starts the job.
3. Please mark your opinion beside the Task Statement on the Task Ranking Form in the column labeled "Required"
1—If a new employee is expected to perform the Task when he starts the job; mark the Task with a "1."
0—If a new employee is NOT expected to perform the Task, mark it with a "0."
Look carefully at the example in Figure 1 and you will see clearly how to mark your opinions on the Task Ranking form.

ID No.	Task No.	Importance	Time Spent	Frequency	Required	
						apr TASK RANKING FORM Name *Linda Newton* [0 7 2 5 1 3]
01	00	*	*	*	*	COMMUNICATING - GIVING AND RECEIVING INFORMATION
01	01	2	3	2	0	Exchanges information with HEAD TELLER concerning supply of money, scheduling, job performance, balance problems, etc.
01	02	3	2	3	0	Exchanges information with BRANCH MANAGER regarding customer problems, work conditions, personal problems, job performance, security, check cashing authority, etc.
01	03	1	1	1	0	Exchanges information with CUSTOMERS concerning deposits, withdrawals, referrals, cross-selling services, complaints, etc.
01	04	4	4	4	1	Reads bank POLICY and PROCEDURES MANUAL to keep abreast of changes in the ways things must be done.
02	00	*	*	*	*	RECEIVING
02	01	1	1	1	0	Receives and verifies the deposit of cash to assure crediting of proper account.
02	02	4	3	3	0	Receives and/or processes credit card payments and/or deposits to assure crediting or debiting of proper accounts.
02	03	2	4	2	0	Receives and processes customer installment loan payments to assure crediting of proper account.
02	04	3	2	4	0	Receives and processes customer commercial loan payments to assure crediting of proper account.
03	00	*	*	*	*	PAYING
03	01	2	1	1	0	Pays out cash for checks drawn on bank when certain specified conditions are met.
03	02	1	2	2	0	Pays out cash for checks drawn on other banks when certain specified conditions are met.
03	03	4	3	3	0	Transfers cash from savings to checking accounts and assures proper crediting to accounts.
03	04	3	4	4	0	Disburses cash directly to customers from their savings accounts following prescribed procedures.

Figure 1. Task Ranking Form

Every Task Statement must be marked with either a "1" or a "0". Do not leave out or skip any Task!

Please be sure you have placed your response in the proper column ("Required") beside the Task on the Ranking form.

Please begin marking Tasks that should be performed by a new employee when he first starts his job.

When you have finished marking the "Required" Tasks, please read the INSTRUCTIONS FOR RANKING TASKS ON IMPORTANCE.

RANK-ORDERING TASKS ON IMPORTANCE

Some Tasks within a Job are much more important to good job performance than others. Certain Tasks if done poorly have almost no effect on whether an employee's job performance is judged as good or bad. Other Tasks are so critical that not doing them or doing them incorrectly would, for instance, cause an employee to be disciplined or fired, equipment to be damaged, quality to be impaired, production to be lost, someone to be hurt or killed, business to be lost, etc.

You are the expert on how your job is done. You know far better than anyone else those Tasks that are the most important to good job performance. Please help us identify the most important Tasks by RANK-ORDERING them within each Duty Area.

Look at example in Figure 1 to see how a bank teller rank-ordered her Tasks within each Duty Area.

REMEMBER!
Rank-order ONLY the Tasks which you perform!
Rank-order the Task Statements WITHIN each Duty Area!

Please read carefully ALL the Tasks listed under the first Duty Area heading. Place a "1" in the "Importance" column on the Ranking form beside the Task which you feel is most important to good performance

Remember: THERE ARE NO RIGHT OR WRONG ANSWERS! Please give your own honest opinion on which Tasks you think are the most important.

Continue rank-ordering Tasks within the first Duty Area until ALL of them are ranked. If two Tasks appear, in your opinion, exactly equal in IMPORTANCE, simply pick one and place it ahead of the other.

Move to the second Duty Area, and again rank-order the Tasks within it using the "Importance" column on your Ranking form. Continue the procedure until ALL Tasks within each Duty Area have been rank-ordered based on your perception of their Importance to good job performance.

After completing ALL the Importance Rankings, turn to the next page and read the INSTRUCTIONS FOR RANK-ORDERING TASKS ON TIME SPENT.

RANK-ORDERING TASKS ON TIME SPENT

Some Tasks within your job require a lot of your time. Certain other Tasks require very little. The relative amount of time you spend performing one Task as compared to another is important!

You are the expert on your job and know far better than anyone else those Tasks which require most of your time. Please help us identify the Tasks on which the most time is spent (relative amount of Time Spent) by RANK-ORDERING the Tasks within each Duty Area. Look at example in Figure 1 to see how a teller rank-ordered her Tasks on Time Spent within each duty area.

REMEMBER!
Rank-order ONLY the Tasks which you perform!
Rank-order the Task Statements WITHIN each Duty Area!

Please read carefully ALL the Tasks listed under the first Duty Area. Place a "1" in the "Time Spent" column on the Ranking form beside the Task on which you feel you spend the most time from among ALL Tasks within the first Duty Area.

Remember: THERE ARE NO RIGHT OR WRONG ANSWERS! Please give your own honest opinion about which Tasks you spend the most time performing.

Next, a "2" should be placed in the "Time Spent" column on the Ranking form beside the second most time consuming Task within the first Duty Area. If two Tasks appear, in you opinion, exactly equal on TIME SPENT, simply pick one and place it ahead of the other.

Continue rank-ordering Tasks within the first Duty Area until ALL the Tasks are ranked on Time Spent. Move to the second Duty Area and rank-order those Tasks using the "Time Spent" column on the Ranking form. Continue the procedure until ALL Tasks are rank-ordered within each Duty Area.

After completing ALL the Time Spent Rankings, turn to the next page and read the INSTRUCTIONS FOR RANK-ORDERING TASKS ON FREQUENCY OF PERFORMANCE.

RANK-ORDERING TASKS ON FREQUENCY

Some Tasks within your job have to be done every few minutes. Other Tasks are performed only once a year. How often you perform one Task as compared with another is important!

You are the expert on how your job is done. Your opinion of which Tasks are most often or most frequently perform is needed. Please help identify the Tasks that are most often performed (relative Frequency of Occurrence) by RANK-ORDERING the Tasks within each Duty Area.

Look at example in Figure 1 to see how a teller rank-ordered her Tasks on Frequency within each Duty Area.

REMEMBER!
Rank-order ONLY the Tasks which you perform!
Rank-order the Task Statements WITHIN each Duty.

Please read carefully ALL the Tasks listed under the first Duty Area. Place a "1" in the "Frequency" column on the Ranking form beside the Task which you most often perform from among ALL the Tasks within the first Duty Area.

Remember: THERE ARE NO RIGHT OR WRONG ANSWERS! Please give your own honest opinion about which Tasks you most frequently perform.

Next, a "2" should be placed in the "Frequency" column on the Ranking form beside the second most often performed task. If two Tasks appear, in your opinion, exactly equal on FREQUENCY, simply pick one and place it ahead of the other.

Continue rank-ordering Tasks within the first Duty Area until ALL the Tasks are ranked on frequency. Move to the second Duty Area and rank-order its Tasks using the "Frequency" column on the form. Continue the procedure until ALL Tasks within each Duty Area are ranked.

After completing ALL the Frequency Rankings, turn to the next page and read the INSTRUCTIONS FOR RANK-ORDERING DUTY AREAS ON IMPORTANCE.

RANK-ORDERING DUTY AREAS ON IMPORTANCE

When Tasks involving similar or common activities are grouped together, they are called Duty Areas. As you were rank-ordering the Tasks of your job, you were working on Tasks within Duty Areas. Now that you have completed rank-ordering your Tasks, it is important to know which of the Duty Areas are more important to good performance on your job. ALL Duty Areas are important, but some are more important than others!

You know far better than anyone else those Duty Areas which are the most important to good job performance. Please help identify the more important Duty Areas by rank-ordering them.

Look at the example in Figure 2 to see how a teller rank-ordered her Duty Areas on Importance

IMPORTANT FIRST STEP
Turn back in your Task Ranking Forms and
carefully review the Tasks listed under each Duty Area!

Please read carefully ALL the Duty Area headings. If there is any doubt in your mind about the tasks a Duty Area represents, look back in your task ranking forms to refresh your memory.

Place a "1" in the 'Importance" column on the Ranking form beside the Duty Area you feel is the most important. Next, a "2" should be placed in the "importance" column on the Ranking form beside the second most important duty area. If two Duty Areas appear exactly equal in IMPORTANCE, simply pick one and place it ahead of the other.

Remember: THERE ARE NO RIGHT OR WRONG ANSWERS! Please give your own honest opinion about which duty areas you think are more important!

Continue rank-ordering Duty Areas until ALL Duty Areas are ranked on Importance.

After completing ALL the Importance Rankings, turn to the next page and read the INSTRUCTIONS FOR RANK-ORDERING DUTY AREAS ON TIME SPENT.

Figure 2. Rank-Ordering Duty Areas

RANK-ORDERING DUTY AREAS ON TIME SPENT

Some Duty Areas require that you spend more time performing Tasks within them than others. The relative amount of time you spend doing work in one Duty Area as compared to another is important

Please help identify the Duty Areas in which the most time is spent by rank-ordering them on the relative amount of Time Spent

Look at the example in Figure 2 to see how a teller rank-ordered her Duty Areas on Time Spent.

IMPORTANT FIRST STEP
Turn back in your Task Ranking Forms and
carefully review the Tasks listed under each Duty Area!

Please read carefully ALL the Duty Area headings. If there is any doubt in your mind about which tasks a Duty Area heading represents, please look back in your Task Ranking forms again to refresh your memory.

Place a "1" in the "Time Spent" column on the Ranking form beside the Duty Area heading in which you feel you spend the most time doing work.

Next, a "2" should be placed in the 'Time Spent" column on the Ranking form beside the second most time consuming Duty Area. If two Duty Areas appear exactly equal on TIME SPENT, simply pick one and place it ahead of the other.

Remember: THERE ARE NO RIGHT OR WRONG ANSWERS! Please give your own honest opinion about the Duty Areas in which you spend the most time doing work!

Continue rank-ordering Duty Areas until ALL Duty Areas are ranked on time spent. After completing ALL the Time Spent Rankings, turn to the next page and read the INSTRUCTIONS FOR RANK-ORDERING DUTY AREAS ON FREQUENCY OF PERFORMANCE.

RANK-ORDERING DUTY AREAS ON FREQUENCY

Some Duty Areas require that work be done in them much more often than others. How often work is performed in one Duty Area as compared to another is important.

Please help identify the Duty Areas in which you most frequently perform work by rank-ordering the Duty Areas on Frequency of Occurrence. Look at the example in Figure 2 to see how a teller rank-ordered her Duty Areas on Frequency.

IMPORTANT FIRST STEP
Turn back in your Task Ranking Forms and
carefully review the Tasks listed under each Duty Area!

Please read carefully ALL the Duty Area headings. If there is any doubt in your mind about which Tasks a Duty Area heading represents, please look back in your Task Ranking forms again to refresh your memory.

Place a "1" in the "Frequency" column on the Duty Area Ranking form beside the Duty Area heading in which you most often perform work.

Next, a "2"should be placed in the "Frequency" column on the Duty Area Ranking form beside the second most frequently performed Duty Area. If two Duty Areas appear exactly equal in FREQUENCY, simply pick one and place it ahead of the other.

Remember: THERE ARE NO RIGHT OR WRONG ANSWERS! Please give you own honest opinion about the Duty Areas in which you most often do work.

Continue rank-ordering Duty Areas until ALL Duty Areas are ranked on Frequency. After completing ALL the Frequency rankings, turn to the next page and read the INSTRUCTIONS FOR WEIGHTING PERCENT OF JOB REPRESENTED.

WEIGHTING PERCENT OF JOB REPRESENTED

One final opinion is needed about your Duty Areas. Please estimate, in your opinion, what portion or percentage of the job EACH Duty Area represents.

Please write in the "Percent of Job Represented" column on your Duty Area Ranking Form, your estimate of how much of the job each Duty Area represents. Naturally, your PERCENTAGE ESTIMATES across ALL Duty Areas MUST TOTAL 100!

Look at the example in Figure 2 to see how a teller estimated the percentage of the job each of her Duty Areas represented.

INSTRUCTIONS FOR RETURNING MATERIALS

After estimating the percent of the job represented by each of your Duty Areas, you have finished the Duty Area and Task ranking phase of the project.

Please go through your Ranking forms very carefully to be sure you have rank-ordered all Tasks and Duty Areas on each measure. Check to be sure you recorded your opinions clearly and accurately in the proper columns on your Ranking Forms.

Place your Ranking Forms inside this booklet and return it to the proper person.

****

How to complete your Task List

Step 1:   Find a pencil and a quiet place. Carefully READ EACH numbered TASK. If it IS NOT PART of your job, pencil a CHECK MARK over the number beside the TASK statement. If the TASK IS PART of your job, make NO MARK, and go on to the next TASK. When finished, each of your job TASKS is identified. Each TASK that IS NOT PART of your job is "CHECKED".

Step 2:   SET APPOINTMENT with your immediate supervisor.

Step 3:   PRESENT your "marked" TASK list to your supervisor. Ask that your list of "perceived" JOB TASKS BE REVIEWED. DISCUSS any TASK on which you TWO DISAGREE. Mutually AGREE whether each TASK IS or IS NOT PART of your job. If you agree a "marked" TASK IS PART of your job,

ERASE the check. If you agree a "marked" TASK IS NOT PART of your job, DRAW A LINE through both the TASK number and statement.

Step 4: Once ALL JOB TASKS are identified, ask your boss to RANK-ORDER the TASKS within each DUTY AREA. Rank-order based upon IMPORTANCE to good job performance. Rankings BEGIN in each DUTY AREA with a "1" for the MOST IMPORTANT TASK. It ENDS with the least IMPORTANT TASK receiving the highest number. Use the line between the TASK number and its statement to indicate IMPORTANCE rankings. Once ALL TASKS are RANK-ORDERED within each DUTY AREA, ask your supervisor to RANK-ORDER the DUTY AREAS. Again, the MOST IMPORTANT DUTY AREA receives a "1" and the LEAST IMPORTANT DUTY AREA receives the highest number. You now have your own JOB DESCRIPTION. You know what your JOB TASKS are and which ones the boss thinks are MOST IMPORTANT.

Step 5: Go back to your quiet place with your new JOB DESCRIPTION. Turn to the back page and read the 9-Point Rating Scale for NEEDS ASSESSMENT. Using this scale, choose the statement which best describes your ability to perform each TASK. WRITE ITS RATING SCALE NUMBER on the line to the LEFT of the TASK number. Remember, "1" means you don't have a clue how to do it, while a "9" indicates you are excellent in performing it. Each JOB TASK TASKS MUST BE RATED.

Step 6: SET APPOINTMENT with your immediate supervisor.

Step 7: REVIEW your confidence level RATINGS on each TASK with the supervisor. ASK FOR TRAINING on any TASK you rated at "4", "3", "2" or "1".

APPENDIX B

Team Building

You Can't Judge A Book By Its Cover Questionnaire

1. My nickname as a child was
2. My favorite recreational activity is
3. My favorite flavor of ice cream is
4. Person who has most influenced my life is
5. My favorite team is
6. Three things I value most in life are
7. My favorite type of music is
8. Was President of the US when I was born
9. The most major accomplishment in my life

Agenda
What is a team?
Group/Team Dynamics
Characteristics of Effective Teams
Barriers to Teamwork
Communication Style Questionnaire
Effective Team Communication
Communication Skill Practices
Review
Action Plan

Training Objectives
List the stages of team development.
Identify the characteristics of effective teamwork.
Identify your communication style and how it helps or hinders team communication.
Demonstrate effective team communication skills

An effective TEAM:
1. Has clearly established goals and objectives that are accepted by team members.
2. Establishes high standards of performance for itself.
3. Allows members to disagree and has an effective way to resolve problems and conflict.

4. Reviews past actions to plan for future improvements.

5. Is cohesive: has a sense of unity.

6. Has members who listen to each other and provide useful feedback.

7. Recognizes individuals for contributions they make.

8. Assists a member when needed to ensure successful completion of team goals.

9. Attaches a high value to new, creative approaches to problem solving.

10. Is flexible because its members influence one another and their leader.

Stages of Team Development

Stage 1: Membership (Forming) Stage 2: Sub-grouping (Norming) Stage 3: Confrontation (Storming)
Stage 4: Shared Responsibility Team
(Performing)

Communication Style Questionnaire

Communication Style Questionnaire

Please mark the response for each of the following statements that "best describe your behavior most of the time."

Be honest and answer how you really behave rather than how you think you should behave. There are no right or wrong answers.

1. When communicating with others, I like to:
   - ☐ a. get quickly to the point.
   - ☐ b. do all the talking.
   - ☐ c. tell only what I want known.
   - ☐ d. go into minute detail.

2. On occasion, I tend to be:
   - ☐ a. short or rather blunt.
   - ☐ b. slow to share or give information.
   - ☐ c. too strict in interpreting what I hear.
   - ☐ d. very subjective in describing things.

3. My communication is usually geared toward:
   - ☐ a. being friendly with people.
   - ☐ b. being precise.
   - ☐ c. being cooperative.
   - ☐ d. getting things done.

4. People have accused me of:
   - ☐ a. being too vague and uncertain.
   - ☐ b. not listening to what is said.
   - ☐ c. putting things off.
   - ☐ d. talking more than I should.

5. In my discussions, people:
   - ☐ a. know I'm looking for the facts.
   - ☐ b. know I don't like being surprised.
   - ☐ c. know my position.
   - ☐ d. can sense my enthusiasm.

6. I prefer conversations which:
   - ☐ a. tend to be positive.
   - ☐ b. tend to be logical.
   - ☐ c. are straightforward.
   - ☐ d. tend to be calm.

7. I prefer conversations that:
   - ☐ a. stimulate me.
   - ☐ b. tend to be optimistic.
   - ☐ c. I perceive to be sincere.
   - ☐ d. I can control.

8. Don't involve me in conversations that:
   - ☐ a. generate stress.
   - ☐ b. lack cooperation.
   - ☐ c. are contrary to my point of view.
   - ☐ d. I can't control.

9. I enjoy it most when I'm:
   - ☐ a. listening to other people.
   - ☐ b. following a set agenda.
   - ☐ c. telling other people what to do.
   - ☐ d. self-assured and confident.

10. My greatest communication flaw is my:
    - ☐ a. demand for every little detail.
    - ☐ b. tendency to respond too quickly.
    - ☐ c. desire to be the center of attention.
    - ☐ d. speaking before knowing the facts.

11. Most co-workers think of me as:
    - ☐ a. friendly.
    - ☐ b. careful.
    - ☐ c. readily accepting change.
    - ☐ d. genuine.

12. The thing I need most is to be:
    - ☐ a. with others.
    - ☐ b. allowed time to make transitions.
    - ☐ c. supported.
    - ☐ d. given candid direction and feedback.

13. The basic concept of communication is to:
    - ☐ a. promote cooperation.
    - ☐ b. gain control over others.
    - ☐ c. influence others.
    - ☐ d. regulate outcomes.

14. In my written communication I tend to:
    - ☐ a. write little or nothing.
    - ☐ b. oversell my point of view.
    - ☐ c. follow the rules.
    - ☐ d. write more than necessary.

15. I work best in a place that is:
    - ☐ a. free-wheeling.
    - ☐ b. sociable.
    - ☐ c. structured.
    - ☐ d. comfortable.

16. I'm motivated by conversations that:
    - ☐ a. challenge me.
    - ☐ b. comfort me.
    - ☐ c. are sociable.
    - ☐ d. acknowledge me.

17. When people are facing stress, I tell them:
    - ☐ a. about the positive aspects.
    - ☐ b. what they should do.
    - ☐ c. to just make the best of it.
    - ☐ d. to remain calm.

18. My greatest communication strength is:
    - ☐ a. my concern.
    - ☐ b. I never meet a stranger.
    - ☐ c. my willingness to make a decision.
    - ☐ d. my willingness to listen.

Communication Style Score Sheet

Statements	<u>1</u>	<u>2</u>	<u>3</u>	<u>4</u>
1	a	b	c	d
2	a	d	b	c
3	d	a	c	b
4	b	d	c	a
5	c	d	b	a
6	c	a	d	b
7	a	b	c	d
8	d	c	b	a
9	c	d	a	b
10	b	d	c	a
11	c	a	d	b
12	d	a	b	c
13	b	c	a	d
14	a	b	c	d
15	a	b	d	c
16	a	d	c	b
17	b	a	d	c
18	<u>c</u>	<u>b</u>	<u>d</u>	<u>a</u>
Totals	——	——	——	——

Directions: Circle your responses and total the number of responses in each column.

Interpretation of Communication Styles

Every person has a set of normal behavior patterns. These patterns are reflecting to others in our personality and the way we communicate. Understanding how we communicate with others can enlighten us regarding how we are perceived. We can then learn to reduce unproductive behavior and better control our communications.

Column 1 - The Director

When communicating, you like to feel in charge, like challenges, difficult assignments and quick action. You tend to be very decisive in conversations.

Communication improvements may be needed because you tend to be too brief, a one-way communicator, a poor listener and sometimes come across as blunt.

You like freedom, power, independence and quick results. Make sure these things work for you rather than against you in communications with others.

Column 3 - The Feeler

When communicating, you like being sincere, being a group member, need appreciation, stability and time to adjust to change.

Communication improvements may be needed because you tend to respond slowly with information, need too much personal attention and are easily turned off by aggressive people.

You tend to want to build roots, to feel needed and to be asked, not told what to do. Be sure these things work for you in your communication.

Column 2 - The Talker

When communicating you like to feel successful in persuading others, being around others, appearing successful, being popular and positive.

Communication improvements may be needed because you tend to talk too much, speak without thinking, oversell your ideas and give more informaiton than is necessary.

You want popularity, influence, acceptance and public recognition. Be sure these things work for you in your communications with others.

Column 4 - The Organizer

When communicating with others, you like to be thorough, to feel you're in a low-risk situation, cooperative,organized and usings standard operating procedures. You're very logical in conversations with others.

Communication improvements may be needed because you tend to be excessively detailed, write long memos, to over-emphasize when putting things in writing and are slow to trust others.

You want thinking time, low-risk situations, cooperative relationships, organization and long explanations. You should overcome negative situations these tendencies can lead you into and use the positive to succeed.

Characteristics of Effective Communication

Hindrances To Effective Communication

Key Principles

Skill Practice Situations

1. A co-worker has left the last three days when she has completed her work. The rest of the team is still trying to get orders out. The team contract says that each member will stay and help until all orders are shipped. How would you handle it?

2. A co-worker says that you keep your work area really dirty. What will be your response?

3. Your supervisor wants you to pull off a project you've been working on for two months and give it to someone else in your work group. You really like this project and want to complete it. How do you approach your supervisor since your work has not been criticized?

4. You work with Claude who consistently (at least one break per day) comes back from break 15 minutes late. You cannot leave until he returns. How would you deal with this?

5. You are a member of a safety process action team. You and one other member of the eight-member group are the only active participants. To get more participation from all members, how would you proceed?

6. You have been selected as a lead operator in your area. Julie, one of your co-workers, has been resistant to your efforts to coordinate activities such as workflow, breaks, etc. How would you address this problem?

Action Plan

Area of Concentration:
What Outcome Do I Want?
What Action Steps Will I Take To Get There?

1.
2.
3.
4.
5.
6.

Appendix D

Secrets of Successful Training

Questions to ask your customer during the initial interview

(Be sure to use open-ended questions)

TARGETING THE PROBLEM:

1. What specific problem have you identified? (Is it behavior, productivity, quality, etc.?)

2. What portion of the problem is due to employee willingness and what portion is due to a lack of skill or knowledge? (IS THIS REALLY A TRAINING PROBLEM? Is it a motivational problem, a lack of supervision, a process or procedural design problem, an equipment problem, etc.?)

3. What specific outcome are you anticipating? (Change in attitude, behavior, skill level, etc?)

4. What was your plan of action when you encountered this kind of problem in the past? (Is this the first time you've seen this particular problem? What have you already tried?)

5. What were the strengths and weaknesses of your plan? (Did it work partially, not at all?)

6. What evaluation method or measurements told you it was a success? Short term? Long term?

7. How will the final decision concerning this training project be made? (Who is the final decision-maker concerning this training project?)

8. What does your upper management think of your approach to this training project? (Has your boss "bought into" your approach?)

9. How will this request affect previous training program development priorities and schedules? (How critical is this problem? Is everything else still due as before or can time line shift?)

TARGETING YOUR TRAINING AUDIENCE:

1. Describe the target group for this training project? (Hourly, salaried-exempt, salaried-non-exempt, combination, cultural composition, age levels, years of service, male/female, etc.?)

2. What education and experience levels are represented in the target group? (Is it six grade and below, high school, college or a combination of levels?)

3. Tell me about the number of people in each target group? (What is the total number of people to be trained in categories broken down as in Question 1?)

4. What is the "current' performance level of me group? (Is this information documented, where and when can it be accessed, how recent is the information, how long have performance records been kept?)

5. What is the 'desired' performance level for the group after training? (What should they be able to do after training, at what level of proficiency, productivity and/or quality?)

6. What Subject Matter Experts (SME's) are available to assist? (What are the resources available within the target group, management, quality assurance, engineering, accounting, research, etc.?)

ESTABLISHING ANY TRAINING HISTORY:

1. Tell me about any previous training the group has received? (How long ago?)

2. Tell me about the people who conducted it? (Us, consultant, corporate, etc.?)

3. How well was it received by this group? (Direct or indirect feedback?)

4. Describe how the training program content was structured? ("Tailored' to your people or "canned"? Generic or job-specific?)

5. How was the material presented? (Seminar, classroom, video tape, slide show, training manual, OJT, etc.)

6. What indicated to you that it was successful? Unsuccessful? (Change in behavior, productivity, quality?)

7. What were the MOST beneficial aspects of this training? (Observable, measurable?)

8. What were the LEAST beneficial aspects of this training? (Observable, measurable?)

DESIGNING THE TRAINING PROGRAM:

1. What other departments within the organization should be involved? (Which departments and whom within the departments?)

2. Tell me your feelings on the involvement of other outside resources? (If so, what organization and specifically, whom within the organization or will you entertain recommendations?)

3. At what level do you want outside resources involved? (Do you want them designing, leading, overseeing, directing, assisting, suggesting, recommending, etc.?)

4. If outside resources are utilized, how will billing be handled? (Who's monitoring and approving consultant's time sheet, coordinating payment, budgetary responsibility for payment, etc.?)

5. What is the time line within which this program must be ready? (When is the project deadline?)

6. What resources are you willing to commit? (Access to personnel, budgetary dollars, equipment, downtime of equipment, assignment of personnel to project, inter-department coordination, political, etc.)

7. What are the restrictions and limitations to size of the group as training is administered? (Will it be one-on-one, a small group, a large group, etc.?)

8. How do you feel about doing the training off-site? (What about facility cost, equipment rental, refreshments, scheduling, coordination, etc?)

9. Where will the training be done? (Will it be done at the trainee's work station, general area of work station, on-line, auditorium, training room, conference room, etc.?)

10. Are then any restrictions on training fane? (Will training time be limited to 2 hours, half a day, a day, a week, two weeks or as much time as need)?

11. What different types of presentation media are you willing to consider? (May we use classroom lecture, platform lecture, audio cassette, training manual, overhead transparency, slide, computer-based, video tape, pencil-and-paper training aids, simulations, role-playing, experiential learning, etc.?)

12. Who win be involved in delivering the training? (Will it be self-taught by trainee, an employee training his replacement, by line instructors, by training department trainers, by consultants, by supervisors or management, etc.?)

13. Are any procedural or other process changes under consideration that might or will impact how the people should be trained? (When is implementation of the change(s) anticipated?)

14. How will incidentals associated with training program administration be paid? (Refreshments, meals, tokens, mileage, door prizes, facility rental, etc.?)

15. Where does training department's responsibility for training program end? (Is it our responsibility for on-going administration, for train-the-trainer and exit, to administer once, to contract for a consultant delivery or to just develop and deliver, etc.?)

16. Would you consider accepting either canned or off-the-shelf generic training packages or programs? (May we use purchased materials just as they arrive in 'as is' condition?)

17. Would you consider accepting either a 'modified" canned or off-the-shelf generic training program or package? (Training department modification of canned or generic program, pay vendor to modify program, etc.)

18. How do feel about the training program being tailor-made to our specific situation and needs? (Built from scratch, using our people, equipment, our situations and experiences, etc.?)

EVALUATING THE NEW TRAINING PROGRAM:

1. How long before the training program would you see the 'pre-test' of each individual's knowledge/performance being administered? (Establish a performance baseline of where the individual is before training.)

2. How long after training would you see the 'post-test' of each individual's knowledge/performance being administered? (Measure the amount of change in knowledge/performance after training.)

ASSOCIATE
TOTAL QUALITY MANAGEMENT
AWARENESS
SURVEY

TO: ALL UNIT ASSOCIATES

In January, a corporate Process Improvement Team was created. The team named itself "GET OUR ASSOCIATES TRAINED SOON" or the "GOATS". As the name implies, our team mission is to help every associate get the training necessary to develop to his or her full potential. One of the ways this is being done is through "**Total Quality Management**" (TQM).

First of all, understanding TQM is important. Therefore, what the **GOATS Team** needs to do is find out how much everyone already knows about TQM. To do this, we ask that you respond openly and honestly to the attached survey. All responses are confidential! Your cooperation and assistance in providing information to us is critical.

There are no right or wrong answers to the questions on the survey. As you will notice, we are not interested in your name. We are interested only in:

[]   **Whether you work in the office or on the warehouse floor.**
[]   **Whether or not you are paid for overtime (Exempt/Nonexempt).**
[]   **At what location you work.**

Please complete this survey. Fifty (50) statements are provided. Each question asks for your opinion in two ways. First, at what level do you **AGREE** or **DISAGREE** with the statement? Second, how **IMPORTANT** or **UNIMPORTANT** is the statement? **Please be sure to mark your opinion on both scales!** If you honestly do not have or know an answer, please mark the "DK" box on the form.

The two scales (Agreement & Importance) are <u>two</u> independent pieces of information. In other words, you may "strongly disagree" with a statement but it may be "very unimportant"
to you. We need to know that! On the other hand, you may "strongly agree" with a statement and it may be "extremely important" to you. Read carefully and give us your opinion. The following is an explanation of the two rating scales:

AGREEMENT   # IMPORTANCE

1—Strongly Agree   1—Very Unimportant (Not Needed)
2—Agree   2—Unimportant
3—Mildly Agree   3—Helps Sometimes
[]—DON'T KNOW   []—DON'T KNOW
5—Mildly Disagree   5—Needed
6—Disagree   6—Important
7—Strongly Disagree   7—Extremely Important (Essential)

Here is an example of how to complete the rating of the question: "Management wants <u>ALL</u> my suggestions for improvement". If you "agree" with the statement and think it is "important", indicate your answer the following way:

Ex: Management wants <u>ALL</u> of my suggestions for improvement.

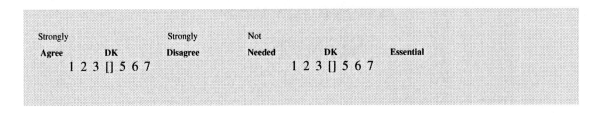

If you "strongly disagree" but "don't know" how important it is, mark your response this way:
Ex: Management wants <u>ALL</u> of my suggestions for improvement.

Strongly		Strongly	Not		
Agree	**DK**	**Disagree**	**Needed**	**DK**	**Essential**
1 2 3 [] 5 6 7			1 2 3 [] 5 6 7		

If you have any questions, please ask for clarification from the person conducting the survey. GOOD LUCK and thanks for your cooperation!

Start of Survey

01.   The facility identification number & company name for my work location is.... (Ask session leader)

——— —— ———   _____

Facility ID #   Company Name

02.   My primary work assignment is in the...(Please mark only one!)
        [] Warehouse Area [] Office Area [] Transportation Area

03.   I am paid...(Please mark only one!)
        [] A salary. [] By the hour.

04.   I have worked here...(Please mark only one!)
        [] Under 6 mos. [] 6—11 mos. [] 1—2 yrs. [] 3—5 yrs. [] Over 5 yrs.

Leadership & Coaching

05.   Management is committed to finding better ways to improve the quality of services we provide.

Strongly Agree	DK	Strongly Disagree		Not Needed	DK	Essential
1 2 3 [] 5 6 7				1 2 3 [] 5 6 7		

06.   Our goals and objectives related to improving service quality are clearly spelled out.

Strongly Agree	DK	Strongly Disagree		Not Needed	DK	Essential
1 2 3 [] 5 6 7				1 2 3 [] 5 6 7		

07.   Adequate resources (i.e., time, money, etc.) are provided for me to improve quality.

Strongly Agree	DK	Strongly Disagree		Not Needed	DK	Essential
1 2 3 [] 5 6 7				1 2 3 [] 5 6 7		

08.   All levels of management are involved in promoting quality.

Strongly Agree	DK	Strongly Disagree		Not Needed	DK	Essential
1 2 3 [] 5 6 7				1 2 3 [] 5 6 7		

09.   I am encouraged to be active in local and national quality-oriented associations and business groups.

Strongly Agree		DK		Strongly Disagree		Not Needed		DK		Essential
1	2	3	[]	5	6	7		1 2 3 [] 5 6 7		

10.   My boss is allowed to reward high-quality performance in many different ways.

Strongly Agree		DK		Strongly Disagree		Not Needed		DK		Essential
1	2	3	[]	5	6	7		1 2 3 [] 5 6 7		

11.   High-quality performance is recognized throughout the company.

Strongly Agree		DK		Strongly Disagree		Not Needed		DK		Essential
1	2	3	[]	5	6	7		1 2 3 [] 5 6 7		

Data Collection & Analysis

12.   Quality standards/indicators are in place for all of our jobs.

Strongly Agree		DK		Strongly Disagree		Not Needed		DK		Essential
1	2	3	[]	5	6	7		1 2 3 [] 5 6 7		

13. Data is routinely collected on how my job tasks are performed.

Strongly Agree	DK	Strongly Disagree	Not Needed	DK	Essential
1 2 3 [] 5 6 7			1 2 3 [] 5 6 7		

14. The data collected on my performance is meaningful.

Strongly Agree	DK	Strongly Disagree	Not Needed	DK	Essential
1 2 3 [] 5 6 7			1 2 3 [] 5 6 7		

15. The data necessary to determine the cause of a quality problem is readily available.

Strongly Agree	DK	Strongly Disagree	Not Needed	DK	Essential
1 2 3 [] 5 6 7			1 2 3 [] 5 6 7		

16. We use quality data to prevent problems, not just fix problems when they occur.

Strongly Agree	DK	Strongly Disagree	Not Needed	DK	Essential
1 2 3 [] 5 6 7			1 2 3 [] 5 6 7		

17. Continuous improvement activities within our company are well-coordinated between groups (i.e., sales/operations/transportation, warehouse floor/office, etc.).

Strongly Agree	DK	Strongly Disagree	Not Needed	DK	Essential
1 2 3 [] 5 6 7			1 2 3 [] 5 6 7		

18.   With regard to continuous improvement, management "practices what it preaches".

Strongly Agree	DK	Strongly Disagree	Not Needed	DK	Essential
1 2 3 [] 5 6 7			1 2 3 [] 5 6 7		

Strategic Quality Planning

19.   My input is used in the company's planning process.

Strongly Agree	DK	Strongly Disagree	Not Needed	DK	Essential
1 2 3 [] 5 6 7			1 2 3 [] 5 6 7		

20.   When planning for the future, we use the quality data we have already collected.

Strongly Agree	DK	Strongly Disagree	Not Needed	DK	Essential
1 2 3 [] 5 6 7			1 2 3 [] 5 6 7		

Associate Involvement

21.   I have the authority to correct any problems I discover.

Strongly Agree	DK	Strongly Disagree	Not Needed	DK	Essential
1 2 3 [] 5 6 7			1 2 3 [] 5 6 7		

22.   I have the freedom to voice my opinion about the cause(s) of quality problems.

Strongly Agree		DK	Strongly Disagree	Not Needed		DK	Essential
1 2 3	[]	5 6 7			1 2 3	[]	5 6 7

23.   My suggestions for quality improvement are seriously considered by management.

Strongly Agree		DK	Strongly Disagree	Not Needed		DK	Essential
1 2 3	[]	5 6 7			1 2 3	[]	5 6 7

24.   I am sufficiently trained how to evaluate and improve quality.

Strongly Agree		DK	Strongly Disagree	Not Needed		DK	Essential
1 2 3	[]	5 6 7			1 2 3	[]	5 6 7

25.   I am recognized by management for suggesting ways to improve quality.

Strongly Agree		DK	Strongly Disagree	Not Needed		DK	Essential
1 2 3	[]	5 6 7			1 2 3	[]	5 6 7

26.   Feedback is provided on how well we are accomplishing our quality objectives.

Strongly Agree		DK	Strongly Disagree	Not Needed		DK	Essential
1 2 3	[]	5 6 7			1 2 3	[]	5 6 7

Quality Assurance of Services

27. Our customer's needs and expectations tell us how to design the delivery of service to them.

Strongly Agree	DK	Strongly Disagree	Not Needed	DK	Essential
1 2 3 [] 5 6 7			1 2 3 [] 5 6 7		

28. We measure quality at every step as service is provided to our customers.

Strongly Agree	DK	Strongly Disagree	Not Needed	DK	Essential
1 2 3 [] 5 6 7			1 2 3 [] 5 6 7		

29. The way my job performance is measured accurately reflects the true quality of my work.

Strongly Agree	DK	Strongly Disagree	Not Needed	DK	Essential
1 2 3 [] 5 6 7			1 2 3 [] 5 6 7		

30. Everybody doing the same job is held to the same quality standards.

Strongly Agree	DK	Strongly Disagree	Not Needed	DK	Essential
1 2 3 [] 5 6 7			1 2 3 [] 5 6 7		

31.   We check the quality of our work on a regular basis.

Strongly Agree	DK	Strongly Disagree		Not Needed	DK	Essential
1 2 3 [] 5 6 7				1 2 3 [] 5 6 7		

32.   We are required to keep a record of every quality measurement we take.

Strongly Agree	DK	Strongly Disagree		Not Needed	DK	Essential
1 2 3 [] 5 6 7				1 2 3 [] 5 6 7		

33.   We track the quality performance of companies that supply us with goods and services.

Strongly Agree	DK	Strongly Disagree		Not Needed	DK	Essential
1 2 3 [] 5 6 7				1 2 3 [] 5 6 7		

34.   The service quality indicators we track are the most stringent in the industry.

Strongly Agree	DK	Strongly Disagree		Not Needed	DK	Essential
1 2 3 [] 5 6 7				1 2 3 [] 5 6 7		

Continuous Improvement Results

35. Our service quality is currently the best it has ever been.

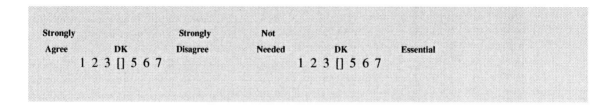

Strongly
Agree   **DK**   **Strongly**   **Not**
                                  Disagree   **Needed**   **DK**   **Essential**
        1 2 3 [] 5 6 7   1 2 3 [] 5 6 7

36. Our competitors are falling behind us in the area of service quality.

Strongly
Agree   **DK**   **Strongly**   **Not**
                                  Disagree   **Needed**   **DK**   **Essential**
        1 2 3 [] 5 6 7   1 2 3 [] 5 6 7

37. The commitment to continuous improvement is actively demonstrated by all company divisions, departments and locations.

Strongly
Agree   **DK**   **Strongly**   **Not**
                                  Disagree   **Needed**   **DK**   **Essential**
        1 2 3 [] 5 6 7   1 2 3 [] 5 6 7

38. Our external suppliers (i.e., carriers, etc.) make a strong effort to cooperate with us in quality improvement.

Strongly
Agree   **DK**   **Strongly**   **Not**
                                  Disagree   **Needed**   **DK**   **Essential**
        1 2 3 [] 5 6 7   1 2 3 [] 5 6 7

39. Productivity Improvement Team recommendations are implemented by Management.

Strongly Agree		DK		Strongly Disagree	Not Needed		DK		Essential
1	2	3	[] 5 6 7			1	2	3 [] 5 6 7	

Customer Satisfaction

40. We constantly monitor customer likes and dislikes with regard to our services.

Strongly Agree		DK		Strongly Disagree	Not Needed		DK		Essential
1	2	3	[] 5 6 7			1	2	3 [] 5 6 7	

41. We are aware of each customers' needs and expectations.

Strongly Agree		DK		Strongly Disagree	Not Needed		DK		Essential
1	2	3	[] 5 6 7			1	2	3 [] 5 6 7	

42. It's almost impossible for defective work (i.e., damage, inventory errors, paperwork errors, etc.) to reach our customers.

Strongly Agree		DK		Strongly Disagree	Not Needed		DK		Essential
1	2	3	[] 5 6 7			1	2	3 [] 5 6 7	

43.   We get regular feedback on customer satisfaction with the quality of our work.

Strongly Agree	DK	Strongly Disagree	Not Needed	DK	Essential
1 2 3 [] 5 6 7			1 2 3 [] 5 6 7		

44.   Our company policies make it easy to quickly resolve customer complaints.

Strongly Agree	DK	Strongly Disagree	Not Needed	DK	Essential
1 2 3 [] 5 6 7			1 2 3 [] 5 6 7		

45.   We pride ourselves on concern for customer satisfaction.

Strongly Agree	DK	Strongly Disagree	Not Needed	DK	Essential
1 2 3 [] 5 6 7			1 2 3 [] 5 6 7		

46.   We make it easy for customers with service problems to get the help they need.

Strongly Agree	DK	Strongly Disagree	Not Needed	DK	Essential
1 2 3 [] 5 6 7			1 2 3 [] 5 6 7		

47.   We record and report all customer complaints the same way.

Strongly Agree	DK	Strongly Disagree	Not Needed	DK	Essential
1 2 3 [] 5 6 7			1 2 3 [] 5 6 7		

48.   We are getting fewer customer complaints about our services.

Strongly Agree	DK	Strongly Disagree		Not Needed	DK	Essential
1 2 3 [] 5 6 7				1 2 3 [] 5 6 7		

49.   We try hard to find out if customers are satisfied with our services.

Strongly Agree	DK	Strongly Disagree		Not Needed	DK	Essential
1 2 3 [] 5 6 7				1 2 3 [] 5 6 7		

50.   Customer satisfaction information is used to improve our service offerings.

Strongly Agree	DK	Strongly Disagree		Not Needed	DK	Essential
1 2 3 [] 5 6 7				1 2 3 [] 5 6 7		

Suggested Group Exercise For Introducing The
ASSOCIATE SUGGESTION PROGRAM

PAPER CUP EXERCISE

OBJECTIVE: To provide associates with an experience that demonstrates the concept of creativity and the power of group creativity.

INSTRUCTIONS: This exercise needs to be presented in two phases.

PHASE 1—Hand out one copy to each associate and ask that they each list as many ideas as they can think of for which paper cups could be used. Set a two minute time period. Have each associate work alone and in silence.

(You can anticipate that the average person will list about 15 ideas. These are usually generated within the first minute and then most people sit rather blank for the second minute with few ideas coming to mind.)

Ask each associate how many ideas he/she came up with during the two (2) minutes. Then take up their list of ideas.

PHASE 2—Put associates into small groups of three to four people. Tell each group to select a group name, the sillier the better.

Tell the groups they are going to compete with each other in listing ideas for using a paper cup. Have each group choose one of its members to record the group's ideas. (Hopefully the associate who can write the smallest and fastest.)

Hand out a second copy of the paper cup exercise sheet to the group recorder. Give the groups three (3) minutes to list as many ideas as they can think of.

Therefore, make two sets of copies of the Paper Cup Exercise on the next page.

LIST as many USES
of a
PLASTIC CUP
as possible!

BE CREATIVE!

Appendix E

Process Map Technical Training Procedure

Training Philosophy:

- Is to utilize a training strategy that gets the trainees involved and actively participating in the learning process.
- The desire is to create an adult learning situation verses the traditional trainer-trainee-teaching environment.
- The strategy promotes teambuilding since sessions are structured around 4-person teams. The trainee is motivated (if not pressured) by the team environment and facilitator (trainer) to actively participate. Leaders are allowed to surface as the team works to accomplish its assignments. The trainer's role becomes less instructive and more facilitative and encouraging. Non-participators in this team learning environment are indicative of poor future team performers. This provides quick insight and feedback on the trainee's future potential as a contributor to the team.
- The strategy employed involves "insight" learning where the trainee personally "discovers the operational process as the training session progresses.
- The approach is designed to work with trainees "fresh off the street" as well as with "seasoned" employees.
- The process maps are based on behaviors the employee must exhibit to keep product successfully moving through the process. Each process map contains a critical path through the process for the product if everything goes according to plan. The most commonly seen process exceptions are also documented as the vehicle to empower and drive decision-making to the operator level and reduce employee dependence on supervisory direction.

Preparation of Training Materials

- Detailed (down to the key-stroke level) behaviorally-based process maps are prepared in conjunction with and validated by Subject Matter Experts (SMEs) for all major operational procedures. SMEs include employees who have demonstrated high levels of both productivity and quality on the job.
- Training materials are prepared from process maps by removing the verbage from every other process step and preparing a "numbered" list of the removed verbage.

Training of Hourly Associates

- Current hourly employees are grouped (based upon their performance & attitude) into 4-person teams. (Ideal team size is 4 persons. 3-person teams may be used but 2-person creates too much pressure while 5 persons generates too little pressure to participate and allows trainees to hang out on the periphery of team involvement.
- One trainer (facilitator) per team is absolutely mandatory.
- Operation Manager serves as the trainer to assure that hourly employees perceive their supervisor as the "process expert". This also provides the Operation Manager with an opportunity to gain valuable insights into employee teambuilding skills and expertise as well as their cognitive and reasoning skills. Fast and slow learners become readily apparent, especially with new hires. The Operation Manager can then decide whether the time and effort required bringing the "slower" new hire up to the desired productivity and quality level is warranted.

Process Map Technical Training Procedure (continued)

Day One

- The training session is scheduled for two hours.
- The facilitator explains the purpose of the training is to establish uniformity in the way things are done within as well as across the shifts. There are many different ways to do something, but one method is usually the most efficient, effective and economical way to accomplish it. This method is termed the "current best approach" (CBA). Our training goal is to identify and share, with all team members, the CBA for each process. Each team member is asked to adopt and adhere (100% of the time) to the existing CBA until such time as a new CBA is developed, documented, trained and implemented.
- The facilitator demonstrates and explains the three basic symbols used in process mapping: task step; question or decision and the branch or option. A task is the smallest meaningful piece of work that can be identified. An example of a task is "changing a tire". The task steps involved in accomplishing the task include "removing tire from trunk", "removing jack from trunk", "jacking car", "loosing & removing lug nuts", "removing tire from axle", etc.
- A rectangular box is used to represent each task step. The rectangular box usually has an arrow coming to it and an arrow coming from it.
- A diamond is used to represent a question or a decision with two options. If used as a question, the diamond usually has an arrow coming into it and two arrows (one for "yes" and one for "no") coming out of it. If used as a decision, the diamond usually has an arrow coming into it and two arrows (one for each option) coming out of it.
- An elongated hexagon is used to represent a branch with three or more options. A branch usually has an arrow coming into it and three or more arrows coming out of it.
- The facilitator then tells the team that he will assist them in process mapping the task of placing a call from a pay phone.
- The facilitator starts by helping the team identify the "starting point" and the "ending point" of the placing a call from a pay phone. Every process begins with an initial step or starting point that initiates the process flow. In this case, the initiating task step is **"locates pay phone"**. It is written in a rectangular box in the upper left corner of the whiteboard. The ending point that completes or wraps up the process of placing a call from a pay phone is **"hangs up & walks away"**. It is written in a rectangular box at the bottom right corner of the whiteboard. There is the beginning and the ending of the process to be flowed.

Process Map Technical Training Procedure (continued)

- The facilitator assists the team members in discussing and identifying the various task steps that must be preformed between the beginning and the end of the process. There is no set number of steps required to do this task but several questions should be introduced during the process to insure learning and understanding. Possible steps and questions include: **Is there a receiver?** (diamond)

> If **yes**—Draw an arrow line (write a "**yes**" above line) to a rectangular box and write in "**pick up receiver**".
>
> If **no**—Draw an arrow line(write a "**no**" above line) back to rectangular box "**locates pay phone**".

> **Dial tone?** (diamond)
>
> If **yes**—Draw an arrow line (write a "**yes**" above line) back to rectangular box "**Dials #**".
>
> If **no**—Draw an arrow line (write a "**no**" above line) down to rectangular box "**hangs up & walks away**".

> **"Busy?"** (diamond)
>
> If **yes**—Draw an arrow line (write a "**yes**" above line) down to rectangular box "**hangs up & walks away**".
>
> If **no**—Draw an arrow line (write a "**no**" above line) down to diamond "**person or answer machine?**"

> > If **person**—Draw an arrow line (write a "**person**" above line) down to diamond "**right person?**"
> >
> > > If **yes**—Draw an arrow line (write a "**yes**" above line) down to rectangular box "**talks**".
> > >
> > > > **"Finished?"** (diamond)
> > > >
> > > > > If **yes**—Draw an arrow line (write a "**yes**" above line) down to rectangular box "**hangs up & walks away**".
> > > > >
> > > > > If **no**—Draw an arrow line (write a "**no**" above line) down to rectangular box "**talks**".
> > >
> > > If **no**—Draw an arrow line (write a "**no**" above line) down to rectangular box "**leaves message**".
> > >
> > > > Draw an arrow line down to rectangular box "**hangs up & walks away**".
> >
> > If **machine**—Draw an arrow line (write a "**machine**" above line) down to rectangular box "**leaves message**".
> >
> > > Draw an arrow line down to rectangular box "**hangs up & walks away**".

- The facilitator passes out a detailed process map to the team.
- The facilitator instructs the team to highlight the "critical" path through their assigned process map (critical path is the flow through the map if everything goes according to plan.)
- The facilitator validates that the "critical" Path is correctly identified.
- The facilitator reviews the non-highlighted sections of the map (non-highlighted sections represent the most common exceptions or problems experienced with the process).
- The facilitator then takes the team (with their highlighted process map) to the warehouse floor & walks the Team through the task steps of the process.
- The facilitator then collects the process map and releases the team.

Process Map Technical Training Procedure (continued)

Day Two

- The training session is scheduled for two hours.
- The facilitator passes out process map (with the statement missing from every other task step) and a scrambled but numbered list of the missing task statements.
- The facilitator instructs the team to reason and logic their way through the process step by "filling in the blank" with the number for the proper task statement on the list.
- The facilitator provides feedback on the team's accuracy at the end of each page of the process map.
- Upon completion of the exercise, the team's "critical" path process map is returned and once again the team is taken back to the warehouse floor for a "hands on" walk-through of the process.

Status of Process Mapping

Warehouse Operational Processes DOCUMENTED:

Receiving
Put-Away
Order Management (Except Air, Forced Orders & HazMat)
Order Management (Air, Forced Orders & HazMat)
Picking (Paper)
Replenishment
Bounce (Paper Picking)
Gaylord Packing
Less-Than-Truck Load (LTL) Shipping

Pre-Pack Operational Processes DOCUMENTED:

Pre-Pack Overview
Scheduler
Accumulation
Set-Up
Work Station Operation
First-Piece Audit

Audit Processes DOCUMENTED:

Fast Pack
Bulk Pack
Pick Error (Fast, Bulk, Gaylord)
Aisle Location Audit
Pre-Pack Set-Up Audit
Pre-Pack "First Piece" Audit

Warehouse Operational Processes TO BE DONE:

Fast & Bulk Packing
RF Picking
Forced Orders
Returns
Inventory Management Control
In-Transit
Export
Cycle Count

APPENDIX F

FACILITATOR'S

KIT

FOR

BRAINSTORMING

JOB ANALYSIS

TASK LISTS

Purpose

The kit explains how to prepare for and conduct a Task Identification Brainstorming Session (JOB ANALYSIS). The Task List is used for job descriptions, selection, training and associate/process performance improvement.

Step 1   Management Orientation

Advise management of project intent pointing out the benefits/uses of the collected data.

Step 2   Identification of Subject Matter Experts (SMEs)

Ask Management to identify four (4) or five (5) incumbents who are knowledgeable **Subject Matter Experts (SMEs)** about how the job under study is done. Composition of the group must be diverse (sex, age, race, minimum six months of length of service, etc.). One or two "**SUPPLIERS**" (people from whom things are received) and one to two "**CUSTOMERS**" (people for whom work is done) must be included. One or two "**supervisors**" may also be included.

Step 3   Notification of SMEs

Prepare and distribute a **MEMORANDUM** describing: Who is involved; why each is involved; location, time & duration of meeting; personal & organizational benefits of involvement; etc. (See Appendix A). If overtime is required for sessions, notify associates and pay it.

Step 4   Location, Equipment and Supply Requirements

Identify a meeting room with adequate & comfortable seating, proper lighting & temperature and clear wall space on which to tape flip chart paper for display. Supplies include: a pad of flip chart paper, easel, markers (4 colors—red, blue, green, black), masking tape, a pad of 2" x 2" Post-Its, a legal pad, a dozen pens or pencils.

Refreshments (Optional): Coffee, juice, sodas, doughnuts, cookies, etc.

Step 5   Pre-Session Preparation

Prepare a flip chart page containing a list (written in four different colors) of action verbs (See Appendix B) ending in "S". List as many action verbs as possible. Reserve meeting room. Adjust temperature. Check markers for proper functioning. Set up easel. Assure adequate number of pages (10 minimum) on flip chart pad. Purchase adequate refreshments. Set up table and chairs. Sharpen pencils. Tape flip chart page of verbs on wall so the associates cannot see it. Write definitions of TASK and DUTY AREA on flip chart page and tape it on the wall. Identify someone to assist you in writing Tasks on legal pad as they are identified during session.

Spend time on the job with incumbents before session begins. This allows "mental imaging" as Tasks are generated during the session. It also develops familiarity with job jargon. Meanings are learned before brainstorming session pressures and distractions.

Step 6   Opening Session Remarks

Welcome. Together we will identify the Tasks which make up the job of _____. You have been selected because you, above all others, have the precise knowledge of what must be done on the job. We ask that you share these insights with us. Once identified, the Tasks can be used:

- • To better select & train new associates.
- • To train & cross-train existing associates.
- • To continuously improve communications & performance among current associates.

Let's begin with definitions. **A TASK is the smallest meaningful piece of work which can be identified.** For instance, "picks up pencil", "uses computer" or "wears safety glasses" are ambiguous and fail to describe meaningful pieces of work. Meaningful results are not accomplished. "Writes reports", "greets customers" and "calculates overtime", on the other hand, convey meaning and describe value-added activities. **A DUTY AREA is a cluster of related Tasks representing a functional area of job responsibility.**

A Task Statement always begins with an action verb ending in "S". Working together, we can identify all the Tasks performed by associates doing the job of _____. We're using a technique known as **"brainstorming"**. Several rules are necessary for this process. First, no suggested Task is unimportant. If it's mentioned, it's written down. Second, a suggestion's worth can not be criticized. Third, every member of the group is equal in rank, so no one is higher than anyone else.

In summary, each person is asked to contribute his or her suggested Task without fear of criticism, censorship or reprisal. Are there any questions? If not, let's begin. (If no one suggests a Task, target a group member and ask for one.)

LOGIC: A group working to list job Tasks has more fun than individuals working alone. People who feel they are making important contributions are eager to share details of their work. When the Task list is complete, it affirms both the job and the person involved.

Step 7   Task Brainstorming and Expectations

Task brainstorming correlates highly with the popcorn cooking process. Both start slowly, accelerate rapidly and gradually end. Sessions usually last from 45 to 90 minutes. Most jobs have 60 to 120 Tasks. As Tasks are suggested, the writing pace sometimes gets feverish. Therefore, request someone to help in the listing process.

Brainstorming may be STRUCTURED or UNSTRUCTURED:

STRUCTURED:

Each SME is given pen and paper. 5 to 10 minutes is given to write down as many job Tasks as possible. Each SME is asked in turn to share a Task from his or her list. Unique Tasks are written on the flip chart until each SME's list is exhausted. The session ends with group consensus that all Tasks have been listed.

UNSTRUCTURED:

One SME is asked to identify a job Task and it is written on the flip chart. The group is encouraged to offer more suggestions which are quickly written on the chart. The assistant keeps track of Tasks identified while the facilitator is busy writing. When a lull occurs, use previously identified Tasks as stimuli to restart the group. For example, "Are there any other Tasks related to this one?" If this fails, use the list of action verbs taped on the wall. Ask the SME's if the verbs bring to mind any previously unidentified Tasks. When no further suggestions are offered, the session is over.

Before dismissing, set a time and date for clustering Tasks into Duty Areas. Thank the group for their participation.

Step 8   Task Editing

The Tasks written on the chart paper are carefully reviewed and edited for clarification. Sometimes worker traits, worker characteristics, job requirements, physical abilities, knowledge statements and skills are listed during the brainstorming. This situation occurs because censorship is prohibited during the session. "Non-Tasks" must be removed during the editing process. Task statements must be clear, concise, meaningful pieces of work. If not, make it so. **The list must contain ONLY Tasks.**

Step 9   Clustering Tasks Into Duty Areas

A technique known as **"affinity diagraming"** is used to cluster Tasks into areas of job responsibility. Simply stated, this means grouping together things which have something in common. SMEs find it very easy to do.

Prior to reassembling the SMEs, write each Task legibly on a separate 2" x 2" Post-It note. Number each Post-It note sequentially (i.e., 1, 2, 3, etc.). Spread the numbered Post-It notes on the meeting room table.

Hang at least 8 sheets of **blank** flip chart paper on the meeting room wall. Most jobs have from 4 to 8 Duty Areas, hence, the 8 separate chart papers. More sheets may be hung during the session, if needed.

Instruct the SMEs to study the Tasks on the table and look for common areas of job responsibility. When similarities are seen, SMEs "STICK" common Tasks on the same sheet of chart paper hanging on the wall. All **"related"** Tasks end up on the same single sheet of chart paper. Most Duty Areas contain 6 to 20 Tasks.

Note: <u>SMEs MUST ACCOMPLISH THE "CLUSTERING" ASSIGNMENT WITHOUT SPEAKING.</u>

When all Tasks are taped on the wall, a consensus has been reached. Ask the SMEs to brainstorm for Duty Area titles. Duty Area titles end with the word **"Activities"**. When a consensus is reached, the best titles are then written at the tops of the hanging charts.

After the session when everyone is thanked, assign an identification number (i.e., **0100, 0200, 0300,** etc.) to each Duty Area. **The first two numbers identify the Duty Area. The last two numbers identify the Tasks within each Duty Area** (i.e., **0101, 0102, 0103, 0104.** etc.). The Task List is then typed using the format shown in Appendix C.

MEMORANDUM

DATE: (At least one week prior to session)

TO: John Doe (Associate)

FROM: You (Facilitator)

RE: Task Brainstorming Session

===

CONGRATULATIONS! You have been identified as a Subject Matter Expert (SME) on the job of _____. Your knowledge and experience with and about this job is needed to help us identify all the Tasks which must be performed to successfully do the job. This information is necessary to help us begin to continuously improve the selection, training and performance of our associates.

On (Day & Date), a meeting will be held at (Location). It will begin at (Time) and will last approximately two (2) hours. The following associates will be involved:

Associate #1	Associate #7
Associate #2	Associate #8
Associate #3	Associate #9
Associate #4	Associate #10
Associate #5	Associate #11
Associate #6	Associate #12

Please be prompt so the meeting can begin on time. If you have any questions, please call me at (Phone Number). I look forward to working with you.

Action Verbs

files	lists	sorts	suspends	collects	lifts
schedules	answers	moves	prepares	counsels	answers
analyzes	adds	drives	subtracts	coaches	reviews
divides	corries	documents	closes	opens	coordinates
checks	advises	confirms	revises	opens	tests
opens	performs	requests	responds	notifies	enters
assigns	trains	informs	completes	puts	introduces
screens	maintains	organizes	corrects	picks	terminates
writes	loads	proofs	packs	inputs	calculates
labels	keys	counts	types	verifies	balances
reads	insures	plans	nails	raises	determines
attaches	chocks	activates	inspects	delivers	explains
lays	places	tastes	samples	rolls	folds
tapes	waxes	cleans	clears	clips	orders
signs	extends	fills	assures	computes	films
disposes	turns	glues	assembles	evaluates	manipulates
finds	paints	greases	switches	winds	lubricates
empties	feeds	erases	sets	passes	distributes
unloads	stacks	seals	changes	phones	communicates
radios	bends	adjusts	washes	sends	receives
fixes	tosses	throws	calls	mixes	reconciles
handles	prints	hooks	squeezes	presses	recommends
sands	primes	forks	points	shoots	aims
copies	confirms	spreads	stops	starts	duplicates
sequences	aligns	frames	builds	sews	eliminates
fuels	pours	jumps	searches	locates	constructs
seeks	stencils	strips	stripes	sharpens	delegates
wraps	dumps	ties	splices	fastens	extinguishes
rips					

multiplies

APPENDIX G

Customer Name
Facility Name
Anywhere, World

8 DAY TRAINING AGENDA

DAY ONE
WEDNESDAY
Date
Training Facility—Street Address

Classroom Training

(8 hours)

Start Time 8:00 am

0.25 hour   TRAINING AGENDA PRESENTATION AND DISCUSSION—Conducted by Trainer.

0.75 hour   ICE BREAKER—(Classroom)—Conducted by Trainer.

Have associates pair up. One associate interviews the other for approximately 5 minutes. The associates are then asked to switch roles so the interviewer becomes the interviewee for the next five minutes. All the things we want them to find out about each other during their interviews are listed on a flip chart: Examples—Name, spouse's name, kids' names and ages, grandchildren's names and ages, city and state of birth, last company worked for and type of job held, hobbies, favorite sports team, favorite musical artist or group, favorite color, etc. Have each pair stand in front of the group and introduce each other by telling what they found out during their interviews. Make sure the coaching staff participates in the interview and introduction process too in order to relax the group.

1.00 hour   YOUR COMPANY'HISTORICAL ORIENTATION—(Classroom)—Conducted by Trainer.

Discuss Your Company's foundation and growth . Explain the background of the Your Company's acquisition. Introduce the stockholder tape as an overview of the five (5) companies making up YOUR COMPANY. Emphasize that YOUR COMPANY is a City-based X year old company and is listed on the New York Stock Exchange. It serves the......industry.

Play the Video: "2002".

Questions and answers.

Discuss the arrival of CEO from Company and his operating philosophy of Total Quality Management. Tell about the subsequent acquisitions of X, Y, Z., etc. and their impact on company growth and market share (approximately what %). Explain the creation of the Productivity and Customer Service department.

Play the Video: "Partners in Growth Through Quality".
Questions & Answers.

Explain the name change to YOUR COMPANY LOGISTICS in June of 1993. Play the Video: "YOUR COMPANY LOGISTICS". Questions & Answers.

0.25 hour   BREAK (10:00 to 10:15 am)

1.75 hours   CUSTOMER OVERVIEW & PARTNERSHIP WITH X LOGISTICS (Classroom)—Conducted by Trainer, Project Manager, Regional VP, Facility Manager, Customer Representative.

Customer Quality Overview Presentation—Customer Representatives.

— Why did Customer create this facility? What is the MISSION of this facility?
— Which Customer businesses utilize this facility to service and supply their customers?
— Why is this facility's picking & shipping accuracies and response times so critical to each of our Client's customers?
— What are the types and levels of service our Client's customers are expecting from X LOGISTICS?
— Why did the Customer chose X LOGISTICS as its partner in this venture?
— What are the requirements and expectations placed on Client vendors & suppliers who ship their materials into this facility?
— What are the critical things for which we need to watch as in-bound materials are received for put-away?
— How and to whom at the Customer should receiving discrepancies be reported?
— How does the Customer define quality (complete, accurate, timely and damage-free) for suppliers & vendors shipping to us?
— How does the Client define X LOGISTICS quality (complete, accurate, timely and damage-free) as we ship to its customers?
— What determines whether X LOGISTICS is doing its distribution job well or poorly?
— What are the Customer's needs, requirements and expectations from X LOGISTICS associates at this facility?
— How can we at this facility contribute to the Cutomer's business growth and success?
— How do we know what the Client's customers like and dislike about X LOGISTICS's service? What satisfies and dissatisfies them?
— What records are kept by the Customer quality? Who collects and uses this information? What is the information used for?
— What are the most common distribution defects or mistakes that occur here at this facility? What is the operational definition for each type of mistake or defect? What proportion of these errors or mistakes are commonly assumed to be an associate's fault? What proportion do we usually attribute to the process or the way we have to do things? How does the Customer arrive at these conclusions?
— By what process do we audit, investigate, evaluate and report problems (coordination with the Customer's Quality Assurance group regarding errors with in-bound materials, incorrect shipping orders & shipping priorities, damaged materials, poor process specifications and the process itself, etc.) at this facility?
— Describe the impact on the Client's customers for the most common mistakes or defects which can occur at this facility. What do they cost in lives, time, money and customer loyalty?
— Who is responsible for quality at this facility? Who is responsible for detecting mistakes/defects? Who is responsible for identifying and correcting the causes of these mistakes or defects?
— Overview of how and from where the Customer's client orders are generated and arrive for processing at this facility.

• X LOGISTICS Presentation—Project Manager, Regeional Vice President, Facility Manager, Operations Manager & Coaching Staff.
An explanation of what X LOGISTICS expects from associates and from the Customer in order for this partnership to be successful.

1.00 hour LUNCH (12:00 Noon to 1:00 pm)
0.50 hour   TEMPORARY SERVICES CO.—Account Representative & Facility Manager.
Explanation of Temporary Services Co. Partnership With X LOGISTICS & What It Means For You.
- Who Are You Working For & For How Long?
- Reporting Procedures For Hours Worked.
- Accident Reporting Requirements & Workers Comp.
- Safety Issues (Back Belts, etc.)
- Pay Day & Check Pick-Up Time and Location.
- Any Special Benefits or Programs You Are Eligible For.
- Questions & Answers.

1.25 hours   X LOGISTICS BENEFITS PROGRAM ORIENTATION OVERVIEW (Classroom)—Explained by X Corporate or Regional Human Resource Representative.

- X LOGISTICS Employee Handbook.
- Counting of Temporary Service Time Towards 90-Day Pre-Benefit Performance Evaluation Period.
- Health (HMO, Conventional)—Costs & Coverages.
- Dental—Cost & Coverage.
- Vision—Cost & Coverage.
- Life Insurance & Supplemental Life Insurance—Costs and Coverages.
- 401(k)—Eligibility and Contributions.
  Tuition Assistance—Eligibility and Participation Requirements.
- Employee Assistance Program.

0.25 hour   BREAK (2:45 to 3:00 pm)

1.00 hour   FACILITY RULES & REGULATIONS—X LOGISTICS POLICIES & PROCEDURES ORIEN-TATION (Classroom)—Conducted by Facility Manager, Operations Manager & Coaching Staff.

Shift schedules, work hours, time cards, UMS cards, breaks, sickness policy, absence & tardiness policies, vacation policy, holiday policy, pay days, benefit claims assistance, etc.
Ice & snow policy.
Emergency exit & evacuation routes and assembly points.
Safety policies and procedures.
Hazardous materials communication.
Accident reporting & emergency treatment—CPR, on-site first-aid and off-site clinic location.
Accident investigation policy & procedures.
Confidentiality of company & customer information.
Ethics & Honesty policies.
Grievance procedures
Smoke-Free environment.
Overtime policies & procedures.
Drug-Free environment.
Sexual harassment policy.
Grounds for immediate termination (theft, drugs, fighting, insubordination, etc.).
Security Access.

1.00 hour ISO 9000 (Classroom)—
Conducted by X Corporate Representative & Customer Representative.

Show Video: "History of ISO 9000".
Discuss the evolution of Europe into a "Common Market". Explain how this creates the need for standardization and a more uniform set of codes or conditions under which commerce can be conducted.
Why is the Customer concerned about ISO 9000.
Provide an overview of certification procedures.
Status of ISO 9000 certification at the Client's Company & at X LOGISTICS.
Why is it important to me as an associate? What should I do and how should it be done?

Stop Time: 5:00 pm

DAY TWO
THURSDAY
Date
Training Facility—Street Address
Classroom Training
(8 hours)

Starting Time: 8:00 am

0.75 hour   ICEBREAKER—Conducted by Trainer.

"YOU CAN'T JUDGE A BOOK BY ITS COVER"—Pass out the Book Cover Sheet. Get the group to generate one additional question to fill out the last blank section on the form. Ask each associate to fill out the form completely. Have each associate stand and read his answers aloud in front of the group. Coaches should lead out during this sharing period to relax the group and reduce their anxieties.

0.50 hour   PROPER LIFTING TECHNIQUES (Classroom)—Conducted by Operations Manager & Coaching Staff.

- •   Start the Video: "Love Your Back—Proper Lifting Techniques."
- •   Stop the video at the segment indicated for lifting demonstrations.
- •   Distribute the proper lifting technique handouts to each associate.

Divide associates into teams of 6 to 10. Have several boxes of varying shapes, sizes and weights available for each group to utilize in lifting practice. Coaches assigned to each group should demonstrate the proper lifting technique with each size, shape and weight of box. The team should then spend at least ten minutes practicing and coaching each member's lifting technique.
Ask the associates to return to their seats and re-start the Video.

Stop the video at the segment designated for exercise demonstrations. Reassemble the teams and their respective coaches. Pair up associates and have the first person stand and hold his arms straight out in front of him with his stomach muscles loose. Have a second person pull down on the first person's out-stretched arms while the first person tries to hold his arms up with his stomach muscles loose. Then instruct the first person to again hold his arms out but this time with his stomach muscles tightened. Again the second person attempts to pull down on the first person's arms. The first person will quickly begin to realize the importance of properly preparing to lift while standing.

Finally, have each team member practice the leg and stomach strengthening exercises shown in the handout.

Discussion, questions & answers.

1.00 hour   FORK LIFT DRIVER TRAINING (Classroom)—Conducted by Operations Manager & Coaching Staff.

Introduction to X LOGISTICS annual fork lift training & certification program (OSHA required). (approx. 5 minutes)

Video: "Safe Fork Lift Operation" (approx. 25 minutes required).

Review the set of Safe Fork Lift Operation overhead transparencies and have the group discuss the significance of each one (approx. 30 minutes)

0.25 hour   BREAK (10:15 to 10:30 am)

0.75 hour   FORK LIFT CERTIFICATION EXAM (Classroom)—Conducted by Operations Manager & Coaching Staff.

Administer the Pencil-and-paper job knowledge test to the entire group (approx. 30-45 minutes required). After everyone has completed the exam, have them exchange papers and then go over the answers to each question. Collect papers and score them for inclusion in each associate's personnel folder.

0.25 hour   OVERVIEW OF FUNCTIONAL PROCESS FLOW OF THIS FACILITY (Classroom)—Conducted by Facility Manager & Operations Manager.

Macro Product Receiving & Put-Away Process Flow Chart & Overview Video: Shows product being received and unloaded, product being inspected & re-packaged, product being placed in receiving staging lanes, material being blind counted, receiving document and blind count being compared by inventory control clerk and material being put-away in racks and bins.

Macro Order Taking & Processing Flow Chart & Overview Video: Shows brief segment of Customer Service Representatives (CSR's) taking orders from customers, placing orders in order processing system, generating pick tickets, placing pick tickets in basket, notifying floor associates of need to pick orders, picking the order, packing & shipping the order and returning paperwork for filing.

0.50 hour   FORKLIFT FLOW CHART EXAMINATION—Conducted by Trainer.

Explain and administer the Forklift Flow Chart Examination. Have associates write their names and dates at the top of the exam. Give the group approximately fifteen minutes to complete the exam. Make sure adequate time is allowed for all to finish. Then and only then have the group put down their pencils. Have the group exchange papers. Walk the group through each question and review the correct answers with the group before collecting the exam papers for scoring. Record the scores for each associate in their personnel file.

1.00 hour   LUNCH (12:00 Noon to 1:00 pm) (Provided by X LOGISTICS at Training Facility).

1.00 hour   EMPLOYEE RELATIONS—Conducted by X Logistics Corporate Labor Relations Director.

Robert A. explains our corporate values, work force diversity, ethics, equal employment opportunities and operating philosophy of mutual respect. He then discusses the chartering and formation of the Atlanta World Parts Center's Values Committee and its mission and purposes (ethics, Associates' Suggestion Program, Total Quality Management Steering Committee). He then explains our union avoidance philosophy, discusses our existing grievance procedures and explains his "open ear" approach to employee relations.

3.0 hours   TEAM BUILDING EXERCISES (Classroom)—Conducted by Trainer.

TEAM BUILDING AND QUALITY HANDOUTS—Distribute the Team Building and Quality handout (blue) folders to each associate. Ask the associates to open their folders and remove the Team Building handouts for use during the afternoon session.

COUNT THE (E's)—Conducted by Trainer.—(approx. 15 minutes)

Count the "E's in the paragraph" used to define a Team. This exercise is done first individually and then is done in groups.

Individual—Each person is asked to count the number of "E's" present in the paragraph and to write down the number on a sheet of paper and turn it over on his or her desks. The Team Definition paragraph is then shown for 10 seconds on the screen via overhead.

Group—The associates are broken into groups of 3 to 5 people and are given 5 minutes to elect a spokes person and plan a strategy on "how to get an accurate count of the "E's" in the Team Definition paragraph. The Team Definition is again shown for 10 seconds on the overhead. The group is then given two minutes to reach a consensus on the number of "E's" present in the paragraph. Each group's spokes person is then asked to report the group's answer and the facilitator records it on the flip chart. (Answer: There are eight (8) "E's" in the paragraph and one "E" in the title.) Facilitator points out the improved accuracy when it's done as a group. Then ask why and discuss!

STAGES OF TEAM DEVELOPMENT—Conducted by Trainer.—(approx. 30 minutes)

Present and discuss the stages of TEAM GROWTH:

Stage 1—FORMING—Members cautiously explore the boundaries of acceptable group behavior. The team accomplishes little!

Feelings: excitement, anticipation, optimism, pride, attachment, suspicion, fear & anxiety.

Behaviors: define task, how to accomplish; determine acceptable behavior; how to deal with problems; what info to gather; discussions of lofty, abstract concepts/issues, symptoms or problems not relevant to task; complaints about organization; task barriers.

Stage 2—STORMING—Members jump in deep water, start to drown, thrash about. Realize task is different & more difficult than imagined. Members get testy, blameful & overzealous, but begin to understand one another.

Feelings: Resistant, attitude fluctuations & pessimism.

Behaviors: Arguing, defensiveness, competition, factions, questioning owner's wisdom, setting unrealistic goals, concern over work load, pecking order, disunity, tension, jealousy.

Stage 3—NORMING—Members reconcile competing loyalties and responsibilities. Accept team norms, roles and member individuality. Conflict is reduced & cooperation improves. They help each other stay afloat. Progress begins.

Feelings: constructive criticism, acceptance & relief.

Behaviors: Achieve harmony, avoid conflict, friendly, confiding, sharing, cohesion, common goals & spirit, establishing and maintaining norms.

Stage 4—PERFORMING—Settled relationships and expectations. Diagnosing and solving problems, choosing and implementing changes. Accept individual strengths and weaknesses. Swim together, effective & cohesive. Get the work done.

Feelings: Satisfaction, understanding & insightful.

Behaviors: Constructive self-change, prevent or work through group problems, close attachment.

CHARACTERISTICS OF AN EFFECTIVE TEAM—
Conducted by Trainer.—(approx. 30 minutes)

Have each person write down at least three things which they think are characteristic of an optimally performing team. Divide the group into three teams. Have them select a leader and recorder. Have each group list the unique characteristics identified by its members on a flip chart sheet. The three (3) team leaders are then asked to present their group's findings.

The trainer then reviews the overhead transparency of Optimum Team Work Characteristics:

- Establishes clear goals and objectives that are accepted by team members.
- Establishes high standards of performance for itself.
  Allows members to disagree and has an effective way to resolve problems and conflict.
- Reviews past actions to plan for improvements.
  Has a sense of unity.
  Members listen to each other and provide useful feedback.
  Recognizes individuals for contributions.
- Attaches a high value to creative approaches to problems.
- Members influence one another and the Team Leader.

The trainer compares and contrasts the group findings with the overhead transparency. The trainer also explains that the group has just performed its first brainstorming session.

0.25 hour   BREAK (3:15 to 3:30 pm)

IDENTIFYING & PRIORITIZING CRITICAL START-UP FACTORS (approx. 30 minutes)—Conducted by Trainer.

Have each associate write down at least three (3) things which must happen, occur or be done in order for the facility start-up to be successful.

Divide the associates into teams of five to ten people. Have each team identify a scribe and a spokes person. Have the scribe document on a flip chart each unique critical start-up factor identified by members of the team. Once all factors are listed, the spoke person should facilitate (using the Nominal Group Technique) the team in reaching a consensus on the rank-ordering of start-up factors from the most important to the least important. The spokes person for each team then present the results to the entire group.

Demonstrate the NOMINAL GROUP TECHNIQUE—The facilitator may allow short, but timed, group discussion of each factor before overall voting begins. When voting begins, each team member is then asked to silently pick and write down three start-up factors he believes are the most critical to the start-up's success. The facilitator next asks each team member to share his choices which are then recorded using "hash marks" on the flip chart beside the start-up factors. The factor with the most votes gets ranked #1, the factor with the second most votes gets ranked #2 and so on. Whenever there is a tie, simply ask each team member to re-cast his vote among the factors which are tied. If re-voting results in a second tie, then and only then does the facilitator cast the deciding vote. Very rarely will the facilitator be called upon to cast the deciding vote. This method is a quick and easy way for groups to reach a consensus without arguing and lengthy debate.

COMMUNICATION STYLES (approx. 30 minutes)

Each person is asked to independently complete the communication style questionnaire. There are no right or wrong answers. Respondents are asked to indicate the answer which best describes how they really feel. Responses are then transferred to the scoring sheet. Point out that each of the four columns must be totaled. The column having the highest number of incidents on the questionnaire is the respondent's dominant communication style. Read the interpretation sheet. Explain that there are no right or wrong styles. We just need to be aware of our dominant style and how it might affect our communication with others.

-Talk about the process not the person.
-Stick with the facts, try not to generalize.
-Actively listen. Ask probing questions, clarify and get the communicator to elaborate.
-Always communicate in a calm tone with the objective of understanding each other.

• HOW TO LISTEN (approx. 30 minutes)

How many of you are good listeners? Let's try a test. Read the following list of number out loud and ask the group to only listen. After you finish, have them write down what they heard.

5, 22, 11, 3, 15, 17, 12, 7, 13

Ask the group:

What was the first number? The last number? The one in the middle?

What can we do to listen better?

-Remain Neutral—Do not give advice, agree or disagree, criticize or interrupt.

-Give Your Complete Attention—Let them know you are listening. Establish eye contact and maintain it.

-Ask About Their Statements—Dig out information, invite them to tell more.

-Restate Main Points—Let them hear their words restated to them.

-Get Agreement—Summarize what you both said. Ask the other person what the nest step should be. Develop a course of action.

DISTRIBUTION OF MAPS—Conducted by Facility Manager.

Instruct the group on how to locate the facility. Be sure everyone feels comfortable with how to find the warehouse. Explain why the starting time is so early and emphasize how critical it is to be on time!

Stop Time: 5:00 pm

DAY THREE
FRIDAY
Date
Facility—Street Address
On-Site, "Hands-On" Training
(4 hours)

<u>Start Time: 6:00 am</u>

0.75 hour   TOUR OF THE FACILITY—Conducted by Facility Manager & Coaching Staff.

Facility Walk-Through—Associates are instructed to assemble at the warehouse. Once the roll is called, associates are then divided into small groups and a coach is assigned to each group as a tour guide. Coaches pass out facility layout maps showing rack and bin locations to each associate. Coaches then walk their groups through the facility. Bin & Rack locations and staging areas and their functions/systems are explained in detailed. All associate questions MUST BE answered. Special attention should be paid to multi-pack locations. Also point out that multiple part numbers are stored at a single location and emphasize the care and concentration required during put-away & picking. At the conclusion of the walk through, the groups are reassembled for the Scavenger Hunt.

1.25 hours   SCAVENGER HUNT—Conducted by Operations Manager & Coaching Staff.

The Hunt—Associates are formed into three or four teams. Each group selects a team leader. Make sure each team member has a facility layout map showing bin and rack locations. Each team leader is given a set of packing tickets listing items to be picked and packed by the group as well as the locations (bins & racks) where the items are stored. Each team has fifteen minutes to develop a strategy or plan on how to best pick the designated parts in the most efficient and effective way. Once team member assignments have been made by the leader, the Facility Manager will start the scavenger hunt. The hunt is timed to see which team most quickly and most accurately gathers its required material in the proper quantities and properly packages the parts for shipment. Prizes (candy bars) are awarded to each team (largest bars to the winners, second place finishers get smaller bars and the third place team receives the smallest bars). Everybody participates and everybody wins!

The Put-Away—A coach is assigned to each team and walks his team through the return to inventory of every item picked during the scavenger hunt. This also becomes a learning exercise. It assures team members begin to learn the locations of bins and racks as well as assuring that all materials are correctly returned to their proper storage locations.

0.25 hour   BREAK (8:00 to 8:15 pm)

1.75 hours   PRACTICAL FORKLIFT/ORDER PICKER DRIVING SKILLS SIMULATIONS—Conducted by
                   Operations Manager & Coaching Staff.

-Set up standardized simulations and/or obstacle courses on which floor associates can demonstrate their skill in handling order pickers and fork lifts, etc.

-FORK LIFT—Have the associate drive through the obstacle course. Then have the associate remove a pallet of finished goods from a designated storage rack using a forklift. Have the associate drive back through the obstacle course and set the pallet down. The associate's skill level is determined by the speed (timed with stop watch) and accuracy (number of pallets knocked over) with which the simulation is accomplished. Reverse the process and have the associate put the pallet back in its proper storage location. This gives a second time and accuracy measure.

-ORDER PICKER—Have associate drive an order picker through a course lined with pallets standing on their edges. Have the associate properly secure himself with the order picker's safety belt and then use the order picker to remove an item from the top shelf of a storage rack. Then have the associate return through the obstacle course. The associate's skill level is determined by the speed (timed with stop watch) and accuracy (number of pallets knocked over) with which the simulation is accomplished. Reverse the procedure and have the associate replace the item back in its proper storage location. This gives a second time and accuracy measure.

1.00 hour LUNCH (10:00 Noon to 11:00 am) (Associates are dismissed for lunch and asked to regroup at the Training Facility at 11:00 am. Associates are on their on for lunch!

DAY THREE
FRIDAY
Date
Training Facility—Street Address
Classroom Training
(4 hours)

Start Time: 11:00 am

0.50 hour   ICEBREAKER—Conducted by Trainer.

Think for a minute about your previous job. Please write down five (5) things (BARRIERS TO QUALITY PERFORMANCE) that prevented you from doing a quality job (doing the right things right).

Divide the group into four (4) teams. Have each team select a leader. The leader should then write down the unique Quality Barriers on a flip chart. He should then facilitate the team in reaching a consensus on rank-ordering the barriers from the largest to the smallest in preventing quality performance. Each leader then presents his team's findings before the entire group. The coach then compares and contrasts the findings of each group.

0.25 hour   OVERVIEW OF CORPORATE VISION & MISSION—Conducted by Trainer.

Introduce the concept of Total Quality Management at X Logistics. Play the first segment of "The Elston Tape".

0.75 hour   The CARD FACTORY—Conducted by Trainer.—(Simulation of the Authoritarian Style of
                 Management).

Prepare a record-keeping sheet to monitor defects (number of spades) in each hand. Also prepare a graph to track defects per production run (every time three hands are produced).

As the Owner of "Winning Hands" explain that the idea of selling a winning card hand was conceived while playing with a "free" deck of cards on a plane flight to Baltimore.

Later market research showed that people would buy an eight (8) card hand which is void in spades.

How do I start the business? First, talk to friends at city hall and have them condemn the front table and four chairs. Proceed to inform the associates seated there that they are being evicted so you can open your business. Place the table in the front of the room with three chairs on one side and one on the opposite side.

Proceed to hire yourself a human resource (HR) manager. Explain that his duties are to help you hire a quality work force to produce "heartless" hands.

Have HR hire an administrative assistant (AA) to keep your production records. Explain the job as keeping records on each production run. Information to be supplied to Administrative Assistant (AA) by Quality Director (QD).

Have HR hire a Quality Director (QD). His job is first to work with HR and hire two Quality Assurance Inspectors (QA's). The QA's are to count the number of hearts in each 8 card hand produced. They then report the number of spades produced by each associate to the QD who the reports it to the AA.

Have HR hire a Production Manager (PM) who then works with HR to hire three (3) Production Associates (PA's) to draw 8-card "heartless" hands. He also hires a supply clerk (SC) to shuffle the deck and provide the cards face down for the PA's to draw.

Have HR hire a Training Manager (TM) whose job it is to make sure everybody on the production line knows what to do.

Start the process and transfer, hire and fire as performance dictates. Do not, under any circumstances, allow anyone to change how you want the business run.

After nine (9) hands are produced, count how many "spadeless" hands you have that you can sell. Declare bankruptcy.

Point out that the process works because some good hands are produce. The problem is obviously poor employee attitude and performance.

Have the group suggest what they see as better ways to operate the company.

Point out that middle management is caught in the middle between upper management and the associates. They are helpless but to do what they are told.

0.50 hour   PROCESS MANAGEMENT—HOW TO SET IT UP IN AN ORGANIZATION—Conducted by Trainer.

Introduce the concept of process management. Talk briefly about how it is implemented.

Show Video: "Stuck On Quality." Implementing a continuous improvement philosophy.

      List the key component
         -Customer focused.
         -Shared responsibility.

Show the second part of "The Elston Tape"—the TQM roll out at the X LOGISTICS.

-Talk about regional owners and steering committees and identification of regional critical success factors.
-Talk about facility steering committee and its identification of facility's critical success factors (getting the most bang for the buck).

0.25 hour   Break (1:00 to 1:15 pm)

0.50 hour   UNDERSTANDING PROCESSES AND THE NEEDS & REQUIREMENTS OF INTERNAL & EXTERNAL CUSTOMERS—Conducted by Trainer.

Introduce the concept of INPUT—TASK—OUTPUT. Also explain the concept of internal & external customers. Discuss identifying customer needs, requirements and expectations.

- Show Video: "The Customer Is Always Dwight".

  -How did SUPERMARVELEX define quality?
  -How did GISCO define quality?
  -How did the WORLD NUT COMPANY define quality?

- Assignment:

-Create an Action Plan to identify the needs and requirements of an internal customer.
-Create an Action Plan to identify your needs and requirements to an internal supplier.

- Show the last segment of "The Elston Tape".

0.50 hour   CORPORATE "GENERIC OVERVIEW" OF THE RECEIVING PROCESS—Conducted by Mike and the Coaching Staff.

Explain the concept of and need for CONTROL POINTS in the Receiving Process. Tell the group to write down the control points discussed in the video they are about to see.

- Show the Video: "In-Bound Process Flow".

- Ask the group to identify the control points emphasized during the video. Write them on the flip chart. Discuss the significance of each control point and why it must be present in the receiving process.

  Examples of
  Control Points: Unbroken seal on truck.
  Blind count of what is on truck.
  Compare the blind count with truck's bill of lading.
  Sign bill of lading to document legal transfer.

0.75 hour   RECEIVING ACTIVITIES—Conducted by Facility Manager & the Coaching Staff and Client Representative.

- Procedures for routine receipt of materials, customer returns, re-packaging of received materials, etc are explained.

- There are different types of paper work used to transfer materials from the Customer to X and the significance of each is thoroughly explained. Pass out and go over completed examples of each type of transfer document.

- The Customer explains how X knows the product is released for put-away into inventory. Explain entry of product information into the inventory control system and what it means to Customer Service Representatives and the Client's customers.

- X explains its Receiving Procedures—Pass out a Warehouse Receiving Process Flow Chart to each associate. Show Receiving Process Video and have a coach narrate and explain what is happening as the video is played. After seeing the video, have various associates read each step and explain why the step needs to be done. Associates should make notes on their flow charts to document clarified points. At the end of the session, the flow chart should be added to each associate's notebook for future reference.

Instruct the group to reassemble on Thursday morning at 6:00 am at the facility.

<u>Stop Time: 3:00 pm</u>

DAY FOUR
MONDAY
Date
Facility—Street Address
On-Site, "Hands-On" Training
(4 hours)

<u>Start Time: 6:00 am</u>

1.25 hours   SCAVENGER HUNT—Conducted by Facility Manager & Coaching Staff.

The Hunt—Associates are formed into three or four teams with at least one X CSR per team. Each group selects a team leader. Make sure each team member has a facility layout map showing bin and rack locations. Each team leader is then given a new set of packing tickets listing items to be picked and packed by the group. A X CSR should be assigned to each group and will show the group how to look up/inquire about the storage locations (bins & Racks) of items within the AMAPS system. Coaches are to oversee the accuracy of this process. Once storage locations are written down on the packing lists for each item, each team then has fifteen minutes to develop a strategy or plan on how to best pick the designated parts in the most efficient and effective way. Once team member assignments have been made by the leader, the Facility Manager will start the scavenger hunt. PARTS WHICH DO NOT HAVE PART NUMBERS ATTACHED TO THEM <u>MUST NOT TO BE REMOVED FROM A RACK OR BIN STORAGE LOCATION DURING THIS EXERCISE</u>! The hunt is timed to see which team most quickly and most accurately gathers its required material in the proper quantities and properly packages the parts for shipment.

The Put-Away—A coach is assigned to each team and walks his team through the return to inventory of every item picked during the scavenger hunt. This also becomes a learning exercise. It assures team members begin to learn the locations of bins and racks as well as assuring that all materials are correctly returned to their proper storage locations.

0.75 hour   TOUR OF RECEIVING AREA AND EXPLANATION OF FUNCTIONS PERFORMED—Conducted by Customer Representative & Facility Manager.

Tour the Receiving storage area and explain what product & materials are stored there, why and for how long. Show associates how Receiving is done and walk them through the paper work procedures. Re-cover the transfer documentation (Customer receiving/QA release forms) to assure associates know where each type comes from and for what purpose it is used. Demonstrate re-packaging.

Next. show where product is staged when it is ready for release for put-away.

0.25 hour   BREAK (8:00 to 8:15 pm)

0.50 hour   RECEIVING IN-BOUND SHIPMENTS FOR THE CUSTOMER WHEN ITS RECEIVING DEPARTMENT IS CLOSED—Conducted by Customer Representative & Facility Manager.

Pass out "Processing In-Bound Receipts for the Customer During Off-Hours" flow chart. Explain the situation and circumstances under which this process is implemented. Walk the associates through the flow chart on the floor and then have them perform the steps of the off-hour receiving process on an actual load. Answers all questions and verify associate understanding of process How(s) and Why(s).

0.75 hour   X WAREHOUSE RECEIVING—Conducted by Operations Manager & the Coaching Staff.

Have associates demonstrate the procedures learned from the classroom on Wednesday. Have them demonstrate when and where to go to begin the process, write in Receiving Control Log, obtain the Blind Tally Sheet, perform a blind count and turn in the paperwork properly. <u>Make sure all associates are comfortable with accurately and legibly writing down the type of product received and the quantity of the product received on the Blind Tally Sheet!</u> Once the product type(s) and quantity(ies) received are written down, the associate should sign/initial the Blind Tally Sheet. Emphasize the need for accuracy and readability of the completed document! Have the associates use their Warehouse Receiving Process Flow Chart to guide them. Have various associates read aloud and explain why each step of the receiving process needs to be done. Associates should make additional notes on their flow charts to document clarified points. At the end of the session, the flow chart should be re-placed in the associate's notebook for future reference.

0.50 hour   "HOT" RECEIPT PROCESSING—Conducted by Operations Manager & the coaching Staff.

Pass out a "Processing Hot Receipts" flow chart to each associate. Explain the situation and circumstances under which "hot" receipts are processed. Walk the associates through the flow chart on the floor and then have them perform the steps of "hot" receipt processing on a specific part. Answers all questions and verify associate understanding of the hot receipt process How(s) and Why(s).

1.00 hour   LUNCH (10:00 to 11:00 am) "ON YOUR OWN"

DAY FOUR
MONDAY
Date
Training Facility—Street Address
Classroom Training
(4 hours)

<u>Start Time: 11:00 am</u>

0.50 hour   FLOW CHARTING—Conducted by Trainer.

PLACING A CALL ON A PAY PHONE—Tell the group they will be responsible for maintaining the "Current Best Approach" (CBA) flow charts for each old process after initial start-up training is completed. Associates will also flow chart any new processes that are developed. Therefore, each associate needs to understand how to create a functional flow chart. To illustrate how a flow is done, first have the group work together to flow chart the process of "placing a call on a pay phone". Emphasize that the process starts when the phone booth is entered and ends when the party answers the phone. Define and demonstrate the action or task "box" and the decision "diamond." Show how a "yes" and "no" arrow come from each decision diamond. Make the flow chart as simple or complex as the group provides the lead. After all questions are answered, ask the group to individually flow out their "getting up" & "getting out of the house" process that they perform each morning.

GETTING UP & GETTING OUT OF THE HOUSE—Ask each person to flow the steps they go through every morning from the time the alarm goes off until they walk out the door headed for work. Have the coaches walk around the room and observe and help associates as they flow chart the "getting up" process. Allow at least 15 minutes for associates to accomplish this activity. When the flow-charting is complete, ask for three or four associates to volunteer to share with the group what they put down on their flow chart. Compare and contrast the various levels of flow charts from MACRO to MICRO. The MACRO level contains few steps and provides only a cursory overview while the MICRO level contains many steps and is highly detailed.

0.50 hour   RECEIVING RECEIPT VERIFICATION PROCESS—Conducted by Operations Manager & the Coaching Staff.

Pass out the Receipt Verification "CBA" Process Flow Chart to all associates. Pick an associate to read the steps of the verification process and ask the associate to explain why each step is performed. This process is performed by the X CSR in the office and serves to verify that what is received by X from the Customer is indeed what was released for X to put-away. The X CSR simply matches what the X associate has written on the blind tally sheet as received with what the Customer has written on their release transfer form as being released to X for put-away. The coach either doing or over-seeing a re-check or re-count resolves any counting discrepancies in the product type or quantity. If the Customer transfer/release document and the X blind tally sheet match, the X CSR looks up the put-away location for the part(s) in the inventory control system. The put-away location(s) is then written on the X blind tally sheet and given back to the associate for use during put-away of the product. The Receipt Verification flow chart should be placed, for quick and ready reference, in the associate's notebook.

0.25 hour   FACILITY LAYOUT MAP REVIEW—Conducted by Trainer.

Ask each associate to open his notebook and remove his facility layout map. (Have extra maps just in case.) Carefully review the layout map with the group. Divide the group into two teams. Have the team members go head-to-head in a contest to place a push pin in the proper location on a map hung at the front of the room. Have the coach read out a location and then see which one of the two contestants finds and first places his push pin in the proper location. This can make learning the storage locations more fun. Each associate should keep his Facility Map in his notebook for quick reference.

0.50 hour   PART PUT-AWAY PROCESS—Conducted by Operations Manager & the Coaching Staff.

Pass out a Put-Away Process "CBA" flow chart to each associate. Start at any place in the room and pick one associate to read the first three steps of the put-away process and explain why each of the steps is necessary. Rotate the picking of associates around the room asking associates to continue reading and explaining the justification for each step. Associates MUST understand about the Receiving Control Log and its purpose. Associates should understand the urgency of getting the product received and put-away into available inventory. The product can only be allocated when product is transferred into the "OH" category in the inventory control system. This up dating of the inventory control system can only occur after all put-away paper work has been turned in and the X CSR enters the storage location(s) into the computer.

The associates should also understand HOW to find new put-away locations. Available put-away locations are in the warehouse and they must be found in the event the primary location is full. They should also understand the critical nature of writing down the actual put-away location in which the product is stored on the blind tally sheet. PUT-AWAY LOCATIONS MUST BE ACCURATELY AND LEGIBLY written on the BLIND Tally Sheet! Associates should also understand the critical nature of quickly comparing what is in the location with what is about to be put into the location to prevent product mixes! Make sure parts being placed into the put-away location match exactly with parts already in the location. Count the parts as they are put-away to verify the accuracy of the quantity received. Write the actual quantity put-away on the blind tally sheet and initial it. Take the completed Blind Tally Sheet back to the X WIP for distribution and filing. Have associates document their notes on the Put-Away flow chart and place the flow chart in their notebooks for future reference.

0.25 hour   BREAK (12:45 to 1:00 pm)

1.00 hour   ROUTINE ORDER PROCESSING—Conducted by Client Representative, Facility Manager & the Coaching Staff.

Explain the mission of the Client and why the facility was created. Emphasize which of the Client's personnel use the order entry system. Discuss where and who can generate orders. Discuss the types of product/equipment handled by each of the Client's business sectors and the critical nature of each. Talk about the Client's warranties and service contracts with its customers. Explain how the Client makes its money.

Discuss criticality of the correct parts reaching its designated shipping location at specified time! Explain what is meant by CAT (Complete, accurate, timely & damage-free) concept.

1.00 hour   MANUAL ORDER PROCESSING—Conducted by Client Representative, Facility Manager & the Coaching Staff.

Why the concern with "manual" orders processing? Due to the critical nature of the business being served, the facility cannot be in a position of failing to respond to the Client's customer's needs. If the inventory control system and/or its OMS processing function goes down (crashes), how will we continue to do business? Talk about the manual order form which can be filled by the Client's CSRs. Also discuss the "hard copy" of the inventory control system and put-away locations as to its whereabouts and how to use it. Explain how orders may be transmitted to the X CSR over a printer, faxed or hand-carried.

Pass out the Manual Order Process "CBA" Flow Chart to each associate. Again have associates read aloud and explain the logic of each step in the manual processing of orders.

Share completed copies of each order form with all associates. Have them highlight the key sections on each order form with which they must be familiar to do their job correctly. Explain the how's and why's of the Sequence Control Logs for each order type and the uniqueness of each business segment's order numbering system. Make sure associates can quickly and accurately identify each business order type by its unique numbering system. (You may want to build a list of twenty order numbers and have the associates indicate under which business system they are placed.) Explain that initially we will run crosschecks until system integrity is verified.

Explain the importance of inventory accuracy in the inventory control system. The Client's CSRs are trying to match customer needs with inventory known to be in the inventory control system of this facility.

<u>Stop Time: 3:00 pm</u>

DAY FIVE
TUESDAY
Date
Facility—Street Address
On-Site, "Hands-On" Training
(4 hours)

<u>Start Time: 6:00 am</u>

2.00 hours   GENERATING, PROCESSING & PERFORMING CYCLE COUNTS—Conducted by Customer Representative, Operations Manager & the Coaching Staff.

Generate a 200-line cycle count printout. Divide the group into the teams equal to the number of coaches present. Make sure each team has a CSR on it. Give each coach a page of lines to cycle count. The coach should make enough copies of the page to give one to half the members of the team. Each coach then takes his team into the racks and bins and begins to demonstrate cycle counting. Once the group feels comfortable with cycle counting, the team should be broken up into pairs. The pairs then cycle count until 8:00 am.

0.25 hour   BREAK (8:00 to 8:15 am)

1.75 hours   PART PUT-AWAY PROCESS—Conducted by Operations Manager & the Coaching Staff.

Utilize the same teams as the first part of the morning. Have the associates open their notebooks to the Put-Away Process "CBA" flow chart. Each coach should review the steps of the put-away process with his team. Make sure the team members can explain why each of the steps is necessary. Once the process is thoroughly reviewed with the team members take the team to the office and get the put-away process started. Associates must fill out the Receiving Control Log accurately and neatly. Associates must understand how urgent it is to get product put-away and into available inventory. The team CSR will transfer the put-away product in to an "in inventory" status in the computer. This up dating of the computer con only occur after all put-away paper work has been turned in and the storage location(s) are entered into the computer. INVENTORY ACCURACY IS ABSOLUTELY ESSENTIAL TO THIS OPERATION! Both the associate who puts the part away and the X CSR who enters the location in the inventory control system must do their job correctly or the part becomes lost in the warehouse. Concentrate and do it right every time. Double-check your work!

Associates should utilize the practice finding empty slots in the event a part's primary location is full. Make sure parts being put-away into a location match exactly with parts already in the location. If parts are placed in the wrong location or if the put-away location is incorrectly recorded, the part is lost! Count the parts, as they are put-away. Write the actual quantity put-away on the blind tally sheet and initial it. Take the completed blind tally sheet back to the office so the CSR can distribute and file all necessary paper work. Have associates document any notes on the Put-Away flow chart and place it back in their notebooks for future reference.
If put-away session runs short of allocated time, resume cycle counting. Cycle counting will increase familiarity with bin and racks pick locations.

1.00 hour   LUNCH (10:00 to 11:00 am) "ON YOUR OWN"

DAY FIVE
TUESDAY
Date
Training Facility—Street Address
Classroom Training
(4 hours)

Start Time: 11:00 am

0.50 hour   PROCESS SIMPLIFICATION—Conducted by Trainer.

Show boss's record of arrival time at work. Identify process owner, the process itself (Getting to Work on Time), the start, the end and the time to accomplish. Pass out the flow-chart that was developed. Unitize the flow chart into its component parts (Getting out of bed, bathroom activities, kitchen activities, dressing, locking up & leaving). Add up the total time to accomplish the process, as it is flow-charted. Record totals for each unit at the bottom of the flow-chart. Have the group review each step on the flow chart and decide whether it should be retained or eliminated. "X" out the process steps that can be eliminated. Then total the times of the steps that remain and see if it is within the acceptable amount of time to get to work.

Remove redundancy, repetition, non-value-added steps from processes.

0.50 hour   CORPORATE "GENERIC OVERVIEW" OF THE SHIPPING PROCESS—Conducted by Operations Manager & the Coaching Staff.

•   Explain the concept of and need for CONTROL POINTS in the Picking and Shipping Process. Tell the group to write down the control points discussed in the video they are about to see.

Show the Video: "OUT-Bound Process Flow".

Ask the group to identify the control points emphasized during the video. Write them on the flip chart. Discuss the significance of each control point and why it must be present in the receiving process.

> Examples of
> Control Points: Unbroken seal on truck.
>   Blind count of what is on truck.
>   Comparison of blind count with truck's bill of lading.
>   Sign bill of lading to document legal transfer.

0.25 hour   ORDER SHIPPING OPTIONS—Conducted by Customer Representative, Operations Manager & the Coaching Staff.

Explain the different types of shipping options available to customers and field technicians:

Silver Streak—(Volume of 50 to 60 orders per day)—Operated in conjunction with Sky Courier allows 45 minutes from the time the order is received by X until our associate places the "picked," "packed" and "weighed" part in the hands of a Sky Courier representative for shipment. The domestic target time for delivery is 6 hours anywhere in the continental US.

Sky Courier receives all Silver Streak orders on its printer. Sky Courier makes the decision of whether to ship the Silver Streak order from one of its 6 depot locations or from this facility. X will not be involved with any of Sky's Depot shipments other than being involved in processing a replenishment order with which to re-stock the depot's inventory (usually handled as a Priority One).

Early Bird—(Volume of 50 orders per day)—Operated in conjunction with Federal Express (Fed EX) allows packages picked up by 9:00 pm at the WPC to be delivered between 7:00 and 8:00 am the following morning in designated zip code locations.

Priority One—(Majority of the order volume per day)—Operated in conjunction with Federal Express (Fed Ex) allows packages picked up by 9:00 pm at the WPC to be delivered by 10:30 am the following morning anywhere in the country.

UPS Ground Shipment—(Very few orders are shipped this way)—Operated in conjunction with United Parcel Service (UPS) assures package delivery within 5 to 7 days.

0.50 hour   CLIENT COMPUTER SYSTEMS—Conducted by Client Representative & Facility Manager.

Explain the role and function of the Client's Computer System. Why was this particular computer system chosen for this facility's order processing and/or inventory control? What are the system's capabilities at the present moment? Discuss the future anticipated systems evolutions.:

Demonstrate to all associates the step-by-step process required to perform the "inquiry" function on the computer system. Also demonstrate the "move" function which is used to transfer product from "in process" status in the system to "in inventory" status which means the parts are ready to be picked from the warehouse inventory and shipped.

0.25 hour   BREAK (12:45 to 1:00 pm)

1.00 hour   PICKING DOMESTIC ORDERS—Operations Manager & the Coaching Staff.

Pass out the Picking Domestic Orders "CBA" process flow chart to each associate. Also pass out the process flow chart Confirming Domestic Orders Picked "CBA". Have each step of the flow charts read aloud and its reason for being explained by associates. Explain how the process begins and what control logs are involved.

Pass out copies of paperwork involved in order picking. Show how the X CSR removes orders from the printer and looks up the pick locations of parts on the inventory control system and then writes it down on the order form. Answer all associates questions with regard to the picking of domestic orders.

Ask each associate to also remove his or her facility layout map for use in the training process also. Review the map with the associates to assure their understanding of bin and rack storage locations.

0.50 hour   DOCUMENTING CHANGES TO PICKING ORDERS—Conducted by Operations Manager & the Coaching Staff.

Pass out the flow chart entitled Documenting Changes To Pick Orders "CBA". Have the steps read aloud and explained. This will detail how the X CSR goes about documenting any changes that are made to pick orders. Who can authorize the changes? What documentation is the Client to provide before the changes are made? Which control Logs are affected?

0.50 hour   RELOCATING PARTS IN WAREHOUSE—Conducted by Operations Manager & the Coaching Staff.

At times it becomes necessary to move parts from one location to another in the warehouse. Certain steps must be followed during the move to assure that parts can be tracked on the AMAPS computer and found later when the parts need to be picked. These steps are outlined in the Relocating Parts "CBA" process flow chart. Each associate must have a complete understanding of the criticality of following this flow chart when relocating parts. The computer cannot figure out where parts really are in the warehouse. The computer only knows what it is told! If you move a part and do not fill out the proper documentation and turn it in to the X CSR for entry into the inventory control system, the computer won't sent you to the right place at picking time.

INVENTORY ACCURACY IS MANDATORY! The X CSR must exercise extreme care when entering the new location into the system also because the computer will not know if the location is entered incorrectly. If the part gets lost in the warehouse, it could be lost for up to one year when it might be found during a cycle count or during a physical inventory when all bins and racks are checked for accuracy. This means a critical part cannot be found when a customer or field technician urgently needs the part within a short time frame!

Stop Time: 3:00 pm

DAY SIX
WEDNESDAY
Date
Facility—Street Address
On-Site, "Hands-On" Training
(4 hours)

<u>Start Time: 6:00 am</u>

1.00 hour   PICKING DOMESTIC ORDERS—Conducted by Operations Manager & the Coaching Staff.

Generate as many picking orders as available. Divide the group into as many teams as there are coaches. Give each team an equal number of orders. The coach should demonstrate the proper picking techniques to each team member. Team members should then pair up and begin practicing to improve their picking skills and accuracy. BEWARE OF MULTI-PACK ITEMS! Multi-Pack items are the cause of many picking errors because it is easy to make a mistake and send too many or too few parts to a customer when filling their order. Some precautions must be taken when shipping multi-pack parts! IF IN DOUBT ABOUT WHETHER TO SHIP A WHOLE PACK OF PARTS OR TO OPEN THE PACK AND SHIP JUST ONE, DON"T HESITATE TO ASK YOUR COACH!!! All paperwork should be completed accurately and neatly. What needs to be turned in to the X CSR should be done in a timely fashion. The paperwork that needs to stay with the part must stay with that part! Every time multiple orders are picked at the same time, the risk of getting the parts cross-shipped to the wrong customer is high.

Ask each associate to also remove his or her facility layout map for use in the training process also. Review the map with the associates to assure their understanding of bin and rack storage locations.

1.00 hour   PACKAGING ORDERS FOR SHIPMENT—Conducted by Facility Manager & the Coaching Staff.

Have picked parts ready with the proper paperwork sitting in the packing & shipping area ready for packing. Divide the group into teams equal to the number of coaches. The coach of each team should demonstrate the proper packaging and box sealing techniques. Each associate should be given the opportunity to practice making, loading and sealing of the shipping boxes.

0.25 hour   BREAK (8:00 to 8:15 am)

1.75 hour   SHIPPING ORDERS (UPS & FEDERAL EXPRESS)—Conducted by UPS & Federal Express
                 Account Representatives & the Coaching Staff.

Pass out Shipping Orders "CBA" process flow chart to all associates. Ask associates to read steps aloud and explain why it is done and what it accomplishes in the process. Explain the weight and size restrictions that apply to Early Bird and Priority One shipments. What is the close out time for daily shipments? What stickers must be applied to each type of shipment? Explain about Saturday delivery and the importance of the "Saturday Delivery" stickers to assure packages will not sit in delivery stations until Monday. Explain the Fed Ex postage meter operation and maintenance upon it. Each associate should feel comfortable with operating this piece of equipment. Make sure the associates place this flow chart back in their notebooks for later reference.

1.00 hour   LUNCH (10:00 to 11:00 am) "ON YOUR OWN"

DAY SIX
WEDNESDAY
Date
Training Facility—Street Address
Classroom Training
(4 hours)

<u>Start Time: 11:00 am</u>

1.00 hour   PROBLEM-SOLVING & BRAINSTORMING—Conducted by Trainer.

Discuss the concept of brainstorming and explain the rules of brainstorming:

Encourage everyone to freewheel; don't hold back on any ideas even if they seem silly at the time; the more ideas the better.
No discussion during the brainstorming. That will come later.
No judgment. No one is allowed to criticize another's ideas, not even with a grown or grimace!
Let people hitchhike—build upon thee ideas generated by others in the group.
Write all ideas on a flip chart so the whole group can easily scan them.

Draw a fish bone on a flip chart. Pick a problem like "picking errors". Have the group brainstorm for causes of picking errors and record them in the appropriate place.

Divide the group into three or four teams and have them use the problem solving procedure on "shipping errors". Have each team select a facilitator to run the team. Have each team present the results of its analysis.

1.00 hour   CREATING & RELEASING BACKORDERS—Conducted by Client Representative, Operations Manager & the Coaching Staff.

Explain why backorders are created. If parts are not in inventory or can not be found in inventory when picking an order, then a "backorder" situation is created. It is critical that the Customer's CSR be notified as quickly as possible especially when picking that parts are not available for shipment. The Customer's CSR must notify the customer or field technician that there is a problem with the part that is urgently needed. The Customer's CSR then must begin trying to locate the part from a manufacturer or "scavenger" the part from a piece of equipment at the factory or in the warehouse. THE PART MUST BE FOUND AND SHIPPED IF HUMANLY POSSIBLE! Backordered parts must be ordered from the manufacturer or in some cases product/equipment may have to be stripped to obtain parts that need to be shipped.

A record must be created indicating that the part was not available and the record will be maintained until such time that the part is received and shipped to fill the order. Backorders will be released for picking and shipment as soon as the parts arrival is acknowledged. Copies of backorder paperwork should be passed out and explained thoroughly. Associates should be instructed to add this information to their notebooks.

0.25 hour   BREAK (1:00 to 1:15 pm)

1.25 hour   PROCESSING & HANDLING INTERNATIONAL ORDERS—Conducted by Client Representative, Facility Manager & the Coaching Staff.

When the Customer's order system comes back up between 2:00 and 3:00 am International orders will usually begin to print since their work day is ahead of ours. INTERNATIONAL ORDERS HAVE TOP PRIORITY SECOND ONLY SILVER STREAKS! Special paperwork is required to ship International orders. Some International orders are held for consolidation prior to shipping overseas. This reduces the overall shipping cost by not having to ship partially filled containers. There is a specified section in the warehouse where International orders are held for consolidation. It is in the shipping area near the canteen.

Pass out the International Orders "CBA" process flow chart to every associate. Have different associates read each step aloud and explain the logic of the step in the overall order process. Ask them to make any clarifying notes on their flow chart and to place their flow chart in their notebooks for future reference at the conclusion of the presentation.

0.50 hour WILL CALLS—Conducted by Client Representative, Operations Manager & the Coaching Staff.

Will calls refer to parts that are to be picked up by the customer at the shipping dock. Make sure no parts are allowed to leave the shipping area until the proper identification and signatures have been obtained.

Stop Time: 3:00 pm

DAY SEVEN
THURSDAY
Date
Facility—Street Address
On-Site, "Hands-On" Training
(4 hours)

Start Time: 6:00 am

1.75 hours   PROCESSING & HANDLING INTERNATIONAL ORDERS—Conducted by Operations Manager & the Coaching Staff.

Have the Customer generate as many international orders as possible when the AMAPS and OMS system comes back up between 2:00 and 3:00 am. Have X CSR and warehouse associates process and handle all paperwork involved with order. If any orders are to be shipped same day, have the orders picked, packed and processed through shipping. Make sure all requisite letters of credit and other customs documents are properly married with product to be shipped. Any of the product that requires consolidation before shipment should be picked and stored in the proper holding area for international consolidation. Make sure all holding tickets and required paper work are married to or separately maintained by X CSR for later shipping requirements. Ask Client Representative to be present during the exercises to assure all associate questions are answered to their satisfaction.

Pass out the International Orders "CBA" process flow chart to every associate. Have different associates read each step aloud and explain the logic of the step in the overall order process. Ask them to make any clarifying notes on their flow chart and to place their flow chart in their notebooks for future reference at the conclusion of the presentation.

0.25 hour   BREAK (7:45 to 8:00 am)

2.00 hours   GENERATING, PROCESSING & PERFORMING CYCLE COUNTS—Conducted by Operations Manager & the Coaching Staff.

Have the Customer generate a 200-line cycle count printout. Divide the group into the teams equal to the number of coaches present. Make sure each team has a X CSR on it. Give each coach a page of lines to cycle count. The coach should make enough copies of the page to give one to half the members of the team. Each coach then takes his team into the racks and bins and begins to demonstrate cycle counting. Once the group feels comfortable with cycle counting, the team should be broken up into pairs. The pairs then cycle count until 8:00 am.

1.00 hour   LUNCH (10:00 to 11:00 am) "ON YOUR OWN"

DAY SEVEN
THURSDAY
Date
Training Facility—Street Address
Classroom Training
(4 hours)

Start Time: 11:00 am

0.75 hour   MEASUREMENT—Conducted by the Trainer.

Prepare a data collection form on which respondents can record their data. Prepare a pareto chart on which to document the collected data.

- Pass out small bags of peanut M&Ms.

Then talk about the process of making a bag of peanut M&M's. How many different colors are present in a bag of peanut M&M's? How are colors placed in the bag? How is the number of pieces a bag contains determined? Show five (5) storage bins with gates at the bottom and weighing belt running underneath them. Ask the group to estimate the number of pieces in each bag. Write their guesses on the flip chart. Have the group open their bags and dump them in a small dish. Proceed to count the number of pieces of each color and the total number of pieces. Have each person come to the flip chart and record his or her data. Look at the data while some one calculates the average for each color and the average pieces per bag.

Have the group come back to the second flip chart and place an "X" on the pareto chart indicating the number of pieces contained in their bags.

If the average number pieces per bag should be 22, does the weighing belt speed need to be adjusted (faster/slower)? If so, which way?

If the average number of pieces is 22 and there are 5 colors, how many pieces (4) of each color should be present in each bag? Do any of the gate(s) need to be adjusted (opened/closed)? If so, which ones and which way?

Let the data tell you what to do to adjust the process!

1.25 hours   QUALITY ASSURANCE, COMPLAINTS, QUARANTINE, DAMAGED PARTS & QUALITY INCIDENT REPORTS—Conducted by Client Representative, Operations Manager & the Coaching Staff.

Complaints—Explain how complaints are received and processed. Make sure everyone understands the roles of the Customer's CSRs, its QA department and X personnel. Complaints must be checked out for proactive reasons. When a shipping error, picking mistake or packing error occurs, we must identify exactly what went wrong to cause the problem. Once the investigation for cause is complete the results will be covered not only with those involved but with all associates in an effort to prevent future mistakes from being made by other associates. Maybe we can even learn from each other's mistakes rather than having to make our own.

Quarantine—When more than two complaints occur on the same part during a month, the part is put on quarantine until QA can carefully check each part in the warehouse inventory for proper operation, whether each part meets specifications, etc. A quarantine on a part means that the part can not be shipped without official release by the Client's Quality Assurance department. Parts may be quarantined in their bins or racks or may be removed to a "holding" area pending QA inspection and release. A QUARANTINE MUST NOT BE VIOLATED!

Quality Incident Report (QIR's) & Damaged Parts—Whenever a part is dropped, it must be assumed to be damaged! The part must be immediately reported using a QIR and then taken to QA for inspection and repair. Whenever a damaged part is discovered, either in a rack or bin or laying in an aisle, a QIR must be filled out and the part turned over to the Customer's QA department for inspection. Completed QIR's should be passed out to each associate. An explanation should then be given of how and why to complete this form. A detailed explanation of the QA release procedure should also be offered.

0.25 hour   BREAK (1:00 to 1:15 pm)

1.00 hour   CROSS DOCK SHIPMENTS—Conducted by Client Representative, Operations Manager & the Coaching Staff.

Sometimes parts are found to be faulty during the Customer's QA department inspections and must be sent back to the manufacturer for repair. Customer personnel will prepare the item for shipment. X will handle the actual shipping of the item through UPS or Federal Express. The Cross Dock Shipment "CBA" process flow chart should be distributed and the steps reviewed and discussed.

1.00 hour   GENERATING MANAGERIAL REPORTS & SYSTEM BACK-UPS—Conducted by Facility Manager & the Coaching Staff.

Pass out the Report Generation and System Back-up "CBA" process flow chart to all associates and have it read aloud and reviewed. This process primarily involves the X CSRs. Explain the hows and whys of backing-up the computer systems utilized in the facility's operation. Assure the X CSRs completely understand these processes. The necessary reports that must be generated to assure adequate information to effectively and efficiently manage the facility's operation. Have the CSRs generate the necessary reports and back-up each of their computer systems.

Stop Time: 3:00 pm

          DAY EIGHT
          FRIDAY
          Date
          Facility—Street Address
          On-Site, "Hands-On" Training
          (4 hours)

Start Time: 6:00 am

4.00 hours   PICKING DOMESTIC ORDERS, PACKAGING ORDERS FOR SHIPMENT & SHIPPING ORDERS—Conducted by Facility Manager & the Coaching Staff.

Ask associates to also remove their facility layout map for use in the training process also. Review the map with the associates to assure their understanding of bin and rack storage locations.

Generate as many International & Domestic picking orders as available. Divide the group into as many teams as there are coaches. Give each team an equal number of orders. The coach should review proper picking techniques with the team members. Team members should then pair up and begin practicing to improve their picking skills and accuracy. BEWARE OF MULTI-PACK ITEMS! Multi-Pack items are the cause of many picking errors because it is easy to make a mistake and send too many or too few parts to a customer when filling their order. Some precautions must be taken when shipping multi-pack parts! IF IN DOUBT ABOUT WHETHER TO SHIP A WHOLE PACK OF PARTS OR TO OPEN THE PACK AND SHIP JUST ONE, DON"T HESITATE TO ASK YOUR COACH!!! All paperwork should be completed accurately and neatly. What needs to be turned in to the YOUR COMPANY CSR should be done in a timely fashion. The paperwork that needs to stay with the part must stay with that part! Every time multiple orders are picked at the same time, the risk of getting the parts cross-shipped to the wrong customer is high. Coaches should float through the warehouse and spot check picks and paperwork at random as associates are picking!

Have picked parts with the proper paperwork ready in the packing & shipping area for packing. Each associate should be given the opportunity to practice making, loading and sealing of the shipping boxes. The coaches must oversee the accuracy and correctness of orders prior to any packaging!

0.25 hour   BREAK (8:00 to 8:15 am)

Associates process packaged parts for shipment by running them through the Federal Express shipping system. Coaches to assure the packages are being processed correctly should monitor the Federal Express machines. Assure the correct stickers are placed on out-going parts. Make sure weight and size restrictions that apply to Early Bird and Priority One shipments are not exceeded. Try to make each associate feel comfortable with operating this piece of equipment.

Glossary

ASTD	American Society of Training and Development
BARS	Behaviorally-Anchored Ratings Scales
CIT	Critical Incident Technique
HR	Human Resources
HRD	Human Resource Development
HRM	Human Resources Management
KRA	Key Results Areas
KSA	Knowledge, Skills and Abilities
PAQ	Position Analysis Questionnaire
PBTA	Process-Based Task Analysis
SHRM	Society of Human Resource Management
SME	Subject Matter Expert
TBJA	Task-Based Job Analysis

ABOUT THE AUTHOR

Mr. Anderson holds a graduate degree in Industrial & Organizational Psychology as well as an undergraduate degree in Management from the Georgia Institute of Technology. His extremely diverse human resources background spans over twenty-five years. The initial steps of his HRD career began in the form of personnel research, training and employment services assignments with state and local governments throughout the southeast. He has experienced start-up situations in both manufacturing and service industries while holding positions in line management, engineering, training and organizational development with DuPont, Johnson & Johnson and GATX Logistics (General American Transportation).

Mr. Anderson provides consultative services in such areas as selection, instructional design, management & leadership training, sales & operator skills training, performance appraisal, re-engineering and organizational culture change for continuous improvement. Client companies serviced include General Motors, Proctor & Gamble, Colgate, Sears, Kimberly-Clark, Monsanto, DuPont, Johnson & Johnson, Weyerhaeuser, Westvaco, J.P. Stevens, J.I. Case, First Union, Alltel, Cummins Engine and Ideon.

With regard to professional organizations, Mr. Anderson helped found the International Personnel Management Association Assessment Council (IPMAAC) and served on its Executive Board and as Program Chairperson for its first international conference. He is a national member of the American Society of Quality Control (ASQC) and the American Society of Training and Development (ASTD). He has served on the Board of Directors for the Northeast Florida Chapter of ASTD. He is also an active member of the National Society For Performance Improvement (NSPI).

For the last six years, he has been associated with the graduate programs at Webster University as faculty coordinator for over forty adjunct professors teaching in the areas of Business, Management, Business Administration, Human Resource Development, Marketing and Computer Resource Management. He also serves as the Departmental Chairperson for Human Resource Development.

Now retired, Mr. Anderson, his wife Margaret and their grandson Ryan live in the mountains of North Carolina.

0-595-32369-3

Printed in the United Kingdom
by Lightning Source UK Ltd.
108952UKS00001B/53